THE WORKING MEN'S COLLEGE

AUSPICIUM MELIORIS AEVI: MDCCCLIV.

Purchased

R.E.Tyler Dec. 1913. C.H.Perry Sc.

WORKING MEN'S COLLEGE

LIBRARY REGULATIONS

RUDYARD KIPLING

RUDYARD KIPLING

Painted by H. Strachey
at Newlands Corner, Guildford, June 15th, 1900

BONAMY DOBRÉE

Rudyard Kipling

REALIST AND FABULIST

LONDON
OXFORD UNIVERSITY PRESS
NEW YORK TORONTO
1967

Oxford University Press, Ely House, London W.1

GLASGOW NEW YORK TORONTO MELBOURNE WELLINGTON
CAPE TOWN SALISBURY IBADAN NAIROBI LUSAKA ADDIS ABABA
BOMBAY CALCUTTA MADRAS KARACHI LAHORE DACCA
KUALA LUMPUR HONG KONG TOKYO

Printed in Great Britain by
Richard Clay (The Chaucer Press) Ltd, Bungay, Suffolk

CONTENTS

PREFACE

Rudyard Kipling, it is now coming to be generally acknow-
ledged, has been more grotesquely misunderstood, misrepre-
sented, and in consequence denigrated, than any other
known writer. I have attempted here to present him as outside
any of the camps into which careless readers have wished to,
indeed have, put him, either in praise or in blame. I say
'careless readers' because I have found that most of those who
so readily label him have not really read him, or have done
so with preconceived notions of what he wished to impart.
Not long ago a distinguished man of letters and lecturer wrote
to me: "People are not only blinded, but *deafened* by prejudice.
If you talk (as I sometimes do . . .) about him, *nobody hears
what you say*. They simply switch off their aids, or have an
automatic cut-out." Thus I have not attempted, except by
occasional incidental remarks, to refute the ill-based accusations
made against him. An unbiased view of the totality of his work
makes such a labour unnecessary.

He must be seen in relation to his day. He was intensely
alert to what was going on around him—more than alert,
knowing it in his bones. Yet he was never thrall to the 'ideas'
that swept across his time; his strong feeling of tradition saved
him from that, though he had an astonishing prophetic vision
of the future. But based on a lively historic sense, he was wary
of accepting the ideological movements that surged around him,
being possessed of that centrality of mind so highly praised by
Bagehot. Thus on one side he stoutly fought the noisy jingoism
of the 'nineties, and on the other was opposed to what was
regarded as 'liberal' thought. For all his intellectual vigour he
was no extremist; and if he cherished the past, he also delighted
in prospects of the future.

It will be seen that I have in no way attempted a biographical
sketch: Professor Carrington has made this unnecessary. Nor
have I tried to analyse his consummate art, since Dr. Tompkins

has brilliantly accomplished that task. What I have tried to do here has been to present Kipling as he appears to me, as he has affected me, spoken directly to me. He has been my constant reading ever since boyhood, and I have already written a good deal about him, both generally, and in some places concentrating on particular aspects; thus I would ask those few who have read my previous essays to forgive me if I repeat myself. And while on the subject of repetitions I would like to add that within the following pages I have occasionally repeated myself, or re-quoted something of Kipling's, but here deliberately, my remarks or quotations being set in a different context, with another application.

I have not read much of the earlier criticism, either English or French, that appeared before his death, this dealing largely with his immature work. It has come to me only in extracts. Inevitably, however, I owe a debt to those who have written since 1936, from Edward Shanks onward, though these have not altered my impressions in any radical respect. Much that I owe is unconscious, but I am aware that I have been influenced, on the biographical side by Professor Charles Carrington's classic biography, and on the creative and artistic side by Dr. J. M. S. Tompkins's delicate and perceptive study. More recently I have profited from Professor C. A. Bodelsen's essays, without always accepting his conclusions, and to a lesser extent from M. Francis Léaud's *La Poétique de Rudyard Kipling*. I would wish to make this general grateful acknowledgement, though on specific points I have drawn attention to valuable illuminations. I have, however, more than once found that I had formed certain views that I later came upon in other people's work published before I had organized my own conclusions, or attempted to make them known. This is inevitable if a writer makes any powerful general appeal; if he has really had something to say, more than one person will have responded.

B.D.

30 December 1965.

ACKNOWLEDGEMENTS

I would first like gratefully to thank Mrs. Bambridge for allowing me to quote so freely from her father's poems; also for reading my script, and correcting me on one or two points of fact, besides, as will be seen, offering suggestions on the question of the fabular element in some of the stories.

I owe a great debt to Dr. J. M. S. Tompkins, who also read my script, corrected me on some points, and gave me great encouragement throughout.

I must also thank Mr. B. W. J. Baxter for allowing me to make use of his thesis *The Poetry in Kipling's Verse*, 1956, which contains drafts of MS. versions of Kipling's poetry in the British Museum. The thesis may be found in the library of the University of Leeds.

I would add that many members of the Kipling Society have given me encouragement, among whom are the President, Mr. R. E. Harbord, the Hon. Secretary, Lt.-Col. A. E. Bagwell-Purefoy, the Assistant Secretary and Librarian, Miss A. M. Punch, and the Hon. Editor of the Kipling Journal, Mr. R. Lancelyn Green. All these have placed facilities at my disposal, enabling me to consult varying texts. To these should be added Professor Charles Carrington.

I am grateful to the University of Leeds for permission to reproduce the portrait by H. Strachey from the Brotherton Collection.

I doubt if I should have completed the work, at all events so soon, without my wife's constant interest, her corrective reading of the text chapter by chapter, and pointing out where the general reader would need explanation. It is to her that my greatest debt is due.

REFERENCES

Bodelsen. ASPECTS OF KIPLING'S ART. By C. A. Bodelsen. (Manchester University Press, 1964.)

Carrington. RUDYARD KIPLING. His Life and Work. By Charles Carrington. (Macmillan, 1955.)

Cohen. RIDER HAGGARD. His Life and Works. By Morton Cohen. (Hutchinson, 1960.)

Cohen. Record. RUDYARD KIPLING TO RIDER HAGGARD. The Record of a Friendship. Edited by Morton Cohen. (Hutchinson, 1965.)

Tompkins. THE ART OF RUDYARD KIPLING. By J. M. S. Tompkins. (Methuen, 1959.)

Other references are given in the footnotes. See also the Guide to Further Reading in Appendix II.

As regards references to Kipling's own work, I have not given page references, as these vary in different editions. I have, however, given the title of the story mentioned or quoted from, or where a book is concerned, the chapter from which the passage is taken.

The volume in which any story quoted from occurs may be found in the list given at the end (p. 219) together with the date of the first publication of the story.

COPYRIGHT NOTICE

PART I

CHAPTER I

General

"A writer impossible wholly to understand"
T. S. Eliot

§1. THE PROFESSIONAL WRITER

Certainly it is difficult to get a unified idea of Rudyard Kipling's complex and enigmatic personality. Reading through his fictional works you find, outstandingly, that he is a writer who can compel your imagination to accompany him from arid villages in Afghanistan to the rich downs of Sussex, from the plains of India to the wildest of Atlantic seas, from Arctic ice to the sweltering African forests. He can impart the chatter of journalists in London, the energy of pioneers in Canada, or the terrible isolation of a lighthouse-keeper. Here is a man who can horrifyingly reveal shocking depths of humanity, show it at its most tender and compassionate, or flash to you a queer vision of an archangelic world. He can go back to ancient Rome, even to pre-history, and forward to the year 2065. His variety is astonishing. It is of no use to read a few stories of one kind and put him in a certain category: you cannot pigeon-hole Kipling—he will catch you unaware. In the same volume a story of deep tragic significance may be followed by one of outrageously extravagant farce. What seizes you continually is the overflowing vitality that gives you the sense of being just there. And through the fiction, the lectures and the letters, there run threads of certain dominating ideas or intuitions, each, perhaps, simple in itself, but which woven together form an intricate, patterned tapestry.

He was temperamentally imbued with an exuberant zest for life, which he found to be "curious—and sudden and

mixed",[1] and an inexhaustible interest and delight in men. To
use his own phrases, he found naught common on the earth,
and more than once thanked Allah for the infinite diversity
of His creatures in His adorable world. He had unceasing
curiosity about what men do, and how they do it. The baggage-
master at his American home used to say that "he had the
darndest mind. He wanted to know everything about everything, and he never forgot what you told him. He would sit
and listen and never stir."[2] In 'Steam Tactics' he speaks of
"the layman's delight in the expert", which he felt and expected his readers to share; and it was for this reason—not to
'show off' as used to be alleged against him—that he so often
in his stories describes technical matters in minute detail. He
was indefatigable in finding out how things are, or were, made,
from ink in the fourteenth century to girder bridges in the
nineteenth: he knew about medieval illumination and old
tobacco jars. He was intent to know how things worked, and
was always almost schoolboyishly excited by the new thing—
motor-cars, wireless, aeroplanes—all unheard of in his youth,
with bounding imagination foreseeing their possibilities. He
had, as Professor Carrington says, "an uncanny skill in picking
the brains of his acquaintances and making convincing pictures, replete with accurate detail, from a few hints picked up
in conversation".[3] He himself tells us that in the Punjab Club

and elsewhere I met none except picked men at their definite work—
Civilians, Army, Education, Canals, Forestry, Engineering, Irriga-
tion, Railways, Doctors, and Lawyers—samples of each branch and
each talking his own shop. It follows then that that 'show of technical
knowledge' for which I was blamed later came to me from the horse's
mouth, even to boredom.[4]

Convincing pictures, yes; but, in sober fact, not always quite
accurate: "I have had miraculous escapes in technical matters,"
he confessed, "which make me blush still. Luckily the men of
the seas and the engine-room do not write to the Press, and my
worst slip is still underided."
      Nor was it material facts alone that he gleaned from the

---

[1] 'The Captive.'   [2] *Carrington*, p. 220.   [3] ibid, p. 168.
[4] *Something of Myself*, III. Other statements by Kipling in this chapter are from
the same source. (References are to chapters.)

people he bewitched into talking to him: he picked up stories from all sources, for as the old priest Gobind told him, as related in the Preface to *Life's Handicap*, "All the earth is full of tales to him who listens, and does not drive away the poor from his door. The poor are the best of tale-tellers, for they must lay their ear to the ground every night." We know the source of a few of his stories. 'The Finances of the Gods', for example, comes from his father's *Beast and Man in India*: 'Little Foxes' was told him—in raw outline, obviously—by an army officer whom he met on board ship, when he "expected no such jewel". He relates also that

. . . in a local train of the Cape Town suburbs I heard a petty officer from Simons Town telling a companion about a woman in New Zealand who 'never scrupled to help a lame duck or put her foot on a scorpion'. Then—precisely as the removal of a key-log in a timber-jam starts the whole pile—those words gave me the key to the face and voice at Auckland [which he had mentioned earlier] and a tale called 'Mrs. Bathurst' slid into my mind, smoothly and orderly as floating timber on a bank-high river.[1]

Incidentally we might wish that this, the most baffling of all his stories, had slid a little less smoothly into his mind, that we might understand the workings.

Added to these sources were the stories or ideas he got from previous writers,[2] for naturally he was something of a plagiarist, as all good writers of necessity are. Shakespeare borrowed from Plutarch among a dozen others; Jonson 'invaded authors like a monarch'; Milton was a notorious thief, and Molière took his good things where he could find them. After all—

> When 'Omer smote 'is bloomin' lyre
> He'd 'eard men sing by land an' sea,
> An' what he thought 'e might require,
> 'E went an' took—the same as me!

> The market-girls an' fishermen,
> The shepherds an' the sailors, too,
> They 'eard old songs turn up again,
> But kep' it quiet—same as you!

---

[1] *Something of Myself*, IV.

[2] For the sources of some other stories see *Carrington*, p. 104 and *Tompkins*, Chapter VIII.

They knew 'e stole: 'e knew they knowed.
They didn't tell, nor make a fuss,
But winked at 'Omer down the road,
An' 'e winked back—the same as us!

(Introduction to 'Barrack-Room Ballads' in *The Seven Seas*)

Sometimes they did tell; but how little Kipling cared is shown by the story he relates of how a reviewer of 'The Wish House' accused him (on grounds it is hard to discover) of borrowing from Chaucer's 'The Wife of Bath', even to the 'mormal on her shinne'. He was unaware of having done so, but was quite content to give himself as "out—caught to leg".[1]

The substance of his stories grew more and more throughout the years to be "the eternal mystery of personality", as one of the characters in 'A Friend of the Family' phrases it—the vulnerable personality of man. Men cannot be protected against themselves, for "That, alas! is the one enemy against which no law can protect any son of Adam; since the real reasons that make or break a man are too absurd or too obscene to be reached from outside."[2] What fascinated him most, especially in his early maturity, was the character and being of the people who did things, for it was what they did that gave them individuality in the Great Game of 'To Be or Not to be' that they played in the face of an indifferent, timeless universe. His individuals had to have an integrity proud and secure in its own fortress—even an integrity of which others might not be proud; they had to be people of action of some kind (women differently from men) because it is through action alone that people reveal what they are, and arrive at a sense of themselves. "'I am Kim. And what is Kim?' His soul repeated it again and again."[3] He discovered the answer only by integrating himself with purposeful action: and for Kipling this can be done solely by men who handle the raw material. We see this when he writes of the Englishmen in India "who live down in the plains and do things other than writing futile reports";[4] and we note that it was the end of

---

[1] *Something of Myself*, Chapter VIII. The 'mormal' actually bothered Chaucer's cook, "That on his schynne a mormal hadde he".

[2] *Letters of Travel*, 'Up the River'.   [3] *Kim*, XIV.

[4] 'A District at Play' in 'The Smith Administration'. *From Sea to Sea*, II.

Strickland when he married and gave up the work at which he excelled through his astonishing knowledge and understanding of the native: "But he fills in his Departmental returns beautifully."[1]

One might reverse Henry James's dictum on Turgenev, and say that there was in Kipling "an impalpable union of the democratic temperament with an aristocratic mind". He could apply to himself the saying "I met a hundred men on the road to Delhi, and they were all my brothers",[2] but what he sought for were the aristocrats. An aristocrat for Kipling was one who, whatever his race, or caste, or creed, had a full man within him, who kept himself whole, and did not set too much value upon his feelings. Those who did this last were always objects of his contempt. He would have agreed with Coleridge, who wrote of 'the thinking disease', namely

that in which the feelings, instead of embodying themselves in *acts*, ascend and become materials of general reasoning and intellectual pride . . . feelings made the subjects and tangible substances of thought, instead of actions, realizations, *things done*: . . . On such meagre diet as feelings, evaporated embryos in their progress to *birth*, no moral being ever becomes healthy.

(Anima Poetæ)

Kipling's typical instance of the destructive effect is that of the wax-moth in 'The Mother Hive', who calls to the bee, "Come here, you dear downy duck, and tell us about your feelings." Or again, in 'Below the Mill Dam' the Waters said to the Black Rat:

If you thought a trifle more about the work you're supposed to do, and a trifle less about your precious feelings, you'd render a little more duty in return for the power vested in you—we mean wasted on you.

For, as we read in 'His Private Honour', "First a man must suffer, then he must learn his work, and the self-respect that that knowledge brings." Those who have his approval are the Ordes and Tallantires[3] of the frontier districts, McAndrew the engineer, the doctors of his later stories, and among women, William the Conqueror in the tale of that name. Then again,

---

[1] 'Miss Youghal's Sais.' [2] Epigraph to *Life's Handicap*.
[3] 'The Head of the District.'

B

there were in *Kim*, Mahbub Ali and Hurree Chunder Moo-
kerjie, besides the Englishmen (the Lama is another matter—
one of the contradictions in Kipling): there were Peachey
Carnehan and Daniel Dravot in 'The Man Who Would be
King', there were forgotten toilers in out-stations: there were
Mulvaney, Ortheris, and Learoyd; Maddingham, the temporary naval officer clearing the sea of mines in 'Sea Constables';
Helen Turrell who had lost her natural son in the war, as re-
counted in 'The Gardener'; Grace Ashcroft in 'The Wish
House'; Pyecroft in many stories; Hobden the labourer—
chorus to the *Puck* stories—with his sardonic smile at the
changes of landlords and the unchangeability of things: even
McIntosh Jellaludin in 'To be Filed for Reference', the sometime Fellow of an Oxford College who had 'gone native'; it
did not matter if they were failures, or tramps, or 'wilful-
missings', so long as they kept themselves whole, though
sometimes only partly, as Dowse the lighthouse-keeper who
went mad because of the infernal streakiness of the tides and
so became 'A Disturber of Traffic', and Love o' Women who
suffered the reward his name implies.

None were obviously successful in the worldly sense, for
Kipling despised success; he has little to say for the high-ups,
the administrators, the people in authority, who as a general
rule—Rhodes was an exception—knew nothing of the matters
they were dealing with. Success or failure, just as with triumph
or disaster, he could "treat those two impostors just the same".
As for himself, he had no desire to be "festooned with the whole
haberdashery of success";[1] a point that is brought out when
Leo, the singer in 'Children of the Zodiac', was disgusted at the
horrible praise that people gave him, and "the silly peacock
feathers that they stuck in his cap, and the buttons and pieces
of cloth that they sewed on his coat".

When talking to men about their work he learnt also about
their characters—what better way could there be since a man's
work is his character? Yet there is a difficulty here, for there
is a limit to men's communication with each other:

What mystery is there like the mystery of the other man's job—
or what world so cut off as that which he enters when he goes to it?

[1] *A Book of Words*, XXIV.

The eminent surgeon is altogether such an one as ourselves, even till his hand falls on the knob of the theatre door. After that, in the silence, among the ether fumes, no man except his acolytes, and they won't tell, has ever seen his face. So with the unconsidered curate. Yet, before the war, he had more experience of the business and detail of death than any of the people who condemned him. His face also, as he stands his bedside-watches—that countenance with which he shall justify himself to his Maker—none have ever looked upon. Even the ditcher is a priest of mysteries at the high moment when he lays out in his mind the levels and fall of the water that he alone can draw off clearly. But catch any of these five minutes after they have left their altars, and you will find the doors are shut.[1]

So, at the age of fifty, with experience to guide him. Nevertheless, it was through conversation that he came to understand Sir John Bland-Sutton, the Sir James Belton of 'The Tender Achilles'; and so he created 'old Mus' Hobden' from one of the men who worked for him in Sussex, "a poacher by heredity and instinct", who, when the Kiplings were shifting some trees, remarked to a suggestion of theirs, "Have it *as* you're minded. *I* dunno if I should if I was you."[2] His unusual power of empathy enabled him to peep through the shut door, and see into people, their motives, their desires, their bafflement.

These abnormal qualities would have been of little avail if he had not been a writer born. From his earliest years he had taken to reading, first in the House of Desolation from the ages of six to twelve, when he was often forbidden contact with other people, so took refuge in books. There he largely read the Bible, of which he had a thorough knowledge, and which he quotes or refers to so often that anyone unfamiliar with it will miss the significance of half his allusions, the source of which he does not always reveal. Even the title of *Many Inventions* is taken from *Ecclesiastes*, though here he gives us the reference. Then, at Westward Ho! his headmaster, 'Crom' Price, a friend of the pre-Raphaelites, gave him the run of his well-stocked library, where he read widely from Chaucer through the metaphysical poets to Swinburne, Mark Twain, together with French classic novels, and set him to précis writing, and revived the school magazine for him to edit.

[1] *Sea Warfare.* 1916. Destroyers at Jutland. IV. 'The Minds of Men.'
[2] *Something of Myself*, VII.

There Kipling wrote a deal of verse, much of it very derivative, a selection from which was published by his parents in India before he left school.[1] During the holidays he would stay with the Burne-Joneses, where he met Swinburne, Rossetti, Browning and others, notably William Morris, his honorary Uncle Topsy, who told the children *The Saga of Burnt Njal* from the back of a rocking-horse. Going back to his parents in India when not quite seventeen to take up a post on *The Civil and Military Gazette* at Lahore, he became a professional writer.

During the first part of what he called his 'Seven Years Hard', under Stephen Wheeler—later a Landor authority—he was kept with his nose to the grindstone, beginning to write on his own in what little spare time he had, his very earliest being monologues dealing with fantastic situations. 'The Gate of the Hundred Sorrows' was published in 1884, to be collected in *Plain Tales* (1888); 'The Dream of Duncan Parrenness', late 1884, is now to be found in *Life's Handicap* (1891); while 'The Strange Ride of Morrowbie Jukes' and 'The Phantom Rickshaw', which originally came out at the end of 1885, written when Kipling was nineteen, were not collected until 1888 in the small Phantom Rickshaw volume, and are now to be found in *Wee Willie Winkie*, where they are revised, and 'introduced' by a narrator who then offers the monologues as written by those to whom the events happened, thus being given the due detachment Kipling came to think proper for the short story.[2] Then in 1886, the more congenial Kay Robinson took over the paper, where, and later on the Allahabad *Pioneer*, Kipling got his chance to write fiction in the form of turnovers. At once the artist emerged, and we can follow his progress.

His tireless curiosity, his zest in all he saw, gave him abundant material. Some he got from his father, but most of the matter for his Indian tales came from his night-wanderings (the night had 'got into his head' from very early days) about remote quarters of the cities he got to know, hidden corners of the bazaars and so on, where he met the strangest people— outcasts, opium addicts, ladies whom he dubbed Fat Vice or

---

[1] *Schoolboy Lyrics.* 1881.

[2] For this paragraph see Louis L. Cornell, in *English Literature in Transition* Vol. 7. No. 4. 1964. Purdue University, Lafayette, Indiana, U.S.A.

Dainty Iniquity, knowing quiet sweltering hot nights on house-
tops, or viewing a "growling, flaring, creed-drunk city". He
would come home "just as light broke, in some night-hawk of
a hired carriage which stank of hookah-fumes, jasmine flowers
and sandalwood: and if the driver was moved to talk, he told
one a good deal".[1] Thus it is that an Indian, Mr. Nirad C.
Chaudhuri, can say, "I think he is the only English writer on
India (in imaginative literature) who will live. Compared with
him Mr. E. M. Forster in his novel [*A Passage to India*] is
pinchbeck." He went also to Simla, and mixed with the idle,
gossiping society of a place which was a holiday resort as well
as a centre of government, where also, as a newspaper man, he
had contact with high official circles, and "saw and heard the
machinery of administration stripped bare". Moreover,
significantly, though under age, he became a Freemason, a
member of a society that ignores colour, caste, and creed. "Here
I met Muslims, Hindus, Sikhs, members of the Araya and
Brahmo Samaj, and a Jew tyler, who was priest and butcher
to his little community in the city (of Lahore). So yet another
world opened to me which I needed."[2] In that way, in many
places, through various channels, he garnered, by sight and
experience and hearsay, the rich harvest for his stories, which
he told with the brevity imposed upon him by newspaper needs,
with comments—which we might call wisecracks—for which he
is often criticized. But a very short story may need to have its
point rammed home.

Passages scattered throughout *Something of Myself* give a
vivid picture of his growth as a professional writer soon to
become the dedicated artist, a Maker, possessed by a Personal
Daemon. He glosses (VIII)

> This is the doom of the Makers—their Daemon lives in
>   their pen.
> If he be absent or sleeping, they are even as other men.
> But if he be utterly present, and they swerve not from his
>   behest,
> The word that he gives shall continue, whether in earnest or
>   jest.

[1] *Something of Myself*, III.
[2] ibid.

Kipling's Daemon came to him early in his Indian days, when once he "sat bewildered among other notions, and said to him: 'Take this and no other.' " The outcome was 'The Phantom Rickshaw', his first serious attempt, he adds, "to think in another man's skin" (VIII). A little later, when he went to Allahabad, he

had an experience which, in my innocence, I mistook for the genuine motions of my Daemon. I must have been loaded more heavily than I realised with 'Gyp', for there came to me in scenes as stereoscopically clear as those in the crystal an Anglo-Indian *Autour du Mariage*. My pen took charge and I, greatly admiring, watched it write for me far into the nights. The result I christened *The Story of the Gadsbys*.

One can agree with his father, who when the story after being over-praised was a little scouted, said, loyally, "It wasn't *all* so dam' bad, Ruddy." (III)

Then we hear of how things went much the same way during his first weeks in America. He "had written a tale about Indian Forestry work which included a boy who had been brought up by wolves",[1] namely 'In the Rukh'; then memories of a childhood's magazine, and a phrase in Haggard's *Nada the Lily* came together. This started him off. "After blocking out the main idea in my head, the pen took charge, and I watched it begin to write stories about Mowgli and animals, which later grew into the *Jungle Books*" (V). But he would not comply with all the 'peremptory notions' of his Daemon, and threw away a couple of the stories. We hear more about these notions later:

My Daemon was with me in the *Jungle Books*, *Kim*, and both Puck books, and good care I took to walk delicately, lest he should withdraw. I know that he did not, because when those books were finished they said so themselves with, almost, the water-hammer click of a tap turned off. One of the clauses in our contract was that I should never follow up 'a success', for by this sin fell Napoleon and a few others. *Note here*. When your Daemon is in charge, do not try to think consciously. Drift, wait and obey. (VIII)

The Daemon is in charge: he cannot be dictated to, and will

---

[1] A not unusual occurrence—apart from Romulus and Remus. It is unlikely that he had heard of *The Epic of Gilgamesh*, where Enkudi is brought up by wolves.

not work where he does not wish to, as Kipling found when he chose a brickyard in which to set a tale about Defoe. But, as he makes Shakespeare say to Ben Jonson in 'Proofs of Holy Writ', "My Demon never betrayed me yet, while I trusted him." Moreover, "Never follow up 'a success'." There was, also, the old Law, "As soon as you find that you can do anything, do something you can't." For it is as John of Burgos said in 'The Eye of Allah': "In my craft, a thing done with is done with. We go on to new shapes after that." It may be noticed that Kipling always had this in mind. In 'The Bull that Thought', the boys in the cattle-yard, playing with Apis, desired him to repeat himself, "which", the narrator says, "no true artist will tolerate".

But though he depended on what might ordinarily be called 'inspiration', Kipling gave a good deal of thought to what the Daemon provided; he by no means let the pen do the writing for him. When he came to ponder on *Rewards and Fairies* he embarked upon it in two minds. How many stories should be authentic, and how many due to 'induction'? Besides, "the tales had to be read by children, before people realized that they were meant for grown-ups"; so he

worked the material in three or four overlaid tints and textures, which might or might not reveal themselves according to the shifting light of sex, youth, and experience. It was like working lacquer and mother o' pearl, a natural combination, into the same scheme as niello and grisaille, and trying not to let the joins show. (VII)

He found writing and all that pertained to it 'glorious fun'; but from the beginning he laboured enormously to be worthy of the guidance he was given. Of his work on the *Pioneer* he wrote:

I made my own experiments in the weights, colours, perfumes, and attributes of words, either as read aloud, so that they may hold the ear, or, scattered over the page, draw the eye. There is no line of my verse or prose which has not been mouthed till the tongue has made all smooth, and memory, after many recitals, has mechanically slipped the grosser superfluities. (III)

Later on he tells us how he would submit the first results of his inspiration to what he called the Higher Editing:

Take of well-ground Indian Ink as much as suffices and a camel-hair brush proportionate to the interspaces of your lines. In an auspicious hour, read your final draft and consider faithfully every paragraph, sentence and word, blacking out where requisite. Let it lie by to drain as long as possible. At the end of that time, re-read and you should find that it will bear a second shortening. Finally, read it aloud alone and at leisure. Maybe a shade more brushwork will then indicate or impose itself. If not, praise Allah and let it go, and 'when thou hast done, repent not'. (VIII)

The instructions continue, reinforcing the advice, and no one can say that Kipling did not work to the utmost limit of his will in framing and polishing his stories. Perhaps he sometimes overdid it, as C. S. Lewis thought, making the style too continuously brilliant; "we need roughage as well as nourishment in a diet; but there is no roughage in a Kipling story". He provides, however, "an almost perfectly satisfactory answer" by reminding his readers that the stories or poems were single items in periodicals, meant to be taken at intervals, and not gobbled down one after another at a sitting.[1]

Kipling's great reward was the joy of the craftsman; it was all, in its deepest sense, 'glorious fun'. There was always "the joy of the working", as he wrote in the Envoi to *The Seven Seas*; moreover he felt that he was dedicated. Addressing the Great Overseer in the Envoi to *Life's Handicap*, he declared:

> One instant's toil to Thee denied
> Stands all Eternity's offence,

going on with his prayer:

> Who, lest all thought of Eden fade,
> Bring'st Eden to the craftsman's brain,
> Godlike to muse o'er his own trade
> And Manlike stand with God again.

There we are conscious not only of the devoted craftsman, but also of the dedicated artist, who finally prays that the vision may not be taken from his ken, that he may need no help from men, but be able to help such men as need.

We see, then, the man enthralled by his imagination, letting it strike out into invented realism; for Kipling was primarily an artist, feeling and seeing by intuition, creating as he let

[1] 'Kipling's World' in *They asked for a Paper* (Bles, 1962)

his formative sensibilities wander. But—adding to the dimension—in common with his own Aurelian McGoggin, "his grandfathers on both sides had been Wesleyan preachers, and the preaching strain came out in his mind". In varying degrees there was always this duality giving substance to his tales. He was eager to *show* raw, naked humanity, from its horror to its near-angelic qualities, but also to suggest, or even state, a moral. Thus he wrote to C. E. Norton at the end of 1896: "As you know I love the fun and riot of writing (I am daily and nightly perplexed with my own private responsibilities before God) and there are times when it is just a comfort and delight to let out with the pen and ink—as long as it doesn't do anyone any moral harm."[1] The duality can be seen as he brought into existence *Stalky & Co.*, which, he said in *Something of Myself*, he designed as 'tracts or parables', but which we find him discussing with his cousin Florence Macdonald who was staying with the Kiplings while he was writing the stories, and was allowed to sit in the room while he did so. "He would write and write: then lay down his pen and roar with laughter: then read a passage aloud to her till she would roar with laughter: 'Come on, Florence,' he would say, 'What shall we make them do now?' "[2]

That kind of duality, lightly indicated by that anecdote, serves in part to account for the structured complexity of the later tales, though even in the earlier stories there is usually more than one level. Kipling could always see, and feel, both sides of a question—or more if there were such. As with Blake, single vision was abhorrent to him, and he scouted the idea of being wedded to a particular line of thought:

> Much I owe to the Lands that grew—
> More to the Lives that fed—
> But most to Allah Who gave me two
> Separate sides to my head. . . .
>
> *I* would go without shirt or shoe,
> Friend, tobacco or bread,
> Sooner than lose for a minute the two
> Separate sides of my head!
>
> ('The Two-Sided Man')

[1] *Carrington*, p. 258.   [2] ibid., p. 250.

He may be the prophet of work, the priest of discipline; but he is also the poet of love, and poet laureate of laughter.

§2. RELIGION

It would perhaps be useful at this stage to seek out the dominating ideas that thread through all Kipling's writings, and from which their pattern is woven; and to see as far as one can the influences that went to mould him. First among these must be his religion, or, if this is too definite a term, his general notion of the universe we live in.

He was born in Bombay on 30 December 1865. His father, John Lockwood Kipling, had at that time been recently appointed Professor of Architectural Sculpture in a new school of art in that city, and it was there that Kipling, with a short break in England, spent the first five and a half years of his life. His Wesleyan-bred parents, though modifying this creed, naturally brought him up to their way of thinking, and gave him his earliest teaching; but he probably learnt as much from his *ayah*, a Portuguese Roman Catholic, who with the infant beside her, would pray at a wayside cross; and from his Hindu bearer, who would sometimes take him into little Hindu temples, where, Kipling tells us, "being below the age of caste, I held his hand and looked at the dimly-seen, friendly Gods".[1] From these he got, one may hazard, that sense, if not of magic, of something inapprehensible in the goings-on of the universe which the West tends to ignore. So he would intuitively sympathize with races quite different from his own, especially with their religions. Though one might not call him initially a *deeply* religious man, from the first he held strong belief that some sort of faith was essential, and understood the need for prayer. When in later years he visited the pagoda at Moulmein, he noted that "those who faced the figures prayed more zealously than the others, so I judged that their troubles were the greater".[2]

Coming to believe that peoples and races had the religion that they could live by, that was in their tradition and their

[1] *Something of Myself*, I.
[2] *From Sea to Sea*, III.

blood, he respected that of others, thinking with his friend,
that great woman Mary Kingsley, that missionaries were a
disrupting danger. In his view, a religion in which a man was
bred was so deeply ingrained that it could not be changed.
"Once a Hindu, always a Hindu," declared Grish Chunder
the Bengali in 'The Finest Story in the World', who, in London,
had "been too well educated to believe in God": while Wali
Dod ('On the City Wall'), bred a Muhammadan, but turned
into a 'Demnition Product' by English education at a Mission
School, flung himself into the wild manifestations of a creed-
drunk city at the period of the Mohurrum; the conversion of
the pagan worshippers of Dungara came to a disastrous end
('The Judgment of Dungara'). Mahbub Ali put this pic-
turesquely for him when he said to Kim: "This matter of
creeds is like horseflesh. . . . Therefore I say in my heart the
Faiths are like the horses. Each has merit in its own country."[1]
But the most cursory reading of *Kim* shows how much
he respected the faith of the Lama; and in that book he speaks
scornfully of the Protestant parson, Bennett, who looked at
the Lama "with the triple-ringed uninterest of the creed that
lumps nine-tenths of the world under the title of 'heathen' ".[2]
The word is given inverted commas, as in the poem he wrote
when in Japan, quoting as heading, evidently from a guide-
book "And there is a Japanese idol at Kamakura".

> O ye who tread the Narrow Way
> By Tophet-flare to Judgment Day,
> Be gentle when "the heathen" pray
> To Buddha at Kamakura! . . .

> And whoso will, from Pride released,
> Contemning neither creed nor priest,
> May feel the soul of all the East
> About him at Kamakura. . . .

He ends with a gently satirical touch at the unimaginative-
ness of the European visitor, and his materialistic preoccupa-
tions:

[1] *Kim*, VIII.
[2] ibid., V.

A tourist-show, a legend told,
A rusting bulk of bronze and gold,
So much, and scarce so much, ye hold
    The meaning of Kamakura?

But when the morning prayer is prayed,
Think, ere ye pass to strife and trade,
Is God in human image made
    No nearer than Kamakura?

Just before he was six years old, he was taken to England and
left in the villa at Southsea he came to call the House of Desolation, where he endured the most hideous torment that a child
can undergo, under the charge of an impercipient woman who,
with her son, bullied him mercilessly under the sanction of the
strictest Evangelical rules, threatening him with Tophet-flare
should he depart, however innocently, from the Narrow Way.
This is told, a little exaggeratedly perhaps, in 'Baa, Baa,
Black Sheep'; and how far the experience sunk in can be
judged by his picturing it again in *The Light that Failed*. This gave
him a lasting distaste for orthodox Christianity, and the generally accepted idea of Hell appalled him. In 'With the Night
Mail' we read of "the men of the old days, each one of them
taught (*that* is the horror of it!) that after death he would
very possibly go for ever to unspeakable torment." It would
seem that the failure of Christianity to eliminate the fear of
death struck him as being a major defect. "Bah! How these
Christians funk death", Dick Heldar exclaims in *The Light
that Failed*;[1] and in 'The Finest Story in the World' we read
of "the western world which clings to the dread of death more
closely than the hope of life"; and in that story too the admirable
Hindu Babu, Grish Chunder, tells the narrator, "You are not
afraid to be kicked, but you are afraid to die." "I am not afraid
to die," he had just said, "because I know what I know." In a
piece written at about the same time, 'One View of the Question', the Muslim in London writing to his brother, says of the
English, "some hold that all war is sin, and Death the greatest
fear under God". How important Kipling held this to be may
be seen from 'The Children of the Zodiac', and its accompany-

[1] XIV.

ing Envoy, which tells us that we're all "bound for Mother
Carey where she feeds her chicks at sea".

Nor was he at all impressed by the behaviour of Christians
when organized. In 'Watches of the Night' we read: "You may
have noticed that many religious people [he means among the
Anglo-Indians] are deeply suspicious. They seem—for purely
religious purposes, of course—to know more about iniquity
than the Unregenerate." We see this again in the early story
'Lispeth', where the heroine is unfeelingly treated, indeed
shockingly lied to, by the Chaplain of the Kotgarh Mission and
his wife, who seemed to have no sympathy or understanding.
"It takes a great deal of Christianity," Kipling comments
sardonically, "to wipe out uncivilized Eastern instincts, such
as falling in love at first sight." In 'They', written some twenty
years later, the narrator tells us:

I was silent reviewing that inexhaustible matter—the more than
inherited (since it is also carefully taught) brutality of the Christian
peoples, beside which the mere heathendom of the West Coast
nigger is clean and restrained. It led me a long distance into myself.

Yet really devoted missionaries he could respect, as he did the
Reverend Justus in 'The Judgment of Dungara', and he seems
to have felt a more sympathetic quality in Roman Catholics.
Father Victor in *Kim* partly understands the Lama, and though
Bennett believed that between him and Father Victor there
was "an unbridgeable gulf . . . it was noticeable that whenever
the Church of England dealt with a human problem she was
very likely to call in the Church of Rome".[1] Again, in 'The
Record of Badalia Herodsfoot' it is the Catholics who do the
better work in the East End slum. His clearest justification of
the Roman Church as against Primitive Methodism is perhaps
Mulvaney's speech to Learoyd in 'On Greenhow Hill':

There's neither high nor low, nor broad nor deep, nor betwixt nor
between wid her, an' that's what I like. But mark you, she's no
manner av Church for a wake man, bekaze she takes the body and
the soul av him, onless he has his proper work to do.

Himself feeling the need for a religion, he had enormous
respect for religion as such, and sympathized deeply with any

[1] *Kim*, V.

attempt in the East to find one, whether Buddhist, Muslim,
Hindu, Sikh, or even Ghurka, as is abundantly shown, not
only in *Kim*, but in many stories told through the mouths of
Indians. Even the worship of Hanuman must be respected,
and in the horrifying story 'The Mark of the Beast', which he
himself describes with significant understatement, as "a rather
unpleasant story", the moral is "Don't trifle with the beliefs of
other people". He would have no mercy on the atheist, and
a terrible fate, in the form of a shattering nervous breakdown, overtook the blatant Aurelian McGoggin, whose creed,
derived from the reading of Comte and Spencer, "only proved
that men had no souls, and there was no God and no hereafter,
and that you must worry along somehow for the good of
humanity".

That did not suffice Kipling: 'worrying along' had no
attractions for him. But where was he to find support? In a
monastery called 'The Chubára of Dhunni Bhagat', where
"Mahomedan, Sikh and Hindu mixed equally under the trees",
all of them old men, Kipling comments, "when man has come
to the turnstiles of Night all the creeds in the world seem to
him wonderfully alike and colourless".[1] At all events, Kipling,
unlike Aurelian McGoggin, was certain that men had souls:
he believed, therefore, that there must be something that
directed them, an Immanent Will, his feeling of this leading
him almost, if not quite, to a sense of predestination. His
autobiographical sketch opens with the words: "Looking back
from this my seventieth year, it seems to me that every card in
my working life has been dealt me in such a manner that I
had but to play it as it came." His ship's engineer, McAndrew
(but he was a Calvinist), felt a more compelling fate as he sung
his hymn:

Lord, Thou hast made this world below the shadow of a dream,
An', taught by time, I tak' it so—exceptin' always Steam.
From coupler-flange to spindle-guide I see Thy Hand, O God—
Predestination in the stride o' yon connectin' rod.

The idea is firmly stated in the poem that heads 'To be Filed
for Reference':

[1] Preface to *Life's Handicap*.

> By the Hoof of the Wild Goat up-tossed
> From the Cliff where She lay in the Sun,
> > Fell the Stone
> To the Tarn where the daylight is lost;
> So She fell from the light of the Sun
> > And alone!
>
> Now the fall was ordained from the first,
> With the Goat and the Cliff and the Tarn,
> > But the Stone
> Knows only Her life is accursed,
> As She sinks in the depths of the Tarn,
> > And alone. . . .

But that, written in 1886, seemed a little too rigidly Calvinistic for Kipling's growing apprehension; and some six years later, in 'The Answer', when a rose in tatters on the garden path murmuring asked why her stem alone of all the bush had been snapped, to her contentment received the reply that it was all willed at the Creation: and "He who questioned why the flower fell", on hearing the answer, "Clutched hold of God, and saved his soul from Hell."

With this sense of predestination went the 'knowledge', to call it so, that everything must come in its own good time. It is no use hurrying the Divine Purpose, and efforts at premature progress will be 'aborted'. Thus the Elizabethan seaman in 'Simple Simon' was unable to put into effect his idea of iron ships: and in 'The Eye of Allah' the microscope had to be destroyed, since, coming too soon "It will be but the mother of more death, more torture [was Kipling thinking of vivisection?], more division, and greater darkness in this dark age." For as the poem 'Untimely' which ushers in the story declares, "Heaven delivers on earth the Hour that cannot be thwarted", a point emphasized in the Horace Ode 31, Bk. V, which rounds off the tale. Virgil prophesied

> Change upon all the Eternal Gods had made
> > And on the Gods alike—
> Fated as dawn but, as the dawn, delayed
> > Till the just hour should strike—

But earlier Kipling had given a still broader, even more all-embracing vision. In 'The Bridge-Builders', the latter part of which constitutes one of the earliest of his Fables, we take part in a *punchayet*, or gathering, of the Indian gods, and are asked to regard the Immanent Will not so much as a directing Being as an enormous process. This conclave regards a thousand ages in the sight of man to be but as yesterday in the immense scale of things. The brevity of human experience is rammed home. The Ganges, together with some of the other gods, is enraged at the insult being offered to the river by the bridge being built over it; but the Buck asks:

'How long has this evil been?'
'Three years, as men count years,' said the Mugger.
'Does Mother Gunga die, then, in a year, that she is so anxious to see vengeance now? The deep sea was where she runs but yesterday, and tomorrow the sea shall cover her again as the Gods count that which men call time. Can any say that their bridge endures till to-morrow?

Ganesh of Good Luck,[1] the Elephant God, declares that all man's constructive efforts are "but the shifting of a little dirt. Let the dirt dig in the dirt if it pleases the dirt". It is all ephemeral. The gods themselves, if they do not change, at least get new names. Once more it is the Buck who states the case;

'Ye know the Riddle of the Gods. When Brahm ceases to dream the Heavens and the Hells and the Earth disappear. Be content. Brahm dreams still. The dreams come and go, and the nature of the dreams changes, but Brahm still dreams. . . . The Gods change, beloved—all save One.

This sense, though now more within the limits of common human imagination, remained with Kipling; and in 1924, in Horace, Ode 22, Bk. V he wrote:

Of earth-constricting wars,
Of Princes passed in chains,
Of deeds out-shining stars,
No word or voice remains.

[1] Whose symbol, the Swastika, also according to Lockwood Kipling, "the cross-fylfot of our western heraldry and the hermetic cross of Freemasonry", Kipling took for his symbol together with the elephant head, renouncing it only when Hitler befouled it.

Yet furthest times receive
And to fresh praise restore,
Mere flutes that breathe at eve[1]
Mere seaweed on the shore. . . .

Glazed snow beneath the moon;
The surge of storm-bowed trees—
The Caesars perished soon,
And Rome Herself: But these

Endure while Empires fall
And Gods for Gods make room.
Which greater God than all
Imposed the amazing doom?

('The Survival')

What greater God? That is the final riddle; to say that
Brahm dreams, and that all is a dream in the mind of Brahm is
not enough. But man is not fated to know the answer. Kipling
seems to have felt this in his very early years, but possibly the
feeling was reinforced by what he must certainly have read in
Rider Haggard's *She*, published early in 1887:

. . . the mind wearies easily when it strives to grapple with the Infinite, and to trace the footsteps of the Almighty, as He strides from
sphere to sphere, or deduce His purpose from His Works. Such things
are not for us to know. Knowledge is to the strong, and we are weak.
Too much wisdom would perchance blind our imperfect sight, and
too much strength would make us drunk, and overweight our feeble
reason till it fell, and we were drowned in the depths of our own
vanity.

In 1893 it was 'The True Romance' that was

A veil to draw 'twixt God His Law
And Man's infirmity,

and in the same year 'The Prayer of Miriam Cohen' contains
almost the identical words as she begs for

A veil 'twixt us and Thee, dread Lord[2]
A veil 'twixt us and Thee:
Lest we should hear too clear, too clear,
And unto madness see!

[1] *Def. Ed.*: 'Mere breaths of flutes at eve'.
[2] *Def. Ed.*: 'good Lord'.

C

We shall never see so far, as we learn from 'The Finest Story in the World'. When the narrator is discussing metempsychosis in relation to the stories Charlie Mears tells of his previous existences, Grish Chunder says: "the door is shut . . . *if* he spoke it would mean that all this world would end now—*instanto*—fall down on your head. These things are not allowed, you know. As I said, the door is shut". In his Rectorial Address at St. Andrews in October 1923,[1] Kipling told his audience, "There seems to be an unscientific objection on the part of the First Cause against being inquired of": and still later in 'Unprofessional', when it is asked "What do you suppose is the good of research?" the answer is: "God knows. Only—only it looks—sometimes—as if He were going to tell." But He does not tell, for it is not good for man that he should know.

"All sensible men have the same religion; but what that religion is no sensible man ever tells." Kipling quotes without acknowledgement Shaftesbury's barbed Achitophel-like jest;[2] but for all its indetermination his religion was of importance to him. He believed, or held a passionate hope amounting to belief, that there was indeed a hereafter. More than once he quotes the verse I Corinthians xv. 32: "If after the manner of men I have fought with beasts at Ephesus, what advantageth it me, if the dead rise not?" In 'They', the narrator tries to get in touch with his dead child, but it would be wrong for him to do so: he must not know. Yet there is a hope that somehow God allows man to cling to him, and he refers more than once to the woman of Tekoah in II Samuel xiv, who said that God doth "devise means, that his banished be not expelled from him"; and he makes this into verse in 'The Rabbi's Song' at the end of *Actions and Reactions*:

> Our lives, our tears, as water,
>   Are spilled upon the ground;
> God giveth no man quarter,
>   Yet God a means hath found,
> Though Faith and Hope have vanished,
>   And even Love grows dim—
> A means whereby His banished
>   Be not expelled from him.

[1] *A Book of Words*, XXIV.   [2] *Letters of Travel*, 'Dead Kings'.

There is one widely disseminated 'superstition', as some would wish to call it, that haunted Kipling from time to time. It is that of 'influences' which pervade the universe, and have something to do with its structure, we also being part of that structure. He first toyed with the idea—that would seem the right term—in the story 'Wireless' (radio was then in its exciting infancy) where the consumptive apothecary writes off his own bat, specifically not from memory, portions of Keats's 'St. Agnes's Eve'. 'How? How?' the agonized narrator asks: like causes must produce like results seems an inadequate answer. In that tale occurs the name of Nicolas Culpeper, the historical personage who is the main figure of 'A Doctor of Medicine' in which he drives the plague out of a village. It was done, actually, by the killing of the over-abundant rats, but Culpeper believed it to have come about through planetary influences: "Mars killed the rats because he hated the Moon", as Una put it, rather simplifying the idea. This seized hold of Kipling's imagination; and the form it took he expressed in the poem which precedes the story, 'An Astrologer's Song', set, with a little fitting in, to the tune of 'O worship the King/ All glorious above'. The first two stanzas run:

> To the Heavens above us
> O look and behold
> The Planets that love us
> All harnessed in gold!
> *What chariots, what horses,*
> *Against us shall bide*
> *While the Stars in their courses*
> *Do fight on our side?*

> All thought, all desires
> That are under the sun,
> Are one with their fires,
> As we also are one;
> All matter, all spirit,
> All fashion, all frame,
> Receive and inherit
> Their strength from the same.

It is, therefore, not surprising that when, in November 1928, he gave an after-dinner speech to The Royal Society of Medicine, he called it 'Healing by the Stars',[1] there arguing that

Nicolas Culpeper, were he with us now, would find that the essential unity of creation is admitted insofar forth as we have plumbed infinity; and that man, Culpeper's epitome of all, is himself a universe of universes, each universe ordered—negatively and positively—by sympathy and antipathy—on the same lines as hold the stars in their courses.

He wove this into 'Unprofessional' written some two years later. The men there—two of them are doctors—take out tissues from patients who have been operated upon, and observe them for what they call 'tides' (this might seem to connect with the idea of the 'opsonic index' that Shaw propagated). Mice, on which experiments are being made—the doctors are studying especially cancer, of which Kipling seems to have had a particular horror—have their cages hung on various compass-bearings. This, from one point of view, is age-old lore. When the Sahiba and her servant massaged Kim in his illness, they laid him "East and West, that the mysterious earth-currents which thrill the clay of our bodies might help and not hinder".[2] That idea Kipling may have got in India, but it seems to be known to the wise old women in our own countryside. "It may be crazy mad"; but as Frost, the ex-naval rating who helps in the research comments grinning: "That's what the Admiralty said at first about steam in the Navy." The whole story, visioning "this swab of culture which we call our world" is a plea for the imagination, since "We can't tell on what system this dam' dynamo of our universe is wound," as one of the characters remarks. But it is perhaps significant that the poem at the end of the story harks back, and reinforces, 'The Astrologer's Song'. Here 'Crystal-eyed Sages of Ionia'

> . . . found one Breath in all things,
>   That blows all things between.
> They proved one Matter in all things—
>   Eternal, changeless, unseen;
> 'That the heart of the Matter was single
>   Till the Breath should bid it bring forth. . . .'

[1] *A Book of Words*. Sussex Edition. Vol. XXV. Not in 1928 Edition.
[2] *Kim*, XXV.

Those, it might be said, were Kipling s religious musings—
one can hardly say beliefs. But they were basic. And besides
these there were others which might be called, rather, ideas,
intellectually arrived at, as in the matter of ghosts such as we
find in early stories—'The Phantom Rickshaw' and 'By Word
of Mouth'; or the mysterious and significant sharing of dreams
we read of in 'The Brushwood Boy' from his early middle
period, followed by curious psychic relationships as in 'The
Dog Hervey' of a slightly later period, and, towards the end,
the Token in 'The Wish House'. Or again there are the
mysteries about the nature of material things, of cold-iron for
example, or the sense that the Gods sell anything—at a price,
as we find it phrased in *A Book of Words* and other places, and
illustrated in 'The Knife and the Naked Chalk'. All such
matters, however, might be regarded as story-tellers' material,
rather than truths that had to be imparted. He himself provides
a warning on this point. "I am in no way 'psychic' ", he declared, perhaps too emphatically, in *Something of Myself* (VIII):
"I have seen too much evil and sorrow and wreck of good minds
on the road to En-dor to take one step along that perilous
track," and he blows up the idea of exotic fashionable forms
of 'spiritualism' in the comic story 'The Sending of Dana Da'.
He may, however, have been tempted at the time of his greatest
griefs, for "The road to En-dor is easy to tread," as he writes
in the poem 'En-dor'. Not only had his father once explained
to him that the once notorious Madame Blavatsky was "one
of the most unscrupulous impostors he had ever met" but the
Pioneer had been "devastated by Theosophy",[1] and his sister
Trix had had sad experiences. He could, perhaps, a little
unwillingly admit, that

> . . . nothing has changed of the sorrow in store
> For such as go down on the road to En-dor.

§3. BASIC INTUITIONS

Apart from this groping after a faith which gave Kipling his
indeterminate religion, there were certain strongly felt—we

---

[1] *Something of Myself*, III.

might say experienced—notions which persisted throughout his life, certain of them more vividly felt in his early days, though never lost: others which, embryonic when he was young, became dominant in his later years. They are fundamental, for though always alert to the inventions and discoveries of his day, which are largely the product of the intellect, yet, as André Maurois said, he had "a permanent, natural contact with the oldest and deepest layers of human consciousness". That is one of the reasons, maybe the main reason, why he dealt so often with the enduring pains and problems of humanity, out of which all religion, all poetry, must arise. These intuitions are seldom markedly the *main* theme of a story, though all Kipling's stories have some idea behind them; they are not, except possibly some early ones, mere anecdotes—but the intuitions are part of the colouring, a thread woven into the main fabric—or 'layers' as he might have preferred to have it phrased, which went to make the whole.

One of the earliest of the recurrent recognitions about life, is that of the loneliness of man. 'Without Benefit of Clergy', so soon as 1890, contains the phrase; "the human soul is a very lonely thing, and when it is ready to go away, hides itself in a misty borderland, where the living may not follow". 'The Courting of Dinah Shadd' of the same year ends with the narrator telling us that, "When I woke I saw Mulvaney, lonely as Prometheus on his rock, with I know not what vultures tearing his liver." When Kipling went back to India he found innumerable examples of loneliness. In 'At the End of the Passage' we meet four men who were "lonely folk who understood the dread meaning of loneliness". Mottram "had ridden thirty and railed one hundred miles from his lonely post in the desert". Lowndes "had come as far": Spurstow "had left a cholera-stricken camp of coolies". Hummil, the host, also lived alone,

and received his friends thus every Sunday if they could come in. When one of them failed to appear, he would send a telegram to his last address, in order that he might know whether the defaulter were dead or alive. There are very many places in the East where it is not good or kind to let your acquaintances drop out of sight even for one short week.

It was loneliness, as much as the infernal streakiness of the tides that drove to madness Dowse, the lighthouse-keeper in 'A Disturber of Traffic', a story written in 1891. In 'The Judgment of Dungara', which came out as early as 1888, we read:

> Do you know what life at a mission outpost means? Try to imagine a loneliness exceeding that of the smallest station to which Government has ever sent you—isolation that weighs upon the waking eyelids and drives you by force headlong into the labours of the day. There is no post, there is no one of your own colour to speak to, there are no roads: there is, indeed, food to keep you alive, but it is not pleasant to eat: and whatever of good or beauty or interest there is in your life, must come from yourself and the grace that may be planted in you.

"The smallest station." We get an idea of what even this can mean from the description in 'A Wayside Comedy'—written in the same year—of "the station of Kashima, which Fate and the Government of India" have turned into a prison. The nearest other station is a hundred and forty-three miles away, one which the people of Kashima never visit, though it contains at least twelve English people. The story of which this is the frame gives the sense of a factually realized *huis-clos*.

Company itself, however, does not abolish loneliness—after all, Mulvaney was companioned enough. We learn this truth *passim* in *The Light that Failed* (1891), specifically when Dick Heldar asks Torpenhow, "Who's the man that says we are all islands shouting to each other across seas of misunderstanding?"[1] and Torpenhow answers, "Well, he's right, whoever he is. ..." The idea does not noticeably recur in the later stories, though it is often implicit. Nevertheless, it is finally, definitely stated in his Rectorial Address at St. Andrews, where he told his hearers that Man was "the loneliest of created beings". That, it may be, is the basis of his sense of man's individuality— even, it is possible, of his own—an individuality which in each case has to contend with an abysmal sense of individual nothingness.

There is an equally important allied theme which runs through all Kipling's work, 'the horror of great darkness'

[1] Had Kipling in mind Thackeray's "You and I are but a part of infinite isolations, with some fellow islands more or less near to us"? *Pendennis*, Chapter XVI.

which he had himself encountered at the age of twenty, and which he rightly calls a 'pivot' experience:

> It happened one hot-weather evening, in '86 or thereabouts, when I felt that I had come to the edge of all endurance. As I entered my empty house in the dusk there was no more in me except the horror of a great darkness, that I must have been fighting for some days. I came through that darkness alive, but how I do not know.[1]

His 'salvation' as he put it, was Walter Besant's *All in a Garden Fair*, which became to him "a revelation, a hope and strength". Such an experience, however, may be engulfing. Hummil, in 'At the End of the Passage' (an appropriate title), does not 'come through'. His Indian servant thus diagnoses the cause of his death: "In my poor opinion, this that was my master has descended into the Dark Places, and there has been caught because he was not able to escape with sufficient speed." In 1907, Kipling told a young audience at McGill University: "There is a certain state into which the soul of a young man sometimes descends—a horror of desolation, abandonment, and realized worthlessness, which is one of the most real of the hells in which we are compelled to walk."[2] The most vivid description occurs in 'The House Surgeon', where as part of a long passage, the narrator speaks of how "my amazed and angry soul dropped gulf by gulf into that horror of great darkness which is spoken of in the Bible . . . despair upon despair, misery upon misery, fear after fear . . ." For the purposes of fiction that overwhelming sense was caused by the wronged spirit of a woman: but Kipling himself had felt a "brooding Spirit of deep, deep Despondency" in a house he had lived in.[3] He recognized this as a state that might be brought about by some definite physical or psychological lesion, as happens with the people of 'In the Same Boat', where it was prenatal: or with Marden in 'The Woman in His Life', where it was the result of war strain. This is told in his last volume, *Limits and Renewals*, where also we read in the final Fable, 'Uncovenanted Mercies', that even with Satan "the glare of the halo he

---

[1] *Something of Myself*, III.
[2] *A Book of Words*, III.
[3] *Something of Myself*, V.

wore in His Own Place fought against the Horror of Great Darkness".

Looking at the stories in which these states of being are described, we see that many of them come about from too much strain imposed upon people, 'the breaking strain'. In *She*, Rider Haggard had written ". . . every man, like every rope, hath its breaking strain". Whether or not Kipling got the phrase or the idea from this it is hard to say, since in April of that year he had written in 'A Bank Fraud' that the Directors of a bank "had tested Reggie up to a fairly severe breaking strain". The notion is introduced in many of his tales, for he seems always to have been interested in how much a man could stand without breaking down: and in 1924, addressing an audience at the Rhodes dinner,[1] he remarked that certain things about a man indicate "his potential resistance under breaking strain". How important the notion was to him appears from his very late (1935) poem, 'Hymn of Breaking Strain':

> The careful text-books measure
> (Let all who build beware!)
> The load, the shock, the pressure
> Material can bear.
> So, when the buckled girder
> Lets down the grinding span,
> The blame of loss, or murder,
> Is laid upon the man.
> *Not on the Stuff—the Man!*
>
> But, in our daily dealing
> With stone and steel, we find
> The Gods have no such feeling
> Of justice toward mankind.
> To no set gauge they make us,—
> For no laid course prepare—
> And presently o'ertake us
> With loads we cannot bear:
> *Too merciless to bear.*

But, since he did not encourage whining, the poem tells us at the end that if a man serves 'the veiled and secret Power', he

[1] *A Book of Words*, XXVI.

> In spite of being broken,
> *Because of being broken,*
> *May rise and build anew.*
> *Stand up and build anew!*

In 'Uncovenanted Mercies', where, as in 'On the Gate' the Order Above reflects the Order Below, the souls of men and women are 'reconditioned' for service as guardian angels, the final stage of the process being, as Satan put it, "a full test for Ultimate Breaking Strain".

For these states of breakdown or blackness, the personal relation, the sympathy of even the closest friends is of no avail, as he stresses in his poem 'The Comforters' which goes with the tale of 'The Dog Hervey'—though there may be exceptions if the comforter also has descended into the Dark Places:

> Until thy feet have trod the Road
>   Advise not wayside folk,
> Nor till thy back has borne the Load
>   Break in upon the broke.

> Chase not with undesired largesse
>   Of sympathy the heart
> Which, knowing her own bitterness,
>   Presumes to dwell apart. . . .

> E'en from good words thyself refrain,
>   And tremblingly admit
> There is no anodyne for pain
>   Except the shock of it.

> So, when thine own dark hour shall fall,
>   Unchallenged canst thou say:
> "I never worried *you* at all,
>   For God's sake go away!"

Yet there *are* anodynes for such dark hours, apart from "the shock of it", for unless there were man could not live at all. And this is part of Kipling's complexity. He was a man who, it is clear, was bitterly aware of 'the accepted hells beneath', to use the phrase Saintsbury borrowed from Whitman when discussing Swift. Rider Haggard tells us that once when he was talking with Kipling "I happened to remark that I thought this was one of the hells. He replied that he did not *think*, he was *certain* of it."[1] But in spite of such a feeling, he had an extraordinary, even extravagant delight in nature, in life, in the doings of mankind in "God's great, happy, inattentive world", as he put it in *Letters of Travel*;[2] and it is upon these two seemingly incompatible foundations that he built the philosophy of life which makes of his stories so shining and so moving a pattern.

[1] *Cohen*, p. 203.
[2] IV, 'Up the River'.

CHAPTER II

Kipling's Philosophy for Living

§1. WORK AND DEVOTION

Arjuna. O Krishna, thou speakest in paradoxes, for first
thou dost praise renunciation, and then praisest thou the
right performance of actions. Of these two, which is the
better? Tell me clearly and with certainty.

Krishna. Verily I say unto thee, that of the two the performance of service is preferable to the renunciation of
action.

Bhagavad Gita, V

Kim put the same question to the Lama: "Then all Doing is
evil?" to which the Lama replied: "To abstain from action
is well—except to acquire merit."[1] But to live the life of detached contemplation is given to very few, and is such a life
meritorious? For as Krishna went on to tell Arjuna: "Nobody
can become perfect by merely ceasing to act. In fact nobody
can ever rest from his activity [which includes mental activity]
even for a moment. All are helplessly forced to act, by the
gunas." Kipling was, of course, familiar with the religious
literature of India, but he must have known from the first
that a life of renunciation was not for him, that some sort of
action was imperative for him. Not that he held any brief for
what he called 'indecent restlessness'; and as to the battle of
life 'a detestable phrase',[2] he stated that "The God who sees
us all die knows that there is far too much of that battle."[3] Yet
he felt in his bones that action must be purposeful. It was of
no use to feel as the child Maisie did in *The Light that Failed*
when she said to Dick Heldar, "Let's find things to do and forget
things," though, and here is another contradiction, it is in
doing things that the sense of loneliness and the horror of great

[1] *Kim,* XII.   [2] *A Book of Words,* III.
[3] *Letters of Travel,* 'On One Side Only'.

darkness can be blotted out. As the Services and Loves sing in 'The Supports', the poem which succeeds 'On the Gate':

Heart may fail, and Strength outwear, and Purpose turn to Loathing,
But the everyday affair of business, meals, and clothing,
Builds a bulkhead 'twixt Despair and the Edge of Nothing.

As Mr. Alan Sandison has recently written, Kipling was acutely conscious of "the wider Necessity which has decreed that man shall live forever at the edge of the pit, snatching his identity from the limbo of non-existence which lies at his feet".[1] Of this the very early 'The Strange Ride of Morrowbie Jukes' is, possibly, a gruesome symbol. The phrase springs to mind again, "First a man must suffer, then he must learn his work, and the self-respect that that knowledge brings." 'Work'—that is the key word!

In his maturer years, when he was facing his blindness, Dick Heldar came to the conclusion that "It is better to remain alone and suffer only the misery of being alone, so long as it is possible to find distraction in daily work:[2] and in 1923 Kipling told the Royal College of Surgeons that "There is no anaesthesia so complete as man's absorption in his own job."[3] But it was more than distraction or anaesthesia that Kipling thought of; it was the purposeful direction of the work. So the Abbot in 'The Eye of Allah' said to John of Burgos, who was smitten with grief for the death in childbirth of the mistress whom he loved, "For the pain of the soul there is, outside God's Grace, but one drug; and that is a man's craft, learning, or other helpful motion of his own mind." But it is more than a drug, for as John, who was an illuminator, had said earlier, "if the shape of anything be worth man's thought to picture to man, it's worth his best thought". Work can even, if the work be worth while, rid a man of the thought of death. So the Bull in 'Children of the Zodiac', who was to suffer death from the Scorpion, tells Leo: "You cannot pull a plough . . . I can, and that prevents me from thinking of the Scorpion." It may even redeem a man from himself, as we learn from the very late tale 'Dayspring Mishandled', where Castorley, the snobbishly

---

[1] *Kipling's Mind and Art*, p. 160.
[2] *The Light that Failed*, XIV.   [3] *A Book of Words*, XXIII.

ambitious man, "could break from his obsession, and prove how a man's work will try to save the soul of him".

But it is not given to everyone to have a craftsman's trade over which he can muse, and "Godlike stand with God again". Dovetailed with work is a man's devotion to something outside himself, bigger than he is, which is not exactly his own job, but one which his fellow-beings have (as a man might put it to himself) demanded of him. This might be called devotion to an outside cause. This we get again and again throughout Kipling's writings, from as early as the tale 'Only a Subaltern', where Bobby Wick's devotion to his men brings him to death from cholera—a rather sentimental tale if you like; Kipling could be sentimental. But then, sentimentality is only a name for an emotion which you don't happen to share, and here Kipling's emotion seems justified. Or there is 'William the Conqueror', where devotion to starving Indian children brings a happier ending. Or again there is Mrs. McKenna, 'Ould Pummeloe' of 'The Daughter of the Regiment'. In 'The Judgment of Dungara', where Justus Krenk and his wife endure all possible loneliness in their devotion to missionary work, we read that the reports about them are silent,

because heroism, failure, doubt, despair, and self-abnegation on the part of mere cultured white men are things of no weight compared with the saving of one half-human soul from a fantastic faith in wood-spirits, goblins of the rock, and river-fiends.

In the same way, the four men in 'At the End of the Passage' established their self-respect through giving themselves wholly to their duties.

Surrendering oneself wholly to a job done for a general cause may also assuage immediate sorrow. In the deeply-felt poem, 'A Recantation', we are told of 'Lyde of the Music Halls', a favourite with the poet's son who had recently died in the war, his 'pin-up girl' as we would say, whom he would come to see whenever he was on leave, that

> Never more rampant rose the Hall
> At thy audacious line
> Than when the news came in from Gaul
> Thy son had—followed mine.

> But thou didst hide it in thy breast
> And, capering, took the brunt
> Of blaze and blare, and launched the jest
> That swept next week the Front

Those who serve mankind find in their devotion an anodyne, "though vultures rend their soul" as the poem goes on to state. But with Kipling, as in life, it is difficult, if not impossible, to distinguish between mere slogging work done as such, devotion to a job which entails a cause, or a craft which takes the whole of a man. One of the most striking and moving expressions of this may be found in the epitaph to the Boer general, Joubert:

> With those that bred, with those that loosed the strife
> He had no part whose hands were clear of gain;
> But subtle, strong, and stubborn, gave his life
> To a lost cause, and knew the gift was vain.

Much, however, of what is to be said as regards devotion will be found when Imperialism is discussed, since 'Imperialism' being a Thing (to use the word of the runes on Weland's sword) beyond mere personal incitement, involves the something greater than self which is, apart from the gift of oneself to another, the only real object of what can be called devotion.

§2. LAUGHTER

> Mirth enlargeth the heart, and disperseth much natural heat with the blood, of which it sendeth a good portion to the face, especially if the mirth be so great that it stirreth a man to laughter. Mirth, I say, maketh the forehead smooth and clear, causeth the eyes to glister, and the cheeks to become ruddy.
> William Vaughan, *Naturall and Artificial Directions for Health.* 1600

> That little twist of brain would ring a chime
> Of whence it came and what it caused, to start
> Thunders of laughter, clearing air and heart.
> George Meredith, *The Spirit of Shakespeare*, 2

> Great Pan! How close we are to that rare old fantasy, that the crack of doom will be a universal shout of laughter.
> 'Hugh McDiarmid', of John Davidson

In *Something of Myself* Kipling tells of how at bedtime the children at the Burne-Jones home would in the evening go to the top landing and "hang over the stairs and listen to the loveliest sound in the world—deep-voiced men laughing together over dinner".[1] Laughter for Kipling was an essential element for living, as an anodyne equal in value with work; but we may well sometimes feel that the laughter with him is excessive. Too often we read of men clinging helplessly to lamp-posts or each other, or rolling incapacitated by the roadside. Not that this sort of laughter is altogether rare. Balfour, the sober statesman, seems to have been given to it. He was full of gaiety, and Mary Gladstone in her journal often speaks of Balfour "laughing immoderately", or of him with his brothers and sister being "overpowered by laughter as usual". With Kipling, such laughter is a privilege almost exclusively reserved for men, and we read in 'A Sea Dog' of the men "who laughed those gross laughs women find so incomprehensible". It might seem that among women only Mrs. Godfrey in 'The Dog Hervey' was allowed it, when she and the narrator "were clinging to each other for support", though the native villagers in 'Little Foxes', "women, mothers and virgins, shrilled shriek upon mounting shriek, and slapped their thighs as it might have been the roll of musketry". Moreover it might seem that if Beaumarchais laughed lest he should weep, so Kipling seemed to roar with laughter lest he should despair.

Laughter, for Kipling was a prime human attribute, as we can judge from two of his Fables. In the earliest one (1891), 'Children of the Zodiac', when Leo and the Girl first came to the earth, they "wondered . . . why people shouted Ha! ha! ha! for no cause". It was only when they became aware that some day they would have to die, being of the House of Cancer, that they decided

never to leave each other for an instant, and when they had come to their decision they looked back at the darkness of the House of Cancer high above their heads, and with their arms round each other's necks laughed, 'Ha! ha! ha!' exactly as the children of men laughed. And that was the first time in their lives that they had ever laughed.

[1] *Something of Myself*, I.

Later the Girl told Leo, "We must learn to laugh, Leo. We have laughed once already." And Leo, when he became the poet, the singer, "made the people laugh till they could laugh no more". The two used to go down to the villagers, who "in the evening gave them food and invited them to dance on the grass, where everybody laughed through mere joy of being able to dance". Laughter to ward off the fear of death has become that of delight in life. In the later Fable, 'The Enemies to Each Other' of 1924, we read that Adam and Eve had "ceased to laugh and are made even with the ox and the camel". So also the four Archangels of 'The Legend of Mirth' had to learn to laugh, being taught by the Seraph, who found them sickened by doubt as to whether they had done their best. He led them on

> Until—the Gates of Laughter opened wide—
> The Four, with that bland Seraph at their side,
> While they recalled, compared, and amplified,
> In utter mirth forgot both Zeal and Pride! . . .

There are, then, many varieties of laughter—the one every young person knows, that of the joy in living, as with the villagers who danced with Leo and the Girl; of companionship and reminiscence, as we get, say, in the Stalky story 'Slaves of the Lamp II': there is also sardonic or ironic laughter, as we find in the bitter story 'In the Pride of His Youth', where the unlucky Dicky Hatt, after slaving away to get passage money for his wife and child to join him in India, hears, first of the death of his child, then of the desertion of his wife, just as he is given a rise in salary which would allow him to do what he has been toiling for so long. When he was told of it, "Dicky burst into a roar of laughter—laughter he could not check— nasty, jangling merriment that seemed as if it would go on for ever." There is the lighter laughter of social comedy we get in many of the early stories, such as those concerned with Simla and Mrs. Hauksbee. Or there is the laughter of light revenge, as in 'Pig' to be treated of later, and 'Steam Tactics' where the too slick-and-sly policeman, out to catch motorists exceeding the speed limit, is, to the utter confusion of his mind, deposited far from home in a private zoo, among kangaroos.

D

In other tales there is the laughter of the mob, destructive not healing laughter, as in 'The Village that Voted the Earth was Flat', or 'Little Foxes', the mob in the first instance being the House of Commons, in the second the happy inhabitants of a district in 'Ethiopia'. Laughter can also be a healer, as will be touched upon in the next section. Again and again we find in various stories moments of tension being relieved by laughter— even lasting hatred as in 'The Wrong Thing', where Benedetto found "the old crust of hatred around his heart was broken up and carried away by laughter". These might be covered by the idea of laughter as enlarged upon by William Vaughan and Meredith.

But what distinguished Kipling is the laughter as described by John Davidson, which has been named as 'cosmic mirth' by Professor C. A. Bodelsen,[1] and which he agrees with Dr. Tompkins to call 'orgiastic'. The latter reminds us of Sir Arthur Grimble's account of the Gilbert Islanders, "convulsed by whole villages, covering the beach or the speech-house floor with their relaxed and palpitating brown bodies" at an angry old woman's vituperations.[2] His own utterances, naturally, provide the clearest clue as to what this kind of laughter meant to him; and as so often in Kipling (and, indeed, in most who write both prose and poetry), he expresses it best in verse. There are three poems especially which are revelatory, the completest, from one point of view being 'The Necessitarian'—a title which strangely links up with his predestinarian views— and goes with the Story 'Steam Tactics':

> I know not in whose hands are laid
>   To empty upon earth
> From unsuspected ambuscade
>   The very Urns of Mirth:

> Who bids the Heavenly Lark arise
>   And cheer our solemn round—
> The Jest beheld with streaming eyes
>   And grovellings on the ground;

[1] *Bodelsen*, Chapter I.
[2] *Tompkins*, p. 38.

Who joins the flats of Time and Chance
  Behind the prey preferred,
And thrones on Shrieking Circumstance
  The Sacredly Absurd.

Till Laughter, voiceless through excess,
  Waves mute appeal and sore,
Above the midriff's deep distress,
  For breath to laugh once more.

No creed hath dared to hail him Lord,
  No raptured choirs proclaim,
And Nature's strenuous Overword
  Hath nowhere breathed his name.[1]

Yet, may it be,[2] on wayside jape,
  The selfsame Power bestows
The selfsame power as went to shape
  His Planet or His Rose.

Every word in this poem, every hypostization, every change in
the definitive text, as in all Kipling's poems must be carefully
pondered, as being rigorously chosen and deftly placed. Much
is self-evident—as the Urns of Mirth; much may be illustrated
from the tales, as when, in 'My Sunday at Home', "I waked
the holy calm of the evening every step of that way, with shouts
and yells, casting myself down in the flank of the good green
hedge when I was too weak to stand." Or in 'The Vortex',
"I prostrated myself before Allah in that mirth which is more
truly labour than any prayer." The Absurd is Sacredly so;
Nature's strenuous Overword gave the same importance to
laughter as to His Planet or His Rose. In 'To the Companions',
the God Himself of Mirth contrives the "glorious, unforgotten
innocent enormities". Appended to 'Aunt Ellen', the most
purely farcical of all Kipling's tales, the poem 'The Playmate'
speaks of when

> . . . all an earnest, baffled Earth
>   Blunders and trips to make us mirth;

[1] *Def. Ed.*: 'His Name'.
[2] *Def. Ed.*: 'Yet, it must be,'.

> Where, from the trivial flux of Things
> Rise unconceived miscarryings,
> Outrageous but immortal. . . .

The Goddess, as she may be called, who produces this out-of-order state of affairs, with their accompanying effects, is not Folly:

> She is not Wisdom, but, maybe,
> Wiser than all the Norns[1] is She:
> And more than Wisdom, I prefer
> To wait on Her,—to wait on Her!

To wait also in the other sense of the term. For this great release from the weight of responsibility, of conforming to the order of the earnest Earth, cannot be brought about by the will; it is a grace which comes upon a man when he lets things be. "I knew," we read in 'My Sunday at Home', "that so long as a man trusts himself to the current of Circumstance, reaching out for and rejecting nothing that comes his way, no harm can overtake him. It is the contriver, the schemer, who is caught by the law, and never the philosopher."

In the most improbable of the stories, those which involve 'cosmic' laughter, the narrator is not so much an agent as one who lets thing be. The narrator's—or Kipling's—'demon', not to be confused with the Daemon we read of in *Something of Myself*—suggests acquiescence. In 'Their Lawful Occasions I' "the Demon of Pure Irresponsibility bade me lower myself from the edge of the wharf to the tea-tray plates of No. 267." In 'The Prophet and the Country' "I found myself (under the influence of the night and my Demon) denying all knowledge of the United States." In 'Aunt Ellen' the Demon is mentioned more than once, especially when "on the higher planes of [my soul] where thought merges into Intuition and Prophecy, my Demon of Irresponsibility sang:—'I am with you once more! Stand back and let me take charge. This night shall be also One of the Nights.' So I stood and waited, as I have before, on Chance and Circumstance which, accepted humbly, betray not the True Believer." So also in 'The House Surgeon', his 'demon of irresponsibility' made him create "the Staffordshire

---

[1] The female Fates recognized in Scandinavian mythology. *N.E.D.*

Moultries". It is noticeable that the Demon tends to appear at the time of the Dawn Wind, of which he speaks in many places, even to the extent of writing a poem upon it. He tells us in 'The Vortex': "To me, as I have often observed elsewhere [and was to do so again in *Something of Myself*], the hour of earliest dawn is fortunate, and the wind that runs before it has ever been my most comfortable counsellor"; he had done so earlier in 'Their Lawful Occasions': "To me that round wind which runs before the true day has ever been fortunate and of good omen."

It is evident that this sort of laughter is no mere negative release: it is a positive affirmation of one side of the Power that made his Planet and His Rose; it is, to quote Professor Bodelsen, "an escape from the bondage of time"; the miscarryings seem to be Nature's criticism of herself, a flouting of the usual order. Moreover, as we read in 'The Tree of Justice' it can counteract the horror of great darkness, and Rahere cheers, as he hopes, the dejected Hugh by telling him that "each man must have his black hour or where would be the merit of laughing?" Kipling as a youth and a young man was renowned for his gaiety, his enormous sense of fun in the usually accepted sense of the term; laughter was one of the necessary elements for living. M. Francis Léaud calculates that one-third of his tales and of his poems have laughter in them. In the earlier ones, more often, though not always, it is the lighter laughter that we are asked to join in with: it is more in the later ones, when the tragic experiences of his life had come upon him, that he asks us to partake of cosmic laughter; and it is to be noted that 'Aunt Ellen' did not appear until 1929, in the last of his collected volumes.

§3. COMPASSION

There are, as has been seen, certain themes that run through all Kipling's work, varying in the interest they provoked in him as he developed. Certainly the idea of pity, in the rather commonplace sense of being ordinarily sorry for someone, appears quite early; but as he grew older it became more frequent and more intense, and is better described by the word 'compassion', as implying something deeper, more emphatic as we might say. As early as *Plain Tales*, in 'Thrown Away' we get pity for The Boy who committed suicide because he had too much taken to heart a rebuke from his commanding officer: it is less acutely portrayed in other stories of the same volume, in, for instance, 'A Bank Fraud' and 'In the Pride of his Youth'. And when in 'A Matter of Fact' the deep-sea monster, torn up by an earthquake is writhing in agony, "we watched, the whole crew, stokers and all, in wonder and pity, but chiefly pity. The Thing was so helpless, and, save for his mate, so alone."

The theme, then, runs through many of the tales, but is perhaps most clearly stated in his three last Fables, beginning with 'The Enemies to Each Other' (1924). When the Archangel Jibrail [Gabriel] went to take from the earth the substances that would make Adam, the earth "shook and lamented and supplicated", and Jibrail being moved by the laments, refrained, as did the Archangel Michael. But the Archangel Azrael tore out the necessary sands and clays. When he was asked why he did not spare, he answered the Supreme Being: "Obedience (to Thee) was more obligatory than Pity (for it)." Whence it was ordained that Azrael should become the Angel of Death. And when the Soul unwillingly went through the agony of entering the body and the event was accomplished, "the Word came: '*My Compassion exceedeth My Wrath*' ". 'On the Gate' (1926) is entirely concerned with compassionate forgiveness for the mass of mankind, that they may enter Heaven rather than be consigned to the Lower Establishment (i.e. Hell), possibly under the ruling Q.M.A., that is, *quia multum amavit*; and we are insistently reminded of the saying of the wise woman of Tekoah when she declared that God "doth devise means that His banished be not expelled from Him". This is even taken to the utmost limit. At the end St. Peter is talking to Death—the Archangel Azrael of the earlier Fable—while they watch the overworked Cherubim and Seraphim going home. He asks:

'Aren't they human?'
'To whom do you say it?' Death answered, with something of a tired smile. 'I'm more than human. *I*'ve got to die some time or other. But all other created Beings—afterwards. . . .'

'*I* know,' said St. Peter softly. 'And that is why I love you, O Azrael.'

'Well, that's *that*—for me!' Death concluded as he rose. 'And yet—' he glanced towards the empty plain where the Lower Establishment had withdrawn with their prisoner. ' "Yet doth He devise means".'

'Uncovenanted Mercies' (which will be touched upon later), the last story in Kipling's final book, has embedded in it for motto a verse from Ecclesiastes iii. 21: "Who knoweth the spirit of man that goeth upward, and the spirit of the beast that goeth downward to the earth?" The phrase there which stands out, repeated and italicized, is "Even Evil itself shall pity".

The tale which most simply shows Kipling's sense of compassion is 'The Gardener', the last story in *Debits and Credits*, and the fact of its being the last indicates the emphasis that Kipling wished to place on it. Here, Helen Turrell, the heroine of the story, had an illegitimate son Michael, whom she passed off as, and who was publicly, if knowingly, accepted as her nephew. It is a fairly complex tale, as it involves also the hideous strain of never being able to tell the truth. Michael is killed in the war, and at the end of the story Helen visits the war cemetery where he is buried. She does not know where to find the grave. The story ends:

A man knelt down behind a line of headstones—evidently a gardener, for he was firming a young plant in the soft earth. She went towards him, her paper in her hand. He rose at her approach and without prelude or salutation asked: 'Who are you looking for?'

'Lieutenant Michael Turrell—my nephew,' said Helen slowly and word for word, as she had many thousand times in her life.

The man lifted his eyes and looked at her with infinite compassion before he turned from the fresh-sown grass toward the naked black crosses.

'Come with me,' he said, 'and I will show you where your son lies.'

When Helen left the Cemetery she turned for a last look. In the distance she saw the man bending over his young plants; and she went away, supposing him to be the gardener.

The story will not make its full impact on anyone who does not pick up the reference to the Fourth Gospel (St. John xx. 15), when Mary Magdalene went to the tomb to find the body of Jesus, and a man who was there spoke to her: but "She, supposing him to be the gardener . . .". It would seem that Kipling's hope of, if not faith in, infinite mercy, was one of the supports by the aid of which he lived. The last stanza of the poem 'The Burden' which rounds off the tale reads:

> One grave to me was given—
> To guard till Judgment Day—
> But God looked down from Heaven
> And rolled the Stone away!
> One day of all my years—
> One hour of that one day—
> His Angel saw my tears
> And rolled the Stone away!

If the death of a loved person produces the emotions which most need the anodyne of compassion, there are other situations which call for this—as the loss of love not through death; and of these also Kipling treats. One example must suffice, that of the Burmese girl in 'Georgie Porgie', here called Georgina, who has for some time been mistress, the devoted wife, even—except for the Church formality—of an Englishman. He is not a very honourable character, and sneaks off, rather than goes, home, promising Georgina that he will come back. When in England, however, he falls in love with a woman whom he marries—he had half intended to do this all the time—and brings her back with him, not to Burma, but to a station in India. Georgina hears where he is, but does not know that he is married; and, believing in her simplicity that she would be welcome to him, and once more govern his household, she pursues him to Sutrain. There an Englishman who knows the circumstances, and is himself rather in love with Georgie Porgie's wife, accidentally meets the abandoned mistress, and shows her her old 'husband' with his bride. Georgina does not interfere, but runs off into the dark.

The Bride and Bridegroom came out into the verandah after dinner, in order that the smoke of Georgie Porgie's cheroots might not hang in the new drawing-room curtains.

'What is that noise down there?' said the Bride. Both listened.
'Oh,' said Georgie Porgie, 'I suppose some brute of a hillman has
been beating his wife.'

'Beating—his—wife! How ghastly!' said the Bride. 'Fancy *your*
beating *me*! She slipped an arm round her husband's waist, and,
leaning her head against his shoulder, looked out across the cloud-
filled valley in deep content and security.

But it was Georgina crying, all by herself, down the hillside,
among the stones of the watercourse where the washermen wash the
clothes.

It is bitterly pitying, the choice of each word reinforcing the
compassionate irony of the tale. It is no mere formal 'being
sorry for' the girl.

There are, however, states of being to which compassion
cannot reach, for which there is no immediate balm, only
oblivion purchased at the price of a different kind of torture.
This Kipling reveals his knowledge of in one of the starkest
of his poems, the 'Hymn to Physical Pain', which goes with the
story of healing, 'The Tender Achilles':

> Dread Mother of Forgetfulness
> Who, when Thy reign begins,
> Wipest away the Soul's distress
> And memory of her sins. . . .

> And when Thy tender mercies cease
> And life unvexed is due,
> Instant upon the false release
> The Worm and Fire renew.

> Wherefore we praise Thee in the deep,
> And on our beds we pray
> For Thy return that Thou may'st keep
> The Pains of Hell at bay!

It is a late poem, a poem one might think, of ultimate despair.
There is evidently no anodyne, in the ordinary sense of the
word, for this state of darkness. But Kipling necessarily was
driven deeper—his affirmation of life was too strong to let
him stay there—and he sought for a more radical cure, something to overcome the ill at its source.

§4. HEALING

From his early days Kipling had been interested in healing, not so much of obvious physical ills, such as cholera, the fatal incidence of which in India had appalled him, though that aspect is not altogether lacking; we see it, say, in 'Only a Subaltern'. Later he could write a story about the driving out of the plague ('A Doctor of Medicine'), as we have seen; he described the discovery of the stethoscope in 'Marklake Witches'. What concerned him most was the sickness of the soul, as described in the 'Hymn to Physical Pain'. We find this interest as early as at the end of 'With the Main Guard', where we meet the three soldiers somehow keeping alive in a night of crushing heat, so maddening that Ortheris thought for a moment that Mulvaney was about to shoot himself—which he would never dream of doing while Dinah Shadd was living—and in which Learoyd is actually in danger of death, writhing with prickly heat, moaning out a prayer to be allowed to die. Then Mulvaney, doggedly, with all vividness, indeed with embroidery, tells a story at once grim and humorous of the regiment in action, until the guard is relieved at four o'clock in the morning. As they walk back to their quarters, Learoyd joins in with Ortheris as he bursts into song. Then Kipling, the narrator, who has been with them, breaks in:

'Oh Terence!' I said, dropping into Mulvaney's speech, when we were alone, 'it's you that have the Tongue!'

He looked at me wearily; his eyes were sunk into his head, and his face was drawn and white. 'Eyah!' said he: 'I've blandandhered thim through the night somehow, but can thim that helps others help thimselves?'

In 'At the End of the Passage' some two years later, we get, as described earlier, the picture of Hummil on the verge of his descent into the Dark Places. In the evening, when the four men are gathered together, and Hummil, foully bad-tempered, is, as he himself says, "seven fathoms deep in hell", Mottram gets up and hammers at a ricketty old piano, and they sing outworn songs, even hymns—and Hummil joins in. As they sit down to their dismally unappetizing meal, the doctor of the party "took occasion to whisper to Mottram, 'Well done,

David!' 'Look after Saul, then!' " was the reply. The allusion, familiar to both, as it would have been to almost everybody at that time, is to the First Book of Samuel (xvi. 23): "And it came to pass, when the evil spirit from God was upon Saul, that David took an harp, and played with his hand: so Saul was refreshed, and was well, and the evil spirit departed from him."

These are merely very simple strokes of the brush, filling in the colour of a story. But later there are tales, extremely complex, of which the major theme is healing. Plain physical ailments, though they occur, are not prominent; in 'The Tender Achilles' the contrived physical cure is only a stepping-stone to the mental one. Then we get mysterious tales of a healing that goes beyond medicine, either bodily or mental, those of a science that is beyond our present science, as in 'Unprofessional', and finally we come to the curative of love, possibly even of God's Grace, or at least that of the Spirit, as in 'Uncovenanted Mercies'. But this is to anticipate, and we may note first some of the stories where the cure is psychological: but even there it is difficult to disentangle themes or issues. Straightforward, however, is, 'In the Same Boat', written in Kipling's middle period, where a man and a woman are cured of their deep depressions (which they try to alleviate by drugs), in the first instance being brought together by a doctor with *imagination*, who differs in kind from the one who works only on the basis of *scientific fact*. All comes right with them when it is revealed to each that the ghastly dreams that haunt them when they are in the tormented depths are the results of shocks their mothers had shortly before they were born. That is an old, if possibly justified commonplace notion, and the tale, so far as that goes, is not enormously interesting, though superbly told, and full of side-issues of the Kipling kind, such as sympathy with the devoted, sensible, hard-worked hospital nurse, who, though liked and respected, and superficially rewarded by formal gratitude, drifts on self-effacingly, from case to case.

Not unnaturally, given the time and the stage of maturity he had reached, it is the shell-shock cases that gave Kipling his most frequent material for tales of psychological healing. We can begin with a simple, but delightfully told one 'The

Miracle of Saint Jubanus' in which the young French peasant, Martin, has lost his balance thanks to his war experience. In the words of the humanely, one might say affectionately depicted *curé* of the village, he was among those returned soldiers who "entered hells of whose existence they had not dreamed— of whose terrors they lacked words to tell". Martin could work, "but the work did not restore. And he would hide himself for an hour or two and come back visibly replunged in his torments." His cure was brought about by laughter, bursts of laughter at the sight of two acolytes and an agnostic schoolmaster apparently dancing wildly down the aisles of the church in the toils of a fantastic umbrella. Here, certainly laughter was 'wiser than all the Norns'.

More penetrating are those tales where Kipling uses what might be called Freudian therapy (he was aware of Freud), the clearing up of complexes, not only by having their causes revealed, as with 'In the Same Boat', but by having to face the experience that is at the root of the trouble. The 'theme' here is often simple enough, so far as healing goes: for sometimes the healing process is merely the pivot about which the story swings. Kipling does not cure all his shock cases. There is, for example, Brother Humberstall, of the Lodge of Instruction attached to 'Faith and Works. (No. 5837. E.C.)' who tells the story of 'The Janeites'. He might have been a Battery Sergeant-Major, but that he had never recovered from being blown up at 'Eatables', as the soldiers used to call Étaples. He does, to be sure, manage to be a hairdresser, living what life he otherwise does in the novels of Jane Austen; but he always had to be fetched home by his mother, because, she says, "He's apt to miss 'is gears sometimes. . . . 'E's liable to a sort of quiet fits like." Or there is the story 'Fairy-Kist'; but here are two cases, one of Jimmy Tigner, who had been tried beyond the breaking strain, so that Keede, the doctor in the tales where Freemasonry provides the frame (and in other doctor stories) had to certify him insane; and the other, that of the main figure, Wollin, suspected of murder because of someone else's accident with a skidding lorry, and who lives in a 'hell' for fear of being consigned to Broadmoor. The poem 'The Mother's Son' at the end of the story tells us what Wollin so deeply dreaded:

> They pushed him into a Mental Home,
>   And that is like the grave:
> For they do not let you sleep upstairs,
>   And you're not allowed to shave.
>
> And it was *not* disease or crime
>   Which got him landed there,
> But because They laid on My Mother's Son
>   More than a man could bear.

Here, too, the breaking strain is implied. For Wollin was haunted by voices that compelled him to go about the country putting in plants. (Incidentally here Kipling shows a great knowledge, if not of botany, at least of the great botanists.) Wollin knows that he's mad, in a sense; at least what we would call 'cracked': but he is cured when it is discovered for him that the cause of his obsession with its accompanying dream of a yellow dog and strange words is his 'memory', to call it so, of the story *Mary Meadows* by Mrs. Ewing. This had been read to him by a nurse when he was in a hospital occasionally attacked by bombers, where for over a year he had been treated for shell-shock and wounds, and had heard the story when full of pain and dope.

The plainest case—too plain, perhaps—of a cure of that sort, namely facing the trouble, is that of Marden in 'The Woman in His Life'. He had worked months underground for the blowing up of the Messines Ridge: back in civil life as an engineer, without close friends, and no woman in his life, he had nights of agony: "but he said not a word of the horror, the blackness, the loss of meaning of things, the collapses at the end . . ." all of which "waked up a certain secret dread which he had held off since demobilisation". He is recommended rest; but as is remarked by his servant and ex-batman, Vincent Shingle, "systematically a peculator, intermittently a drunkard, and emphatically a liar":—"If you stop runnin' machinery without slowin' 'er down, she'll lift herself off the bedplate." Kipling adds: "machinery suddenly arrested has no resources in itself. But the human mechanism has." Drink, and driving a car at speed do not help much; and Shingle found the answer by providing his master with a black Aberdeen bitch, Dinah, which Marden at first thought to be an hallucination, 'seeing things'. What happens at the end of this charming, if rather doggy-sentimental story, where Shingle is the real psychiatrist, is that Marden has to follow Dinah into a badger's holt, where she had got trapped, and has to crawl to her as though in a mine at Messines. Facing the terrifying actuality cures him of the Terror.

The greatest tale of all in this group, on all counts a magnificent one, is 'A Madonna of the Trenches', which again has for setting the Masonic Lodge of Instruction, and is, together with the healing theme, one of Kipling's most moving love stories. Strangwick, the main character, has a breakdown at the Lodge. He had been a 'runner', that is, a carrier of messages, at the front in France, and he babbles of communication trenches buttressed with skeletons and floored with corpses. He grows hysterical about what they looked like, and how the bodies creaked when trodden on in frosty weather. But Keede, the 'round, torpedo-bearded G.P.' who is Senior Warden of the Lodge, and happens to have been in the same unit as Strangwick, guesses that this is not his real trouble; he is 'playing up to mislead', and using the horror to screen himself from something more terrifying. He gets Strangwick to tell what is the root of his disorder. What emerges is that Sergeant Godsoe, Strangwick's platoon sergeant, whom he has known all his life and called 'Uncle', has for years been in love with Strangwick's aunt, Bella Armine; but they have kept apart because each was married. They long for the time of their union, namely when they shall both be dead. Bella, who is dying of cancer, writes to tell Godsoe when she expects to die; and on that day her appearance manifests itself to Godsoe, who kills himself so as to rejoin her. Strangwick also sees her, and sees Godsoe talking to her. It is too much for him:

'He was lookin' at 'er an' she was lookin' at him. I saw it, an' me soul turned over inside me because—because it knocked out everything I'd believed in. I 'ad nothin' to lay 'old of, d'ye see?' . . .

'You see . . . there wasn't a single gor-dam thing left abidin' for me to take hold of, here or hereafter. If the dead do rise—and I saw 'em—why—why *anything* can 'appen.'

That had been the real shock—not the *poy-looz* laid six deep each side and stuffed under the duck-boards. At the front, when in semi-delirium, he had asked what advantage it was for him to fight beasts of officers if the dead do not rise—a phrase which Keede points out he had picked up wrong from the burial service, and afterwards corrects to 'beasts at Ephesus'. Stating his trouble under the influence of a soothing drug puts Strangwick on the way to normal health. There is a great deal more to the story, as is brought out by the accompanying poem 'Gipsy Vans': but the most moving poem, applied to the other sex, is 'Azrael's Count', which follows 'Uncovenanted Mercies'. Another depth is indicated by the quotation from Swinburne's 'Les Noyades'—it is odd we may think that Godsoe should quote from it—which heads the tale:

> Whatever a man of the sons of men
>   Shall say to his heart of the lords above,
> They have shown man, verily, once again,
>   Marvellous mercy and infinite love.

Reinforcing the theme is a fragment of that strange play 'Gow's Watch', that Kipling sometimes added instead of a poem.

"Marvellous mercy and infinite love." In the conversation when Kipling told Haggard that this world was certainly one of the hells,[1] they came to talk about the only sons that each had lost, Kipling in the war, Haggard many years earlier; and when Haggard suggested that "this love for our sons was what the Prayer Book calls 'Inordinate Affection' ", Kipling answered, "Perhaps, but I do not care for ordinate affection; nor do you." Inordinate affection, love, is the ultimate compassion, that is the final salve.

Kipling brings this out more plainly, perhaps, in that very complex, human, and moving story 'The Wish House', written with that extraordinary amalgam of realism and fable of which he was master. The story is developed with consummate art, containing within it the whole substance of a novel, to use Dr. Tompkins's apt summing-up of Kipling's later manner; but though intricate, its meaning is evident to anyone who reads it with attention. The clue is given with a clarity unusual with

[1] See p. 33.

such introductions, in the poem preceding the tale 'Late Came the God', where the woman wounded, 'past cure or relieving', the grief

Daily renewed and nightly pursued through her soul to her flesh—
Mornings of memory, noontides of agony, midnights unslaked for her,
Till the stones of the streets of her Hells and her Paradise ached for her. . .

And she builded an Altar and served by the light of her Vision—
    Alone, without hope of regard or reward, but uncowed,
Resolute, selfless, divine.
    These things she did in Love's honour. . . .
What is a God beside Woman? Dust and derision!

Mrs. Ashcroft, the elderly pensioned housekeeper, dying of cancer, but 'big-hearted enough for three', as she is told by her old companion and fellow-sinner Mrs. Fettley (who, we learn at the end, is going blind) relates how for love of a man who had left her she took his ills upon herself by asking the mysterious Token of the Wish House to be allowed to do so. The man is cured of a wasting illness without ever guessing the reason of his cure. How should he? Mrs. Ashcroft has never said a word to a soul until now, and as the story comes out her friend responds with ever-increasing understanding. Mrs. Ashcroft tells Mrs. Fettley:

'I cried an' I cried. An' *you* know, Liz—for you've been with me in my throes—it takes summat to make me cry.'
'Yes; but chile-bearing is on'y just pain,' said Mrs. Fettley.

And later, when she is saying how long she had endured 'God's croolty':

'But the pain *do* count, don't ye think, Liz? The pain *do* count to keep 'Arry where I want 'im. Say it can't be wasted, like.'
'I'm sure of it—sure of it, dearie. You'll 'ave your reward.'
'I don't want no more'n this—*if* de pain is taken into de reckonin'.'
''Twill be—'twill be, Gra'.'

Again it is an illustration of the Gods being willing to sell anything you ask—at a price.
    And this tender story concludes with a poem which takes in much more than this particular instance of human misery,

covering to stretch the black hells which sometimes engulf a man's soul. It is of when Rahere, jester to King Henry I—and who afterwards, historically, became a monk, founded an Abbey and 'Barts' Hospital'—"fell upon an evil mood":

Then a Horror of Great Darkness sunk his spirit and, anon
(Who had seen him wince and whiten as he turned to walk alone)
Followed Gilbert the Physician, and muttered in his ear,
'Thou hast it, O my brother?' 'Yea, I have it,' said Rahere.

'So it comes,' said Gilbert smoothly, 'man's most immanent distress.
'Tis a humour of the Spirit which abhorreth all excess. . . .'

So Rahere, followed always by Gilbert, "wandered dumb and far", till at Smithfield, "where the crowded gallows are", he came across "a leper and his woman, very merry, breaking bread".[1] He was "mere corruption swaddled man-wise", she was whole and clean, and each delighted in the other.

'So it comes,—it comes,' said Gilbert, 'as it came when Life began.
'Tis a motion of the Spirit that revealeth God to man
In the shape of Love exceeding, which regards not taint or fall,
Since in perfect Love, saith Scripture, can be no excess at all.'

That sort of love is the farthest possible limit of devotion.

If these things were, as would appear, the elements of Kipling's philosophy of living, it may be possible to see in what way he built them into his vision of life as it presented itself to him in its actuality, as it was humanly lived.

---

[1] Kipling evidently either remembered or in 1924 re-read Swinburne. Both 'Les Noyades' and 'The Leper' belong to the first series of *Poems and Ballads*.

'A Madonna of the Trenches' and 'The Wish House' were first published within five months of each other.

CHAPTER III

The Framework of Living

§*1. THE INDIVIDUAL*

Unless you come of the gipsy race
That counts all time the same,
Be you careful of Time and Place
And Judgment and Good Name:
Lose your life for to live your life
The way that you ought to do;
And when you are finished, your God and your wife
And the Gipsies'll laugh at you!

Gipsy Vans

It is part of 'the riddle of Kipling' to determine the value he put on the individual in relation to society. Is a man to be judged by what he is—or by what he does? And is not what he does precisely what he is? Man must build himself up, yes, but to be what? In 'His Private Honour', when the unfledged officer, Ouless, inadvertently strikes Ortheris, the problem as to what should happen was resolved by a man-to-man fight, by which Ortheris's honour was salved, and Ouless's manhood achieved by his regarding the private as his equal. But, it is stressed, each had to solve his problem alone, as a man who is a man realizes. When it was suggested to Ortheris that it was his right to get Ouless cashiered if he chose, he answered with deep scorn: "My right! My right! I ain't a recruity to go whinin' about my rights to this and my rights to that, just as if I couldn't look after myself. My rights! 'Strewth A'mighty! I'm a man." But what is a man? "I am Kim. I am Kim. But what is Kim?" we remember. But there the question occurred to a youth without roots when he found himself involved in circumstance. The answer is primarily, but only primarily, himself.

To gain, or to preserve, his individuality, a man must follow his loudest urgings. So we find it in the poem 'The Explorer' (1898)

> . . . a voice, as bad as Conscience, rang interminable changes
> On one everlasting Whisper day and night repeated—so:
> "Something hidden. Go and find it. Go and look behind the Ranges—
> Something lost behind the Ranges. Lost and waiting for you. Go!"

Nor did the explorer name one river, claim one single acre nor keep the smallest nugget of the great country discovered.

To be "careful of Time and Place, and Judgment of Good Name" is fatal, making man into a dull indistinguishable pattern, or even a prig. In 'The Tender Achilles', the surgeon Wilkett had, as he thought, tarnished his reputation by having had to carry out hurried operations at a Casualty Clearing Station in France. Keede reports:

Then he wrung his hands and said, 'To whom much has been given, from the same much shall be required.' That annoyed me. I hate bookkeeping with God! It's dam' insolence, anyhow.

'The Penalty', the poem which succeeds the story begins:

> Once in life I watched a Star;
>   But I whistled, 'Let her go!
> There are others, fairer far,
>   Which my favouring skies shall show.'
> Here I lied, and herein I
> Stood to pay the penalty.

For there can be no book-keeping with God. In the same tale an error has to be made deliberately in the storing of blood samples, so as to rescue Wilkett (this is one of the healing stories), and the trick was carried out by a woman who loved Wilkett. "It wasn't a job," Keede comments, "to trust to a man. A man would have said that he had a reputation or something to lose." The female of the species balances her values far more surely than the male. Maximus, however, in 'On the Great Wall' says to Pertinax, "One must always risk one's life, or one's soul—or some little thing." He, of course, was gambling, to become Emperor of a united Rome.

When he gave his Rectorial Address at St. Andrews in October 1923, the subject Kipling chose was 'Independence', and he told his young audience to remind themselves of the deep instinct: "At any price that I can pay, let me own myself," and never to sacrifice that privilege for worldly advantage. He concluded his address by quoting—without giving the reference—from Ecclesiasticus xxxvii. 13, 14: "And make the counsel of thy heart to stand; for there is none more faithful unto thee than it. For a man's soul is sometime wont to bring him tidings; more than seven watchmen that sit on high on a watch-tower." That the thought was insistent is shown by his having, some five years earlier, written as Dedication of *The Years Between*:

> Seven Watchmen sitting in a tower,
>   Watching what had come upon mankind,
> Showed the Man the Glory and the Power,
>   And bade him shape the Kingdom to his mind.
> 'All things on Earth your will shall win you'
>   ('Twas so their counsel ran)
> 'But the Kingdom—the Kingdom is within you,'
>   Said the Man's own mind to the Man.
>   For time, and some time—
> As it was in the bitter years before
> So it shall be in the over-sweetened hour—
> That a man's mind is wont to tell him more
> Than Seven Watchmen sitting in a tower.

Although the poem has its particular references, being written at the end of the First World War, it contains a contradiction ever active in Kipling—the two different sides to his head. For a man, most likely, only finds himself by giving himself, by some form of devotion to something outside, unless it be to his craft, learning, or other motion of his own mind—and that is a force that drives a man. It may come as an impulse from the Kingdom that is within him; but that too is a continual surrender of himself, which is right so long as a man does not distort himself for "Judgment and Good Name". Kipling, almost despairingly, expresses the conflict in 'At His Execution' at the end of 'The Manner of Men'—one of his latest tales, it may be pointed out. "I am made all things to all men," St. Paul begins, to conclude:

Since I was overcome
  By that great Light and Word,
I have forgot or forgone
  The self men call their own
(Being made all things to all men)
    So that I might save some,
    At such small price, to the Lord,
  As being all things to all men.

I was made all things to all men,
  But now my course is done—
And now is my reward—
  Ah, Christ, when I stand at Thy Throne
With those I have drawn to the Lord,
  Restore me my self again!

Man, the lecture on 'Independence' argues, began to lose his individual self from the moment that as a primitive ape he descended from his personal balance on the branches to associate himself "with his fellows on the flat for predatory or homicidal purposes". Then, later, here and there it came over one or other of the apes that "he desired above everything to escape for a while from the sight and sound and smell of his tribe". "The power that possessed him", we read later, "was a desire to own himself for a while", and do what he wanted to do "without the advice, interference, or even privity of his tribe." It may not always be easy. Dick Heldar in his childhood days *learned* "the power of being alone", which he needed later when he had to face his blindness. And to escape the tribe is becoming increasingly difficult:

The past few years have so immensely quickened and emphasised all means of communication, visible and invisible, in every direction, that our world—which is only another name for the Tribe—is not merely 'too much with us', but moves, shouts, and moralises about our path and our bed through every hour of our days and nights.[1]

So "the power of the Tribe over the individual has become more extended, particular, pontifical", yet there are still those who say, "at any price that I can let me own myself".

But naturally, inevitably, he was concerned with the relation of the individual to society, the constant interplay of various

[1] *A Book of Words*, XXIV.

conflicting emotions, impulses, intuitions, the everlasting conflict between the self and the framework which makes possible
the realization of self. Kipling's sense of the importance of
society has been too heavily stressed; for however much he
felt that man should give himself to something greater than
himself and lose himself in the giving, he felt also that man
hankers after being himself—which perhaps he can be only
after giving himself—and this may be the meaning of 'At His
Execution'. But whatever the outcome, he would have agreed
with Henry V when he said to some of his soldiers, "Every
subject's duty is the king's, but every subject's soul is his own."

§2. *SOCIETY*

"It is only when the conception of the individual has
been reached, that the idea of responsibility begins."

A. H. Sayce

"The fashion in which we are all linked together and
made responsible for one another."

('Thrown Away')

A day or two after speaking at St. Andrews, Kipling spoke to
a gathering at University College, Dundee, and said:

I find myself in an awkward position. But I am consoled by the
thought that I am not the only person who has said one thing one
day and another the next. My Rectorial Address dealt entirely
with the advantage of independence as a possession necessary and
desirable in itself. Today I come before you, equally convinced of
the necessity and desirability of interdependence combined with
association and union. As is usual in such a dilemma, I defend myself by the time-honoured formula: "I have nothing to add, and
nothing to retract." Circumstances, as the doctor, the pure scientist,
and the pure politician tells us, alter cases.[1]

A clear instance of this is when he wrote:

How in all time of our distress,
And our deliverance too,
The game is more than the player of the game,
And the ship is more than the crew!

('A Song in Storm')

[1] *A Book of Words*, XXV.

for the 'circumstance' there was a naval unit in *Sea Warfare* in the 1914–18 War, when, if the ship perished, so would each member of the crew. It is not so much, however, that circumstances alter cases, as that the cases themselves are fundamentally interwoven.

His philosophy of the subject was by no means simple, founded not only on his experience and his reading, but also on what he saw around him. It was not basically an intellectual idea, since he was an artist who arrived at things intuitively. It arose from his sense of man as an individual, then as man in association, society being necessary to the individual, just as individuals make up society, "For the strength of the Pack is the Wolf, and the strength of the Wolf is the Pack," as he stated in 'The Law of the Jungle', and then to a wider union. In what follows I am deeply indebted to Lord Annan's enlightening essay, 'Kipling's Place in the History of Ideas'.[1]

From Kipling's sense (Lord Annan uses the word analysis) "came a conception of history and politics far more disturbing than that of the imperialism which is supposed to be the compass of his imagination". For, in line with Continental sociologists—Durkheim, Weber, and Pareto—and far ahead of any English thinkers on the subject, "he saw society as a nexus of groups; and the patterns of behaviour which these groups unwittingly established, rather than men's wills or anything so vague as class, cultural or national tradition, primarily determined men's actions". First among these groups, was, unavoidably, the family, of which Kipling was intensely conscious. For him, at any rate, after his return to India, his parents, his sister, and himself constituted 'the family square', the 'magic square', the perfect geometrical figure, each side sustaining the other. In that square the functions of each person are pretty obvious; they are biologically determined. And that is the society you cannot help belonging to. But what about the other societies?—the non-compulsory ones—school first, then your trade or profession, and then your nation? And within these societies again you get what may be called the 'in-groups', in which we all largely live; research stations, regiments, Masonic Lodges, cliques or even gangs, all clubs of

---

[1] *Victorian Studies*, Vol. III. Reprinted in *Kipling's Mind and Art*.

various kinds. We get perhaps, the clearest description of such a group in his address to a Naval Club in 1908:[1]

... where men of all ranks work together for aims and objects which are not for their own personal advantage, there arises among them a spirit, a tradition, and an unwritten law, which it is not very easy for the world at large to understand, or to sympathise with.

This kind of in-group Kipling first experienced in Study No. 5 at Westward Ho! as described in the Stalky stories. Here we get a very small in-group, ready to manoeuvre against the larger group, the school itself (in the matter of smoking, say, or breaking bounds) though recognizing it; rejoicing in flouting other small in-groups, such as the solemnly 'good' prefects, but always supporting, obeying the ways of, its own in-group. Within this small society each member had his own particular function: Beetle provided the material for 'English', M'Turk looked after the Latin, and Stalky was responsible for the mathematics. But money, clothes, all belongings, were shared. The Law here, naturally, was limited from lack of experience. As Baloo told Mowgli, "young wolves will only learn as much of the Law of the Jungle as applies to their own pack and tribe".[2]

Then between the ages of, roughly seventeen and twenty-four, Kipling was forcedly aware that he belonged to a larger in-group, that of the Anglo-Indians, "a society which politically, nervously, physically, and spiritually quivered on the edge of a precipice,[3] in, one might add, the middle of a far larger group, or rather, agglomeration of groups. Each had its own religion, its customs, its castes, its own morality or rules for living. These could never coalesce, though they might 'mix', since each group's rules were the outcome of centuries of tradition. And not always even mix. In 'The Debt' there is a 'lifer' "who had unluckily shot a kinsman a little the wrong side of the British frontier. The killing was a matter he could no more have shirked than a decent Englishman his club dues." At the opening of that shocking—deliberately shocking—story, 'Beyond the Pale', which first appeared as early as September

[1] *A Book of Words*, XIII.
[2] *The Jungle Books*, 'Kaa's Hunting'.
[3] Annan, op. cit.

1884, when Kipling was not yet nineteen, he warns that "A man should, whatever happens, keep to his own caste, race and breed." In the touching story, written two years later, 'Without Benefit of Clergy', the happy union of an English official with an Indian girl is blotted out by what seems to be the Fate that broods over India, or, indeed, the world. Only perhaps in a story of the same year, 'Yoked with an Unbeliever' is the attitude modified: an Englishman settles down happily with a Burmese wife. But then, circumstances alter cases.

Nevertheless the theme throughout Kipling's Indian stories is "East is East, and West is West" though sometimes the twain can meet. They have different rules and customs, different standards of excellence, though one not necessarily better than the other; conformity with these is essential, as Kipling illustrated in his second address quoted above and it is, of course, the theme of the *Jungle Books*. You abandon these rules or customs at your peril, since they are the basis of protective civilization, which is a very thin crust, as we living in this century know only too well. In that early, and powerfully imaginative story, 'The Strange Ride of Morrowbie Jukes', Kipling shows us a scrap-heap of people who should be dead, but who revived on their way to the burning-ghats, and have been thrown into a derelict sandpit, from which there is no escape, and in which they can just sustain life. Being severed from their tradition, they behave like Yahoos. And every society, if it is to endure, has its own structure of individuals (this is vaguely suggested in *Stalky*). We get this again and again, but perhaps its plainest statement is in 'An Error in Fourth Dimension' where Wilton Sargent learned from a ditcher on his estate, that "every man with whom he came into contact had a decreed position in the fabric of the realm". Since this was so, Kipling respected the ditcher, believing him to be of equal importance with himself in the architecture of society. But he had no belief in 'the equality of man' in the cant use of the phrase, and with T. H. Huxley would have been prepared to argue for the natural inequality of men. After all, one ditcher might be better than another, though each would have respect for the other, as in 'Friendly Brook'. Nor did Kipling believe that such a structure could fundamentally change. "Remember always," he told his audience in his Rectorial Address, "that except for the appliances we make, the rates at which we move ourselves and our possessions through space, and the words which we use, nothing in life changes."

Permanence—as human beings measure permanence—was the guarantee of the in-group, willed by the in-group. And it may be that because it symbolizes and fortifies such societies that Kipling had so great a liking for ritual. Each group has its own ritual—the Church, the officers' mess, the school, the House of Commons, and, above all, the Masonic Lodge. The word occurs often enough in various tales or lectures, sometimes as meaning the reassuring habit of a craft or calling, as with Mr. Cashell, the dispensing chemist in 'Wireless', who "believed in all the ritual of his craft. Three superb glass jars—red, green, and blue" etcetera; and for Shaynor, the consumptive minor Keats, "the censing of the gay, seven-tinted wench with the teeth was an established ritual which cost something". Mr. Burges, the tobacconist of 'In the Interests of the Brethren', remarks, as he sees to the clearing up of a pipe: "There's a procedure, a ritual in all things": he likes "the ritual of handling things", in short he is a confessed Ritualist, since "All ritual is fortifying. Ritual's a natural necessity for mankind. The more things are upset, the more they fly to it." Even in everyday life it can be a support, as Kipling found in the solitary days of his Indian period, learning that "if one broke the ritual of dressing for the last meal one was parting with a sheet-anchor".[1] Nor, he insists, is this an affectation.

It was this feeling of ordered permanence, or at least of very slow organic growth, of societies, that made him deeply suspicious, even contemptuous of, social reformers—an aspect of his mind to be developed later—those he had met seeming to him to be mainly intolerable shams. "Western civilisation", he says in Letters of Travel,[2] "is a devastating and a selfish game. Like the young woman from 'our State', it says in effect: 'I am rich. I've nothing to do. I must do something. I shall take up social reform.' " And in 'One View of the Question' Shafiz

[1] Something of Myself, III.
[2] IV, 'Egypt of the Magicians'.

Ullah Khan in England writes home to his brother of those who "for all their unrest at the agonies of others . . . abandon no whit of soft living". Not that he was averse from reform, or at any rate betterment, carried out by people who really knew, who were involved in the issues; and one of the reasons for his friendship with Rider Haggard was the latter's great work, official and unofficial, in improving the lot of the cottage-dwelling country labourer.

§3. THE LAW

> Society is impossible unless those who are associated agree to observe certain rules of conduct towards one another; its stability depends on the steadiness with which they abide by that agreement.
>
> T. H. Huxley, *Evolution and Ethics*

What has so far been said leads naturally to a consideration of what Kipling meant by 'The Law', a term there has been a good deal of discussion about. Obviously, without law of some kind, civilization could not exist. But it is not the law of mere brute force, referred to in the poem 'For all we have and are' that Kipling wrote on the outbreak of war in 1914:

> Once more we hear the word
> That sickened earth of old:—
> "No law except the Sword
> Unsheathed and uncontrolled."

His 'Law' was not there to sicken earth, but to keep it healthy; nor was it the same sort of Law that belonged to earth of old, but one suited to civilization as it had developed. It might change in the long process of time, it might vary between one culture and another, but law of some kind there must be, otherwise there is no freedom, for men need to know within what limits they are free, so as to be sure of what they can do without fear. Dick Heldar, in *The Light that Failed* says that the Nilghai "might have condensed the whole of his lumbering nonsense into an epigram: 'Only the free are bond, and only the bond are free.' " In the wolf-pack, after Akela had been deposed, there was anarchy; but in due course, at the meeting

where Mowgli handed in, so to speak, his resignation, one
tattered wolf howled: "Lead us again, O Akela! Lead us again,
O Man-cub, for we be sick of this lawlessness, and we would
be the Free People once more." In a later *Jungle Book* tale,
at a meeting of "young wolves", Akela told them that they
ought to gather themselves together and "follow the Law,
and run under one head, as befitted the Free People".[1]

Nor can the Law be tampered with, or imposed from without.
In 'The Prophet and the Country' we hear from the American,
Tarworth, how Female Presumption fixed Prohibition on his
country, and he foresaw dire results. Kipling, however, had in
mind only the immediate consequences, the activity of the
bootleggers, with the result that he described in the Horace,
Ode 20, Bk. V, 'The Portent'. The whole must be quoted:

> Oh, late withdrawn from human-kind
> And following dreams we never knew!
> Varus, what dream has Fate assigned
> To trouble you?
>
> Such virtue as commends the law
> Of virtue to the vulgar horde
> Suffices not. You needs must draw
> A righteous sword;
>
> And, flagrant in well-doing, smite
> The priests of Bacchus at their fane,
> Lest any worshipper invite
> The God again.
>
> Whence public strife and naked crime
> And—deadlier than the cup you shun—
> A people schooled to mock, in time,
> All law—not one.
>
> Cease, then, to fashion State-made sin
> Nor give thy children cause to doubt
> That Virtue springs from iron within—
> Not lead without.

Yet there may be moments—circumstance again altering the
case—that inbred custom must give way to a greater necessity,

---

[1] 'Tiger! Tiger' and 'Red Dog'.

so that order can reign. In 'The Tree of Justice', one of the stories that tells of the unification of England, when Saxon and Norman were welded into Englishmen—partly by the great De Aquila, prototype of Kipling's wise administrators—the following conversation takes place. Henry I is speaking:

'I'll never quarrel with Anselm, or his Pope till they quarrel with my England. If we can keep the King's peace till my son comes to rule, no man will lightly quarrel with our England.'

'Amen,' said De Aquila. 'But the King's peace ends when the King dies.'

'That is true. [Another is speaking.] The King's peace dies with the King. The custom then is that all laws are outlaw, and men do what they will till the new King is chosen.'

'I will amend that,' said the King hotly. 'I will have it so that though King, son, and grandson were all slain in one day, *still* the King's peace should hold over all England! What is a man that his mere death must upheave a people? We must have the Law.'

What Kipling felt to be essential to the Law is made plain in the *Jungle Books*, where it is far from what we often casually refer to as 'jungle law'. There it brings into play the virtues of loyalty, keeping your promises, courage, and respect for other people. When, for example, there is drought, since all animals must drink, the carnivorous leave alone the deer and so on at the watering-place. Emphatically "the head and the hoof of the Law, and the haunch and the hump is—Obey!" But obey what? or whom? and why obey? Nietzsche, in *Beyond Good and Evil* (188) would seem to some extent to chime in with Kipling, answering his questions if one may slightly distort his approach:

. . . this tyranny, this arbitrariness, this severe and magnificent stupidity, has *educated* the spirit; slavery, both in the coarse and the finer sense, is apparently an indispensable means even of spiritual education and discipline. One may look at every system of morals in this light: it is 'nature' therein which teaches to hate the *laisser-aller*, the too great freedom, and implants the need for limited horizons, for immediate duties—it teaches the *narrowing of perspectives*, and thus in a certain sense, that stupidity is a condition of life and development. [One might compare Bagehot here.] "Thou must obey some one, and for a long time: *otherwise* thou wilt come to grief, and lose all respect for thyself"—this seems to me to be the moral imperative of nature, which is certainly neither 'categorical' . . . nor does it address itself to the individual (what does nature care for the individual!), but to nations, races, ages, and ranks, above all, however, to the animal 'man' generally, to *mankind*.

(Trs. Helen Zimmern)

"Lose all respect for thyself", as a result of coming to grief. Thus it can be suggested that fear was the origin of the Law. In the 'How Fear Came' story of the *Jungle Books* we read:

'Then Tha called us together and said: "The first of your masters has brought Death into the Jungle, and the second Shame. Now it is time there was a Law, and a Law that ye must not break. Now ye shall know Fear. . ."'

We may note that Sulinor, the Dacian-Scythian trader in 'The Manner of Men', a man of no great virtue, recounts how Paul, St. Paul as we know him,

said to me: Serve Caesar. You are not canvas that I can cut to advantage at present. But if you serve Caesar you will be obeying some sort of law. . . . If you take refuge under Caesar at sea, you may have time to think. . . . What concerns you *now* is that, by taking service, you will be free from the fear that has ridden you all your life.

Here, of course, Caesar is not a Nietzschean 'someone', but Rome, the Empire, with its inherited traditions, its Law, which protects, and therefore frees from fear. (Though the fear, in this case—the tale is rather rambling—seems, a little incongruously to be of the Beasts, such as St. Paul had encountered at Ephesus.)

Looking back to what Meon said to his fishermen and ploughmen and herdsmen,[1] that "a faith which takes care that every man shall keep faith, though he may save his soul by breaking faith, is the faith for a man to believe in", it could be inferred that the Law resolves itself into a matter of faith, or at least "such Virtue as commends the law of virtue to the vulgar horde". And again, though it is imperative to adhere to the Law if there is to be any liveable society, there is still the individual, for whom, in the long run, society exists.

[1] 'The Conversion of St. Wilfrid.'

Moreover, a man's own soul, as we have seen, may bring him clearer tidings of the Law than the Seven Watchmen. In 'The Miracle of Purun Bhagat' we meet Purun Dass, a high-caste Brahmin, at one time Prime Minister in a well-run Indian State. He was knighted; then, suddenly, "so far as the world's affairs went, he died". He became a holy man, going about with a begging bowl; and making his way north to his native hills he passed through Simla:

The last time he had come that way it had been in state, with a clattering cavalry escort, to visit the gentlest and most affable of Viceroys. . . . This time Purun Bhagat paid no calls, but leaned on the rail of the Mall . . . till a native Mohammedan policeman told him he was obstructing traffic; and Purun Bhagat salaamed reverently to the Law, because he knew the value of it, and was seeking for a Law of his own.

But there may be a trap in this, a forgetfulness of humility. As the Lama said to Kim:[1]

Friend of the Stars, thou hast acquired great wisdom. Beware that it do not give birth to pride. No man having the Law before his eyes speaks hastily of any matter which he has seen or encountered.

It is probable, however, that by 'the Law' the Lama did not mean the kind of agreed behaviour Kipling normally implied by the term, but rather, some decree as to the nature of existence as interpreted by Buddha. Kipling's meaning of the word as he currently used it may be deduced from two early stories, 'A Wayside Comedy' and 'Georgie Porgie'. In the former we read "that all laws weaken in a small and hidden community where there is no public opinion". When the number rises to twelve—the Jury-number—"fear and consequently restraint begin, and human action becomes less grotesquely jerky". In the latter, where we are concerned with people living beyond the fringes of our own European society, Georgie Porgie, as we have seen, behaves badly; for where "the Queen's law does not carry, it is irrational to expect the observance of other and weaker rules".

We see everywhere in Kipling, then, that for him the Law was a matter of traditional social agreement, which it was

[1] *Kim*, XI.

essential to observe. In the last of the Canadian 'Letters to the Family' (1907),[1] after speaking of the "spirit of sane and realised nationality", he goes on to explain:

The people, the schools, the churches, the Press in its degree, and above all, the women, understand without manifestoes that their land must now as always abide under the Law in deed and word and in thought. This is their caste-mark, the ark of their covenant, their reason for being what they are.

The Law is the relentless spirit of the breed, that oversees and controls.

In his interesting book on Kipling, Edward Shanks regards the assault of the Winged Hats and the Picts on the Wall, as an attack on civilization, and therefore the Law, and it is significant that the poem at the end of 'The Winged Hats' is 'A Pict Song', of which the second stanza runs:

> We are the Little Folk—we!
> Too little to love or to hate.
> Leave us alone, and you'll see
> How we can drag down the Great![2]
> We are the worm in the wood!
> We are the rot at the root!
> We are the germ in the blood!
> We are the thorn in the foot!

The Little Folk—the lesser breeds without the Law. It is such folk, at home as well as abroad, that Kipling would seem to have meant by the phrase (there are conflicting views on this, the only point of agreement being that he emphatically did not mean people with darker skins than our own). Kipling never explained his meaning, it was not his habit to do so, but he was wryly aware of the misinterpretation at one time common—at least if we can judge from his single reference when, in *Something of Myself*[3] he speaks of the piratical American publishers from whom he had so much suffered, as "lesser breeds without the (Copyright) Law". They were not conforming with the customs of the tribe.

[1] *Letters of Travel*   [2] *Def. Ed.*: 'State'   [3] VIII.

CHAPTER IV

The Empire

§1. THE VISION

It was probably at Westward Ho! that Kipling first got his
idea of the Empire, which must have meant chiefly India,
schoolmate as he was with boys most of whom, like himself,
had parents there in one or other of the services, and were
themselves destined for such. Not that they were 'patriotic' in
the vulgar sense, but that 'things were like that'. They disliked
talking about 'the Empire'; they were allotted to a job in a
scheme of things that they accepted. It was devotion, 'service'
in the real sense of the term, as declared in the Incantation, to
call it so, at the beginning of *Stalky & Co.*:

> Some beneath the further stars
>   Bear the greater burden:
> Set to serve the lands they rule,
> (Save he serve no man may rule),
> Serve and love the lands they rule;
>   Seeking praise nor guerdon.
>
> ('A School Song')

That was what the school taught them; but it was never
rubbed in, though it might be implied, as it was by the classics
master, Mr. King (W. Crofts) in 'Regulus', when "he fetched
up, full-voiced upon—'*Dis te minorem quod geris imperas*' (Thou
rulest because thou bearest thyself as lower than the Gods)";
and when later in the same story he dictates from memory to
the erring Winton who had incurred 'lines', he repeats, dic-
tating from memory, the passage from the *Æneid* VI. 851:

> Tu regere imperio populos Romane memento
> Hae tibi erunt artes pacisque imponere morem,
> Parcere subjectis et debellare superbos . . .

F

which may be translated, "Roman! let this be your care, this
your art; to rule over the nations and impose the ways of peace,
to spare the underdog, and pull down the proud." Thus when
the jingoistic M.P. in 'The Flag of their Country' comes to
lecture to the school, they feel nothing but disgust at the 'Jelly-
bellied Flag-flapper'. They were outraged, for "the reserve of a
boy is tenfold deeper than the reserve of a maid".

Kipling, it seems, had no special desire to go to India on
leaving school. "Ruddy thirsts for a man's life and a man's
work", his father said, but he would rather have made his
way in London. In India he became vividly aware of the complex mixture of in-groups, as previously described; but what
struck him most forcibly was the life led by the Anglo-Indians.
"My world was filled with boys, but a few years older than I,
who lived utterly alone, and died from typhoid mostly at the
regulation age of twenty-two. . . . Death was always our near
companion."[1] Many of the people he met, and those he most
admired, devoted themselves completely to their tasks in almost
unbearable conditions, hoping for no reward beyond their pay,
and no recognition for endless patience and unwearying self-
sacrifice. These were the men who did the real work—not the
administrators, the bureaucrats, for whom Kipling always had
a hearty dislike, partly because they did not know how things
were done. This he holds up for scorn in 'The Bridge-Builders',
months of office-work being destroyed at a blow, "when the
Government of India, at the last moment, added two feet to
the width of the bridge, under the impression that bridges
were cut out of paper, and so brought to ruin at least half an
acre of calculations". But chiefly he disliked them for their
ignorance of the life of the people they were supposed to
administer, a point beautifully brought out in 'Tod's Amend-
ment', where the child of six years old, who chatters to the
people in the bazaar as his *ayah* takes him round, tells the senior
members of a committee about to issue new laws on land tenure
exactly where they are wrong. The Legal Member "did not
know that no man can tell what natives think unless he mixes
with them with the varnish off". Kipling's heart warmed to
such men as Lowndes in 'At the End of the Passage', who tried

[1] *Something of Myself*, III.

to inject some idea of just and beneficent rule into the king of an impoverished native State, resisting bribes of money or women, and in constant danger of being poisoned, as Kipling himself had once been.[1] That such men were no figment of Kipling's imagination is evidenced by the remark made to Mrs. Gathorne-Hardy by Lady Ottoline Morrell, who with her husband, very 'left' in politics, visited India in 1935:

> She told me how she had visited several small princely states, and in each one she found one obscure Englishman, officially, I suppose, no more than an adviser, devoting his life, selflessly, and without glory, to the good of the people he was responsible for. I remember in particular one she spoke of who, attached to a difficult prince, was slowly and with tact and gentleness leading him to act for the good of his people.

"Ottoline", we are told, "came back with a high admiration of the British in India."[2]

Or there were men such as the typical Yardley-Orde of 'The Head of the District', who had tried to keep a wife on his pay, and was now dying. He was "dipped—awfully dipped", but his colleague, Tallantire, told him quietly that his friends would arrange her passage home. Orde ruminates:

> It's not nice to think of sending round the hat: but, good Lord! how many men I lie here and remember that had to do it! Morten's dead—he was of my year. Shaughnessy is dead, and he had children. . . . Evans is dead—Kot-Kumharsen killed him! Ricketts of Myndonie is dead—and I'm going too. "Man that is born of woman is small potatoes and few in the hill." That reminds me, Dick; the four Khusru Kheyl villages in our border want a one-third remittance this spring. That's fair; their crops are bad.

Even when he is dying, hoping to see his wife before he does so, his thoughts are on his responsibilities, with 'his people'.

Here then, seen as a whole, was a Thing bigger than man's self for which a man could renounce himself; power had been given to the English, but as the runes on Weland's sword say, speaking of gold, which is power,

[1] ibid.

[2] *Ottoline. The Early Memoirs of Lady Ottoline Morrell.* Ed. by Robert Gathorne-Hardy (Faber, 1963), p. 58.

> It is not given
> For goods or gear
> But for The Thing.

The most extensive statement of what he saw in India is that given in 'On the City Wall':

> Year by year England sends out fresh drafts for the first fighting-line, which is officially called the Indian Civil Service. These die, or kill themselves by overwork, or are worried to death, or broken in health and hope in order that the land may be protected from death and sickness, famine and war, and may eventually become capable of standing alone. It will never stand alone, but the idea is a pretty one, and men are willing to die for it, and yearly the work of pushing and coaxing and scolding and petting the country into good living goes forward. If an advance be made all credit is given to the native, while the Englishmen stand back and wipe their foreheads. If a failure occurs the Englishmen step forward to take the blame.

The theme of saving from famine is presented in 'William the Conqueror', headed by a quotation from Donne's 'The Undertaking':

> I have done a braver thing
> Than all the worthies did;
> And yet a braver thence did spring,
> Which is to keep that hid.

The voluntary slavery to which the people in that story, including William herself, surrender themselves is not kept hid, it is just accepted unnoticed. All work themselves to the bone, even to a state of collapse, to save as many as possible of the people of the district from starvation, against infuriating odds too, as when the people refuse to eat wheat because they are used to rice. The English helpers had been called from other work, some in districts more bearable for Europeans in the hot season, work which they wanted to do—making dams, building railways, or simply administration—work giving the personal satisfaction of construction.

Here, then, Kipling saw people serving the land they ruled, and he also saw them loving it. He noted of the Maharajah of Jeypore that "In the latter years of his reign, he was supplied with Englishmen who made the State their fatherland, and

satisfied themselves with its progress as only Englishmen can."[1]
'Only' is a pardonable exaggeration. How they had come to
serve and rule did not for the moment matter to him; what
appealed to him was the devotion that he so frequently saw in
action, and it may be that it was then that the thought came to
him that an institution, in this case the Empire, that could call
forth such devotion must be admirable. Moreover he could see
the good that was being done for the sheer physical well-being
of the people in matters of food, health, and the cessation of
inter-State wars—the imposition of the ways of peace. Education, to be sure, he was sceptical about, at any rate as carried
out on the old Macaulay lines: he felt it was futile to urge
Indians drearily through Wordsworth's *Excursion*, or Grish
Chunder's 'cram-book on Wordsworth', seeing that they could
have no inkling of its ethos. He was wary about commercial
exploitation, as we see from 'The Enlightenments of Pagett,
M.P.', feeling that a little would not do any harm, but not at
all seeing it as an important factor in the Imperial build-up.
Nor was he greatly impressed, it would seem, from the insight
into government that he met with at Simla; as a journalist this
insight could not have been negligible, though possibly not so
complete as he then thought.

At all events he got to know the vast complexity of India,
with its agglomeration of racial and religious groups, and on
that basis built up his conception of the Indian Empire (as
apart from the idea of the British Empire), and he seems to
have had what was possibly an early-Victorian view, arising
out of the philosophy

of which Edmund Burke was the most forceful exponent. It argues
that societies evolve organically, upon the basis of their own traditions and necessities, and that to impose alien institutions and controls undermines stability and the restraining force of the moral
code.[2]

Thus he very understandably reacted against the attempted
application of 'advanced' Western ideas forced upon a totally

---

[1] *From Sea to Sea*, Letters of Marque, IV.

[2] J. W. Davidson, 'The Idea of Empire' in *Ideas and Beliefs of the Victorians*. B.B.C.
Third Programme talks (Sylvan Press, 1947).

different culture by people largely ignorant of that culture, acting upon abstract ideas. 'In 1885', he tells us in *Something of Myself* (III)

a Liberal Government had come into power at Home and was acting on liberal 'principle' which so far as I have observed ends not seldom in bloodshed. Just then, it was a matter of principle that Native Judges should try white women. Native in this case meant overwhelmingly Hindu; and the Hindu's idea of women is not lofty. No one had asked for any such measure—least of all the Judiciary concerned. But principle is principle, though the streets swim.

He would have approved Talleyrand's dictum, "Whenever a man talks to me of principle, I know him for my enemy." Not that the high bureaucrats in India were much better than the people in power at home, as we find by going back to 'The Head of the District'. There "the Very Greatest of All the Viceroys" appointed as successor to the deceased Yardley-Orde at the head of an Afghan frontier district—therefore Muslim—a highly educated Hindu. "The very simplicity of the notion was its charm ... did anybody see any objection to the appointment, always on principle, of a man of the people to rule the people?" The Khusru Kheyl saw every objection to being ruled by "A Bengali of Bengal—an eater of fish from the South", "a black man". Naturally Tallantire, as Orde's second in command, had to try to see it through. But a friend in the next district told him; "If you keep things straight . . . he'll get all the credit. If anything goes wrong, you'll be told that you didn't support him loyally." The whole story develops the theme in a finally convincing manner.

Kipling, then, saw the Indian Empire, so long as it was allowed to develop 'organically' under humane and understanding guidance, without interference from people who had no sense of its nature, as a great and beneficent service to be performed. Then, in March 1889, at the end of his 'seven years hard' on newspapers, he left India for England, by way of the Far East and the United States. A rendering of what he saw—a popular journalistic account written for *The Pioneer*, is given in *From Sea to Sea*; and though going blatantly as a globe-trotter did not much enlighten him—even if it produced that notable poem 'Buddha at Kamakura'—the conversations that he had with Japanese and Americans on the way their countries were run certainly helped him to form his political views. The mere sight of such different places as Burma, Hong Kong, Japan, San Francisco and Chicago did much to enlarge his views as to the diverse ways in which people have to live, and adjust themselves to conditions. Then, in 1891, after his first success in London, his health drove him abroad to warmer climes. He first took a trip to Naples, where he talked much with Lord Dufferin, a former Viceroy of India who had befriended him there, and learnt something of the problems of government as seen from the upper rather than the journalistic end, something he had not quite realized from the latter. Soon after he journeyed to South Africa, where he did not stay long, then to New Zealand where he enjoyed himself for a very short time, and finally to Australia, which he visited for only a few days. Then home by way of India for a brief visit to his parents at Lahore.

The death of his great friend, and collaborator in *The Naulahka*, Wolcott Balestier, brought him hurriedly back to England, where, soon, afterwards, he married Carrie Balestier and went to live at Vermont. But as part of their honeymoon trip they went across Canada, as recorded in *Letters of Travel* (he had passed through it on his original journey home); but the only significant comment would seem to be where he says in the chapter 'Across a Continent':

The Canadian has no special love for England—the Mother of Colonies has a wonderful gift for alienating the affections of her own household by neglect—but, perhaps he loves his own country.

It would not seem that until after his return to England in 1896, after his unhappy American experience, he began to think generally about the Empire, what it stood for, and what it might mean.

The idea of Empire, though usually associated with the reign of Victoria, dates back at least as far as to the speech of Cranmer in *Henry VIII* (v. 5). Speaking of Elizabeth's successor, he says:

> Wherever the bright sun in heaven shall shine,
> His honour and the greatness of his name
> Shall be, and make new nations.

This is more than simple patriotism;[1] the point lies in the words "wherever the bright sun in heaven shall shine . . . shall be and make new nations". Denham in *Cooper's Hill* speaks of when the Thames, through shipping

> Visits the world, and in his flying tow'rs
> Brings home to us, and makes both Indies ours;
> Finds wealth where 'tis, bestows it where it wants,
> Cities in desarts, woods in cities plants.

Later, Dryden in *Annus Mirabilis*, with reference to London, says:

> she will behold
> From her high Turrets, hourly Sutors come:
> The East with Incense, and the West with Gold,
> Will stand, like Suppliants, to receive her doom.

Similarly Pope, at the end of Windsor Forest, prophesies that

> The Time shall come, when free as Seas or Wind
> Unbounded Thames shall flow for all Mankind,
> Whole Nations enter with each swelling Tyde,
> And Seas but join the Regions they divide;
> Earth's distant Ends our Glory shall behold,
> And the new World launch forth to seek the Old.

'Glory' may perhaps strike a rather strident note: but "The shady Empire shall retain no Trace/Of War or Blood". It is to be a liberty-bringing rule:

> Oh stretch thy Reign, fair *Peace*! from Shore to Shore,
> Till Conquest cease, and Slav'ry be no more:
> Till the freed Indians in their native Groves
> Reap their own Fruits, and woo their Sable Loves.

That was to be the general note. Dyer in 1757, glorifying the wool-trade in *The Fleece*, brings the pax Britannica to view: 'Tis England's delight "to fold the world with harmony". Trade, moreover, "brings arts as well as gains". Beyond that, the British would enlighten pagan nations, and, under the auspices of the S.P.C.K., bring Christianity to them. The South

---

[1] It is quite outside the writings in prose and verse expressing simple love of the countryside, or of its people—"This land of such dear souls, this dear, dear land" sentiment, which abounds.

Sea Bubble had given a shock to the purely commercial side. The growth of the idea of Empire cannot be followed here in any detail, but it may be indicated, since, consciously or not, it must have affected Kipling's attitude. The American rebellion, as it was then thought of, made people think in clearer terms. We get Burke saying to the British Colonists in North America:[1] "Armed as you are we embrace you as our friends and as our brethren by the best and dearest ties of relation", and that those who hold to the foundation of common liberty "whether on this or on your side of the ocean, we consider as the true, and the only true, Englishmen." Earlier in the address he had sketched out a "whole empire . . . likely to be at least as powerful as any nation, or as any combination of nations, which in the course of human events may be formed against us". In 1774 and 1775, on various occasions,[2] he had spoken of the "*imperial character*, whose business it is to coerce the negligent, to restrain the violent, and to aid the weak and deficient". (*Parcere subjectis et debellare superbos.*) Speaking in 'Conciliation with America' he defined an empire as "the aggregate of many states under one common head; whether this head be a monarch, or a presiding republic". At the end we get the famous phrase, "a great empire and little minds go ill together".

Much happened in the next hundred years to affect political thinking—the French Revolution, the Napoleonic wars, the Indian Mutiny. The way the attitude crystallized itself was perhaps best expressed by Trollope in 1872:

We are called upon to rule [the colonies] as far as we do rule them, not for our glory, but for their happiness. If we keep them we should keep them—not because they add prestige to the name of Great Britain, not because they are gems in our diadem, not in order that we may boast that the sun never sets on our dependencies, but because by keeping them we may assist them in developing their own resources. And when we part with them, as part with them we shall, let us do so with neither smothered jealousy nor open hostility, but with a proud feeling that we are sending a son out into the world able to take his place among men.[3]

[1] *The Works of Burke*, World's Classics ed. Vol. V.   [2] ibid., Vol. II.
[3] Quoted by J. W. Davidson, *Ideas and Beliefs of the Victorians.*

But in the same year Disraeli launched what might be called boastful Imperialism, to be fostered by Rhodes and Chamberlain, the latter proclaiming the superiority of what he called, in the jargon of his day, the Anglo-Saxon race. (It is clear that he had never read Defoe's *The True-Born Englishman*.)

I believe in this race, the greatest governing race, so proud, so tenacious, self-confident and determined, this race which neither climate nor change can degenerate, which will infallibly be the predominating force of future history and universal civilisation.[1]

He also held the notion of federalism. But it must be added that he was a great and just administrator, whom Mary Kingsley could thank for his humanitarian work in West Africa.[2]

If, in Seeley's phrase, England seemed "as it were, to have conquered and peopled half the world in a fit of absence of mind", it was bringing hard and humane thinking to the problems that this engendered. The great missionaries, such as Livingstone (apart from his propagation of Christianity), provided enormous help, the whole result being something that in the main the nation had good reason to be proud of: famine relief, the abolition of the slave-trade, medical knowledge, peace-making in several parts of the world, and in really backward parts, such as Africa, a certain degree of civilized order.

Kipling, then, in the 'nineties, with a great knowledge of India, and only a very fleeting view of the rest of the Empire, found himself with some experience, and the inherited ideas adumbrated above, meeting with men whose notions were based largely on theory, and only a vague realization of what it implied. He was certainly attracted by the notion of Imperial Federation, of a number of independent nations bound together by a sense of likeness in outlook, their ships flying over the sea like shuttles, weaving the clan together, rather than the kind of Empire described by Trollope. Speaking to Canadians in 1907, he told them:

I *have*, I confess it now, done my best for about twenty years to make all men of the sister nations within the Empire interested in each

---

[1] Quoted by Alfred Cobban, *Ideas and Beliefs of the Victorians*.
[2] Jack Simmons, ibid.

other. Because I know that at heart all our men are pretty much alike, in that they have the same aspirations, and the same loves, and the same hates; and when all is said and done we have only each other to depend upon.[1]

'Sister nations', not a main state and colonies on the Burkean pattern. In April '97, he had written on the occasion of Canadian Preferential Tariff:

> A Nation spoke to a Nation,
>   A Queen sent word to a Throne:
> "Daughter am I in my mother's house,
>   But mistress in my own. . . ."
>
> ('Our Lady of the Snows')

But the Nations must get to know each other so as to understand each other. At the Rhodes dinner at Oxford in 1924 he said, speaking of Rhodes that he

so arranged what he called his "game" that each man, bringing with him that side of his head which belonged to the important land of his birth, was put in the way of getting another side to his head by men belonging to other not unimportant countries.[2]

So much for the 'colonies' in the old sense of the word; rather a federation of such as were composed of British emigrants—Canada, Australia, New Zealand, and, in part, the South Africa of his earlier days—the Five Nations. But what, say, of India, or the Sudan? There he believed with Chamberlain, but without his arrogance, that the English had a knack of ruling, gently, with understanding and self-abnegation, with devotion to the job, as attested by many stories besides those already referred to. He believed that many of his countrymen had a genius for governing because they understood the people they had to deal with—not the ignorant high-ups of Simla (though not all were ignorant) but the Ordes, Hummils and so on. Not that he thought one race superior to another: the East had in some ways a better religion than the West: Gunga Din was a better man than the average Tommy: the Sudanese Fuzzy-Wuzzy and the Zulu were worthy of admiration as fighting men. There is no feeling at all of racial superiority in Kipling: what he felt profoundly was that at the moment

---

[1] *A Book of Words*, V.   [2] ibid., XXVI.

the British knew how to rule. *At the moment*, for it was only for the time being that this faculty was granted:

> We were dreamers, dreaming greatly, in the man-stifled town;
> We yearned beyond the sky-line where the strange roads go down.
> Came the Whisper, came the Vision, came the Power with the Need,
> Till the Soul that is not man's soul was lent us to lead.
>
> ('The Song of the Dead', 1893)

The Power was lent, not given, us to lead.

Unfortunately, just during this decade, England was swept by a tide of jingoism. This has been endemic throughout our history, from Drayton's 'The Battle of Agincourt', through Thomson's 'Rule Britannia', some of Wordsworth's sonnets, and Tennyson's 'Riflemen Form!'; at this time we still had the jingo song of 1877 itself, with its now forgotten lines,

> We don't want to fight, but by Jingo! if we do
> We've got the men, we've got the ships, we've got the money too.

There were 'Tommy Atkins', 'Soldiers of the Queen', plenty about 'the dear old flag', A. C. Benson's 'Land of Hope and Glory', and many others, even from Meredith.[1] There was no troubling memory of Maiwand or Majuba, where the invincible English had suffered disastrous defeats. There was a general mood of optimism, and of a complacency that appalled Kipling, apart from the jingoism he had always hated from the days of the 'jelly-bellied Flag-Flapper'. The 1897 Jubilee, for which *The Times* asked him to write a poem, gave him an opportunity for preaching humility. Already in the 1893 'Song of the English' he had written:

> Fair is our lot—O goodly is our heritage!
> (Humble ye, my people, and be fearful in your mirth!)

and now, in his famous 'Recessional' he made the point more precise:

> If, drunk with sight of power, we loose
>   Wild tongues that have not Thee in awe,
> Such boastings as the Gentiles use,
>   Or lesser breeds without the Law—

[1] See also 'The Red White and Blue' in *Essays and Papers* presented to C. A. Bodelsen, 1964.

ending: "For frantic boast and foolish word—Thy mercy on Thy people, Lord!" Yet he was afraid that this might be misinterpreted, writing to Haggard on 10 July:

How any nation save ourselves, with a fleet such as we have at present, would go out swiftly to trample the guts out of the rest of the world; and the fact that we do not seem to show that even if we aren't very civilised, we're about the only power with a glimmering of civilisation in us. . . . But my objection to that hymn is that it may be quoted as an excuse for lying down abjectly at all times and seasons and taking what any other country may think fit to give us. What I wanted to say was:—"Don't gas but be ready to give people snuff"—and I only covered the first part of the notion.[1]

He need not have been afraid; the 1914–18 war showed that.

Moreover he reminded his readers that the Empire, whatever it might be, was not eternal, and that in due course all our pomp would be one with Nineveh and Tyre. Always there was with him the realization of what the gods had said at their *punchayet* on the island in the Ganges, a sense he was to frame memorably in one of the finest of his poems, written in relation to 'A Centurion of the Thirtieth', when Rome was losing its grip on Britain:

> Cities and Thrones and Powers
>   Stand in Time's eye,
> Almost as long as flowers,
>   Which daily die. . . .

Power had been lent us to lead; while we had this, and the vision, we were fated to continue. But the task—for task or trust it was—could be passed on, as stated in the poem he addressed to the United States when they took over the Philippine Islands in 1899:

> Take up the White Man's burden—
>   Send forth the best ye breed—
> Go bind your sons to exile
>   To serve your captives' need;
> To wait in heavy harness
>   On fluttered folk and wild—
> Your new-caught, sullen peoples,
>   Half devil and half child.

[1] *Cohen, Record,* p. 33.

All this was to be done, the next stanza says,

> To seek another's profit,
> And work another's gain.

It goes on, as though with a prevision of future disillusion:

> Take up the White Man's burden—
> The Savage wars of peace—
> Fill full the mouth of Famine
> And bid the sickness cease;
> And when your goal is nearest
> The end for others sought
> Watch Sloth and heathen Folly
> Bring all your hopes to nought.

In 'liberal' circles, the phrase 'the white man's burden' gave scope for glowing self-righteousness and the laughter of contempt. 'The white man!' What snobbery! What conceited self-gratulation! Well, the races at that time technologically equipped to do the needed work happened to be what we call 'white-skinned'. 'A white man' came to mean someone who respected and lived by the best traditions of honesty and responsibility which constituted the Law of his tribe. His 'burden'! Oh yes, exploiting the native to make fortunes out of him, which might have been a cogent criticism seen from the City end, and not on the ground. Kipling, of course, was aware of this attitude, and visits it with scorn-inspired comedy. We get this early when Hummil, in 'At the End of the Passage', reads to his worn-out companions in their hell, the report of a speech in Parliament:

And I assert unhesitatingly that the Civil Service in India is the preserve—the pet preserve—of the aristocracy of England. What does the democracy—what do the masses—get from that country, which we have step by step so fraudulently annexed? I answer, nothing whatever. It is farmed with a single eye to their own interests by the scions of the aristocracy. They take good care to maintain their lavish scale of incomes, to avoid or stifle any inquiries into the nature and conduct of their administration, while they themselves force the unhappy peasant to pay with the sweat of his brow for all the luxuries in which they are lapped.

There was, something, of course, in these criticisms; there are always flaws in every human activity. If some foolish people did think that to be white was better than to be what we now call 'coloured', the Ordes and Tallantires did not think so: nor did Findlayson in 'The Bridge-Builders' in regard to Peroo, and no one laughs at the idea of 'the burden' if he has ever seen one of those who carry it worn out physically and nervously by the lonely task of bringing health and peace to countries ravaged by sickness and famine, torn by tribal wars.

No doubt Kipling was proud of what the Empire had done, even if imperfectly; but his criticism was not lacking. The two different sides of his head, his far-reaching sympathy, even suggested the thought expressed in 'A Pict Song':

> Rome never looks where she treads.
> Always her heavy hooves fall,
> On our stomachs, our hearts, or our heads;
> And Rome never heeds when we bawl.

He can be regarded as having been an Imperialist, though not in the sense usually ascribed to him; and it may be noted that throughout *Something of Myself* he always refers to his 'Imperialism' in inverted commas. But up to the time of the Boer War he held a moderate belief in his vision of Empire. Then came disillusion.

§2. DISILLUSION

For the Boer War revealed a weakness at the very heart of the concept. The response of many individuals was splendid—one thinks of the City Imperial Volunteers—and the Colonies set a magnificent pattern of the idea of Federation in practice. At home, in contrast, there was a baffling inertia; not only were there too many people killing Kruger with their mouths, but nothing was being done for the soldiers, or their dependants, whence the vigorously compelling 'The Absent-Minded Beggar' which brought in many thousand pounds for the relief of soldiers' families. At any rate the idea of the Boer War was repugnant to Kipling, seeming to him merely years "where the senseless bullet fell". He deplored

> . . . the set folly and the red breach
> And the black waste of it all
>
> ('The Settler', 1903)

but seeing that it had been entered upon, he could not abide the mismanagement of the directing powers. The private soldier was eminently good, but he was untrained and ill-led; most of the senior officers had to be 'Stellenbosched', as the phrase then was for removing from command. When it was over he had the vision of English and Boer uniting to build up a fine and adept community, and expressed disappointment when a later Liberal Government gave back the Transvaal and the Orange River Colony (as it had come to be called) to the Boers, as thus "we put them in a position to uphold their primitive lust for racial domination",[1] a point of view we have come to appreciate in the last few years. His poems of the time are either in sympathy with the soldiers

> (Boots—Boots—Boots—Boots—movin' up an'
> down again)—
> There's no discharge in the war!

or 'Bridge-Guard in the Karroo'; show fellow-feeling for the Colonials, as in 'Lichtenberg', or appreciation of the fighting qualities of the Boer, as in 'Piet'—("I've known a lot o' men behave a dam' sight worse than Piet"), or the already quoted epitaph on General Joubert. Or they condemn the ineptitude of the higher ranks, as in the verses 'Stellenbosch'. His stories are as outspoken. In 'The Captive', that admirable American, Laughton O. Zigler, tells the narrator about certain Boers:

They could fight in their own way, and don't you forget it. But I guess you will not. They fought to kill, and by what I could make out, the British fought to be killed. So both parties were accommodated.

He also recounts how the English lord whom he met in Cape Town

. . . had his knife into the British system as much as any American. He said he wanted revolution, and not reform, in your army. He said the British soldier had failed in every point except courage.

In the story the relation between the opposing British and Boers is that of friends: the discussion between the eventually captured Van Zyl and the English general ruthlessly shows up the British weaknesses, particularly in the latter's frank statements.

---

[1] *Something of Myself*, VI.

Even the image of the subaltern has faded. The once irritatingly perfect youths of the Anglo-Indian stories have become the designedly irritating half-wits of 'The Outsider' and 'Folly Bridge', tales not to be found in the library editions. In the former, one character says of a regiment using the old ideas of warfare:

". . . It's the same old brand—Badajos, Talavera, Inkerman, Toulouse, Tel-el-Kebir—" (They will learn in time) "When half the men are in Pretoria and half the rest are wounded—if that's what you mean! I'm *so* sick of that 'in time'." "The Colonel will die— I wish he was dead now—'fighting heroically' in some dam'-fool trap he's walked into with his eyes open."

In the second, the public school and Sandhurst subaltern, through snobbery and sticking to rule, holds up urgent expert work on a bridge. There, a more intelligent Colonel deals with him promptly.

What goaded him most, however, were the comments of the pro-Boer factions in England. 'The Comprehension of Private Copper' gives us a sample, when one of the characters summarizes what has been written in the banned *Jerrold's Weekly* taken from the captive 'Renegid' Englishman fighting for the Boers:

'You're the aristocrat, Alf [Copper]. Old Jerrold's givin' it you 'ot. You're the uneducated 'ireling of a callous aristocracy which 'as sold itself to the 'Ebrew financier. Meantime, Ducky'—he ran his finger down a column of assorted paragraphs—'you're slakin' your brutal instincks in furious excesses. Shriekin' women an' desolated 'omesteads is what you enjoy, Alf . . . Halloa! What's a smokin' 'ektacomb?'

This is reported as being "excerpts from the speeches of the accredited leaders of His Majesty's Opposition": it is a variant of what Hummil read to his fellows in 'At the End of the Passage'. The theme is recurrent in Kipling. In 'Little Foxes' (1909) its statement is mercifully shortened: we hear only a little of what the M.P. there had said—a sentence or two about good revenue-payers being habitually flogged to death (but the poor man had been naughtily guyed)—and the sins of Imperialism. Kipling was always scornfully impatient of critics

G

who did not know, from a distance of a few thousand miles, what actually went on ("What should they know of England, who only England know?"), and during the South African War was bitterly indignant.

It was after that war that he incurred his greatest unpopularity by lashing out at what he considered the stupidity, the unfathomable stupidity, complacency, and lack of responsibility of the English, heralded by 'The Lesson' of July 1901, with its slightly varied refrain, "We've had a jolly good lesson, and it serves us jolly well right!" He expressed the belief that it would "do us no end of good", and concluded:

It was our fault, and our very great fault—and now we must turn it to use.
We have forty million reasons for failure, but not a single excuse.
So the more we work and the less we talk the better results we shall get.
We've had an Imperial lesson. It may make us an Empire yet!

It was rousing, it was challenging, and aroused no antagonism. But the reception of the virulent poem 'The Islanders' of January 1902 was markedly different. Its very first line was a stabbing mockery of self-satisfied complacency:

No doubt but ye are the People—your throne is above the King's. . .

where most readers of that day would have recognized the first phrase as that addressed by Job to his comforters (Job xii. 1), and been able to add the remainder of the verse, "and wisdom shall die with you". The poem begins with a description of the sense of false, effortless security in which the English lived, their thankless treatment of the men who guarded them while they slept, the soldiers whom they "thrust out of sight and away", who were trained and cared for less than "your horses and the dogs ye feed and prize". Then came the lines that gave unutterable offence:

But ye said, "Their valour shall show them"; but ye said, "The end is close."
And ye sent them comfits and pictures to help them harry your foes:
And ye vaunted your fathomless power, and ye flaunted your iron pride,

Ere—ye fawned on the Younger Nations for the men who
could shoot and ride!
Then ye returned to your trinkets; then ye contented your
souls
With the flannelled fools at the wicket or the muddied
oafs at the goals.

And he warned them that the happy life they had led

. . . was not made with the mountains, it is not one with
the deep.
Men, not gods, devised it. Men, not gods, must keep . . .

and he asked, prophetic phrases:

Do ye wait for the spattered shrapnel ere ye learn how a
gun is laid?
For the low, red glare to southward when the raided coast-
towns burn? . . .
Will the rabbit war with your foemen—the red deer horn
them for hire?
Your kept cock-pheasant keep you?—he is master of many
a shire.
Arid, aloof, incurious, unthinking, unthanking, gelt,
Will ye loose your schools to flout them till their brow-beat
columns melt?
Will ye pray them, or preach them, or print them, or ballot
them back from your shore?
Will your workmen issue a mandate to bid them strike no
more?

the bitter pun at the end involving organized labour as the
earlier lines had brought in the land-owning gentry. The
vituperative abuse was too much! Kipling was shouting too
loud. Such an attack could do no good; it was too general,
and was by no means to "say acceptable things". Nobody pays
much serious attention to a man who is obviously in a rage.

Later, in calmer mood, able to point more deftly at particular
targets, he attacked the War Office, in two poems, first
'Rimmon', in October 1903, in which the War Office is clearly
implied to be the House of Rimmon. It refers to the commission
which had been set up under Lord Esher to examine into
military organization, and had issued what was judged to be a
whitewashing report:

> Hushing the matter before it was known,
> They returned to our fathers afar,
> And hastily set Him afresh on His throne
> Because he had won us the war.

That penultimate stanza expresses the sorrowful bitterness of those who, as an earlier stanza described:

> . . . remember the sacrifice,
> Dead men an hundred laid—
> Slain while they served His mysteries
> And that He would not aid—

It is a moving, somewhat cryptic poem, unlike the almost gay 'The Song of the Old Guard' of a year later, verse of scoffing plainness, a brilliant adaptation of Francis Quarles's 'Song of Anarcharsis' in *The Shepherds' Oracle*, the chorus chanted by the generals being that chanted by the Bishops at whom Quarles had aimed his poem two hundred and fifty years earlier. The first stanza will give the flavour:

> "Know this, my brethren, Heaven is clear
> And all the clouds are gone—
> The Proper Sort shall flourish now,
> Good times are coming on"—
> The evil that was threatened late
> To all of our degree
> Hath passed in discord and debate,
> And, *Hey then up go we*!

Each stanza is more entertainingly preposterous than the last. But those poems did not reach the great mass of general readers whose ire had been aroused by the shockingly true indictment of 'The Islanders'.

Already there was growing in Kipling a sense, not exactly of resignation, but of acceptance of the truth to which he had given perhaps rather detached expression in 'Cities and Thrones and Powers'. If the War Office was beyond hope, so were other departments of state, made impotent by democracy. He wrote to Haggard from Cape Town at the end of January 1902:

> . . . the question of food supply is as you say *the* vital one. You have the figures and facts and the influence: and for goodness sake

keep hammering at it. What makes me sick is what makes you sick—
the way, to wit, in which the responsible politician admits the cold
truth of one's contention and then explicitly says that he doesn't
dare 'go in advance of public opinion' and so on.[1]

Later in the same year he writes to his fellow thinker in these
matters of the "ornate velvet-plush lies" the politicians—and
others—tell; and even six years later his anger at politicians
breaks through his acceptance: "They are all such a set of
flagrant and persistent liars that I *can't* believe in their rectitude
over anything." He asks to be forgiven for seeming a pessimist.[2]
Nevertheless just after the war he had the heart to make
public utterances urging action, as in *The Five Nations* of 1903,
with its 'Dedication' "Before a midnight breaks in storm", and
'The Dykes', a poem of lament which begins "We have no
heart for the fishing—we have no hand for the oar". We have
failed to keep up the protective dykes: "We are too far from
the beach, men say, to know how the outworks stand." It is
all poetically felt, in a way that 'The Islanders' was not, the
penultimate stanza sorrowfully according that:

> Now we can only wait till the day, wait and apportion our
>   shame.
> These are the dykes our fathers left, but we would not look
>   to the same.
> Time and again were we warned of the dykes, time and
>   again we delayed:
> Now, it may fall, we have slain our sons, as our fathers we
>   have betrayed.

It was in a spirit of what might be called nostalgia that he
wrote the Roman stories of *Puck of Pook's Hill*, lingering with
Pertinax and Parnesius, those old-time versions of Tallantire
and Orde; and we feel a special note creeping in when Pertinax,
after writing his cheerful letter to Maximus, turns to Parnesius
and says: "And now . . . we be two dead men, my brother.
Let us go to the Temple";[3] and they go to worship Mithras.
As a matter of fact they were not fated to die, but what they
had lived for was to go.

---

[1] *Cohen*, p. 197.   [2] *Cohen, Record*, p. 67.
[3] 'The Winged Hats.'

Time and again Kipling warned England of her dykes, as in 1896 with "The earth is full of anger", and he did so again in 1903 with "Before a midnight breaks in storm". There was now and again some optimism in his utterances; but it was rather in his moods of deep pessimism that his astonishing prophetic sense manifested itself, as in 1909, the 'gloomy prognostications', Professor Carrington calls them, of 'The City of Brass'. In that poem, ruthlessly upbraiding as 'The Islanders', but more nobly phrased, he reproves his countrymen for their moral flabbiness; and these lines, foreseeing the future, fill us with sad astonishment:

> As for their kinsmen far off, on the skirts of the nation,
> They harried all earth to make sure none escaped reproba-
> tion.
> They awakened unrest for a jest in their newly-won borders,
> And jeered at the blood of their brethren betrayed by
> their orders.
> They instructed the ruled to rebel, their rulers to aid them;
> And, since such as obeyed them not fell, their Viceroys
> obeyed them.
> When the riotous set them at naught they said "Praise the
> upheaval!
> For the show and the word and the thought of Dominion
> is evil!"
>
> They unwound and flung from them with rage, as a rag
> that defiled them,
> The imperial gains of the age which their forefathers piled
> them,
> They ran panting in haste to lay waste and embitter for
> ever,
> The wellsprings of Wisdom and Strength which are Faith
> and Endeavour.
> They nosed out and digged up and dragged forth and
> exposed to derision
> All doctrine of purpose and worth and restraint and pre-
> vision:
>
> And it ceased, and God granted them all things for which
> they had striven,
> And the heart of a beast in the place of a man's heart
> was given . . .

To anyone living in the seventh decade of this century, bearing
in mind, say, the once ordered African states, the accuracy of
the picture is disturbing. Then another mood would supervene,
and a sense of the unattainability of man's ambitions would
pervade his mind, as when, in 1907, he wrote 'The Four Angels',
ending:

As Adam was a-working outside of Eden-Wall,
He used the Earth, he used the Seas, he used the Air and all;
  Till out of black disaster
  He arose to be the master
    Of Earth and Water, Air and Fire,
    But never reached his heart's desire!
      ('The Apple Tree's cut down!')

 These were indeterminate years, and the stories written in
that decade, collected in *Actions and Reactions* indicate a gradual
change, a growing acceptance. We get two of the old 'Imperial'
kind, 'Little Foxes' already referred to, and 'A Deal in Cotton',
both illustrating how the English official, by understanding the
people he has been sent to watch over and guide, induces or
tricks them into more ordered, more civilized behaviour, in
the former an abandonment of dishonest land-snatching, in
the latter slave-trading, which, while itself being stamped out,
is used against cannibalism. In both stories the result contributes
to the development of the area, the great men on either side
honouring each other. But spasmodically vocal was the irrita-
tion Kipling always felt at the uninterest of the English, the
mismanagement in high places, and the complacency. But the
rather strident cry of the early (1891):

 Winds of the World, give answer! They are whimpering
  to and fro—
 And what should they know of England who only England
  know?—
 The poor little street-bred people that vapour and fume
  and brag,
 They are lifting their heads in the stillness to yelp at the
  English Flag!
      ('The English Flag')

(where 'in the stillness' conveys the prophetic note), gave

place in the middle of 1914 to the more humorously scoffing 'Jobson's Amen':

> "Blessèd be the English and all their ways and works.
> Cursèd be the Infidels, Hereticks and Turks!"
> "Amen," quo' Jobson, "but where I used to lie
> Was neither Candle, Bell nor Book to curse my brethren
> by. . . ."

He could also extend the humour, and laugh a little at his earlier vision of Imperial Federation, and there is a certain realism in its possible justification as, not "the ties of common sentiment" so much as "the ties of common funk", as both stated and allegorically shown in his half-farce, 'The Puzzler'.

He still had hopes of some sort of Empire, however loosely federated, but these seem to have turned to the colonies, especially Canada, as shown in three lectures which he gave there during a visit in 1907 and printed in *A Book of Words*. Speaking of 'Imperial Relations', he said of the Boer War:

> And out of that great gathering of our men on the plains of South Africa there was born, I think, a treaty of mutual preference between the various members of that Empire which—I am no diplomatist myself—I think regular diplomatists will find it difficult to annul.

Earlier in the lecture he had spoken of "the idea of our Empire as a community of men of identical race and identical aims, united in comradeship, comprehension and sympathy" as no new thing. Speaking at Winnipeg on 'Growth and Responsibility', in praise of its astonishing growth of fifteen years, he enlarged on

> . . . men who are labouring with their brains and the sweat of their bodies to build up new cities, and to make firm the outworks of civilisation.
>
> These things are not accomplished except by the hardest of toil, high courage, eternal sacrifice, and very often bitter disappointment.

His feelings towards the Canadians are made plain in 'Letters to the Family'[1] written as newspaper articles during this tour, where he could afford to mix taunts at the apathy of the mother country. The first letter, 'The Road to Quebec' opens with:

[1] *Letters of Travel.*

It must be hard for those who do not live there to realise the cross between canker and blight that has settled on England for the last couple of years.

and he goes on to say that the people who had voted for the Liberal Government would never have done so if they "had only known what they were going to do". In 'Newspapers and Democracy' he related that when he asked "What is the matter with the English as immigrants?"

The answers were explicit: 'Because the English do not work. Because we are sick of Remittance-men and loafers sent out here. Because the English are rotten with Socialism. Because the English don't fit with our life. They kick at our way of doing things. They are always telling us how things are done in England. They carry frills!'

He glowed at what he saw done. Describing 'A People at Home', he gives a loose to all his romanticism, a romanticism of hard work and accomplishment.

I wonder sometimes whether any eminent novelist, philosopher, dramatist, or divine of today has to exercise half the pure imagination, not to say insight, endurance, and self-restraint, which is accepted without comment in what is called 'the material exploitation' of a new country. Take only the question of creating a new city at the junction of two lines—all three in the air. The mere drama of it, the play of human virtues, would fill a book. And when the work is finished, when the city is, when the new lines embrace a new belt of farms, and the tide of Wheat has rolled North another unexpected degree, the men who did it break off, without compliments, to repeat the joke elsewhere.

In 'The Fortunate Towns' he refers to a town he "had first heard discussed nigh twenty years ago by a broken-down prospector in a box car".

'Young feller,' said he, after he had made a professional prophecy, 'you'll hear of that town if you live. She's born lucky.'
I saw the town later—it was a siding by a trestle bridge where Indians sold beadwork—and as years passed I gathered that the old tramp's prophecy had come true, and that Luck of some kind had struck the little town by the big river. So, this trip, I stopped to make sure. It was a beautiful town of six thousand people, and

a railway junction, beside a high-girdered iron bridge; there was a public garden with trees at the station. A company of joyous men and women, whom that air and that light, and their own good-will, made our brothers and sisters, came along in motors, and gave us such a day as never was.

The old vision of Empire still haunted Kipling—even though the Luck in this case was a find of natural gas.

The outbreak of the First World War, the nearness of which he prophesied only a few months earlier in 'The Edge of the Evening' (others, of course had foreseen it) rallied all his old feelings, stirred all his old passion. Here, now, the mature civilization, the well-tried Law, was threatened. The crisis called forth a great patriotic poem, stern, unvisionary, almost bitter, and a challenge to courage:

> For all we have and are,
> For all our children's fate,
> Stand up and take the war.
> The Hun is at the gate!
> Our world has passed away,
> In wantonness o'erthrown.
> There is nothing left to-day
> But steel and fire and stone!
> Though all we knew depart,
> The old Commandments stand:—
> "In courage keep your heart,
> In strength lift up your hand."
>   . . .
> Comfort, content, delight,
> The ages' slow-bought gain,
> They shrivelled in a night
> Only ourselves remain. . . .

The phrases are typical of what he had said for so long: the world "in wantonness o'erthrown"; "the ages' slow-bought gain": yet any person at all aware of history would appreciate the deep feeling behind them. To an age such as our own, where these things seem to go unrecognized in favour of the hypostasized abstractions which Kipling loathed and of which he too clearly saw the potential evils, calling down we might say the judgement of the Gods of the Copy-book headings, the final stanza of the poem will seem distasteful, smacking of rhodomontade. Yet there is a sense of actuality in:

> No easy hope or lies
> Shall bring us to our goal,
> But iron sacrifice
> Of body, will, and soul.
> There is but one task for all—
> One life for each to give.
> What stands if Freedom fall?
> Who dies if England live?

Perhaps only those old enough to remember the shock—and the challenge—of those years can appreciate the stark cogency of that utterance.

Kipling's stories of the war are not concerned, except by far-fetched implication, with all-embracing ideas. They deal, rather, with individual experiences, on the fringe, shall we say, of happenings. There is no such story as 'The Taking of Lungtungpen', or 'With the Main Guard', but, rather, purely personal ones such as 'A Madonna of the Trenches' (already mentioned), 'A Friend of the Family', or, in lighter mood, 'The Janeites'. One naval story, 'Sea Constables', is harsh enough, and will be treated under 'Realism', as will the one about a woman, 'Mary Postgate', both having been stupidly execrated through profound misunderstanding: another about a woman, 'The Gardener', has already been described under the heading 'Compassion', a few poems deal with the Navy in action, such as 'The Verdicts'. A short one about submarines, 'Tin Fish', may be quoted from *Sea Warfare*:

> The ships destroy us above
> And ensnare us beneath.
> We arise, we lie down, and we move
> In the belly of Death.
>
> The ships have a thousand eyes
> To mark where we come . . .
> But the mirth of a seaport dies
> When our blow gets home.

For the rest his poems at this period are documents expressive of his private feelings—the deeply felt epitaphs, showing his mastery of the epigram, or the courageous 'A Recantation' quoted earlier.[1]

His great war poem, expressing all the agony of the individual giving himself to something greater than himself, is the searing poem 'Gethsemane', which must be quoted in full.

> The Garden called Gethsemane
>   In Picardy it was,
> And there the people came to see
>   The English soldiers pass.
> We used to pass—we used to pass
>   Or halt, as it might be,
> And ship our masks in case of gas
>   Beyond Gethsemane.
>
> The Garden called Gethsemane,
>   It held a pretty lass,
> But all the time she talked to me
>   I prayed my cup might pass.
> The officer sat on the chair,
>   The men lay on the grass,
> And all the time we halted there
>   I prayed my cup might pass—
>
> It didn't pass—it didn't pass—
>   It didn't pass from me.
> I drank it when we met the gas
>   Beyond Gethsemane.

In those days everyone would have recognized the reference to Christ's agony in the garden (Matthew xxvi. 36–39, Mark xiv. 32–36).

But if that was the torture of those who actually fought, there was also the grief of those who had suffered loss, as he had done. A universal poem, neither personal nor political, which would apply to anybody in any country at war with another, is 'The Children', a lament which seems at first sight to come rather incongruously in connection with 'The Honours of War', that account of a rag in an officers' mess, a story which, for all its unlikelihood, breathes a sense of the liking the responsible old have for the irresponsible young:

[1] See p. 36

These were our children who died for our lands: they were
   dear in our sight.
We have only the memory left of their home-treasured
   sayings and laughter.
The price of our loss shall be paid to our hands, not
   another's hereafter.
Neither the Alien nor Priest shall decide on it. That is our
   right.
   But who shall return us the children?

One may, no doubt, exact expiation from the enemy, but it
will not balance the irredeemable account: that is beyond the
power of politics. One political poem, however, Kipling did
write in connection with the war, a poem in a sense comparable
with 'Rimmon' and 'The Song of the Old Guard', but far more
heartfelt. It was born from Kipling's anger at the bungling
which led to so many casualties in Mesopotamia, about which
'Stalky' wrote a report so scathing as to earn his dismissal,
which he accepted without surprise. The first stanza reads:

They shall not return to us, the resolute, the young,
   The eager and whole-hearted whom we gave,
But the men who left them thriftily to die in their own dung,
   Shall they come with years and honour to the grave?

The last stanza sums up the whole passionate argument:

Their lives cannot repay us—their death could not undo—
   The shame that they have laid upon our race.
But the slothfulness that wasted and the arrogance that slew,
   Shall we leave it unabated in its place?
                              ('Mesopotamia. 1917')

We did, as might have been forseen, and as Kipling could only
too faithfully realize. Though he had himself suffered irre-
parably from the war, there had been much in it to hearten
him; the splendid reaction of the young men, their courage and
their endurance, together with the response of the Colonies,
whose men came over in their thousands to fight with the mother
country. But the bungling and the politicians brought disillusion that was almost final. He was growing to be satisfied
with close actuality rather than with far-reaching ideas. He
came to abandon politics—"a dog's life without a dog's

decencies" as he described it[1]—and was more and more
content to find his support in the sense of home.

§3. HOME

"Home is where one starts from."

East Coker

"To explain Kipling's . . . feeling for Sussex, as merely the
nostalgia of a man without a country . . . would be a mistake,"
thus T. S. Eliot in his essay prefacing *A Choice of Kipling's
Verse*; yet there is no doubt that Kipling felt that a man must
have his roots somewhere, must belong. Even as late as 'Letters
to the Family' of 1907 he could write, "It must be pleasant to
have a country of one's very own to show off", even if he there
meant a country that one had oneself built up, for by that time
he had already made Sussex his centre. He had had no home
to start from—infancy in India, the House of Desolation,
Westward Ho!, hardly mitigated by visits to the Burne-Joneses
and Poynters, then 'seven years hard' in another part of India.
Such shiftings could not give him the sense of home; he had
belonged to many 'in-groups', yet none was specifically his
own. Nor could the vast Empire of his vision be in any intimate
sense a home.

In 1896, to all intents and purposes driven out of Vermont,
he lived for a time at Torquay, not overmuch drawn to it,
and then at Rottingdean, which he liked for its family associa-
tions—Burne-Joneses, Baldwins, Macdonalds, and so on. His
last visit to the United States, during which his much-loved
daughter Josephine died, was turned by his brother-in-law to a
decisive defeat in that direction, and he returned to live finally
at Burwash, in the house named 'Bateman's', now famous. It
took him a little time to feel that he had come home. At the
end of November 1902 he wrote to C. E. Norton:

> We left Rottingdean because Rottingdean was getting too popu-
> lated, though we didn't want to part from Aunt Georgie. Then we
> discovered England which we had never done before . . . and went
> to live in it. England is a wonderful land. It is the most marvellous
> of all foreign countries that I have ever been in.[2]

[1] In 'The Village that Voted the Earth was Flat'.
[2] *Carrington*, p. 369.

And to Rider Haggard on the publication of his *Rural England*: "I am slowly discovering England which is the most wonderful foreign land I have ever been in."[1] He was discovering it largely through the primitive motor-cars, Locomobiles, which he jumped at as soon as they were produced, not only because they were exciting feats of engineering and technology, but because they enabled him to go about and really see at least a part of England.

First, it would seem, it was the countryside itself that enraptured him, and some of his best descriptive writing intrudes, but always with point, into such diverse tales as 'They', 'The Prophet and the Country', and 'The Eye of Allah'. We can in a moment compare the intimacy of these descriptions with what he wrote in 1895 as part of the setting of 'My Sunday at Home':

It was the very point of perfection in the heart of an English Mayday. The unseen tides of the air had turned, and all nature was setting its face with the shadows of chestnuts towards the peace of the coming night. But there were hours yet, I knew—long, long hours of the eternal English twilight—to the ending of the day. I was well content to be alive . . . and to love my country with the devotion that three thousand miles of intervening sea bring to fullest flower. And what a garden of Eden it was, this fatted, clipped, and washen land! . . . And the joy of it was that it was all mine alienably— groomed hedgerow, spotless road, decent greystone cottage, serried spinney, tasselled copse, apple-bellied hawthorn, and well-grown tree. A light puff of wind—it scattered flakes of may over the gleaming rails—gave me a faint whiff as it might have been of fresh cocoanut, and I knew that the golden gorse was in bloom somewhere out of sight. Linnæus had thanked God on his knees when he first saw a field of it. . . .

He used the palette-knife generously here, in the worst Dick Heldar manner. It is a brilliant picture, but we feel it is rather that of a visitor, not of an inhabitant. We note the three thousand miles of intervening sea, and that the delights of the country are only 'alienably' Kipling's: whereas in the almost as lavish pictures in 'They' of 1904, we get the sense that Kipling really belongs: this is his country, and in turn belongs to him *in*alienably:

[1] *Cohen*, p. 197.

One view called me to another; one hill-top to its fellow, half across the county. . . . The orchid-studded flats of the East gave way to the thyme, ilex, and grey grass of the Downs; these again to the rich cornland and fig-trees of the lower coast . . . I found hidden villages where bees, the only things awake, boomed in eighty-foot lindens that overhung grey Norman churches; miraculous brooks diving under stone bridges. . . .

A quick turn plunged me first into a green cutting brim-full of liquid sunshine, next into a gloomy tunnel where last year's dead leaves whispered and scuffled about my tyres. . . .

The description proceeds, and there are other landscapes in the story, which is perhaps a little two crowded in this respect. Yet even though you feel that this is Kipling's own country, he gives the sense that he is showing it to you; he is not content just to be of it, silently, as though his position were taken for granted. The very size of the landscape is against it. But when we come to 'The Prophet and the Country' of 1924, the very smallness of the picture, the kind of thing noticed, gives the sense that he is just 'there'; nothing astonishing is presented; it is all to be expected:

. . . night shut down on us.

A rounded pile of woods ahead took one sudden star to its forehead and faded out; the way-waste melted into the darker velvet of the hedge; another star reflected itself in the glassy black of the bitumened road; and a weak moon struggled up out of a mist-patch from a valley. Our lights painted the grass unearthly greens, and the tree-boles bone-white.

A similar description of the dawn follows later in the story. As a contrast to this vignette there is a brief passage in 'The Eye of Allah' of two years later which really gives the sense that the narrator is at home:

They walked quietly back along the leads, three English counties laid out in evening sunshine around them; church upon church, monastery upon monastery, cell after cell, and the bulk of a vast cathedral moored on the edge of the banked shoals of sunset.

All these descriptions, at whatever stage of familiarity, indicate an intense appreciation amounting to love, different in tone from earlier pictures, say of the Himalayas in *Kim*.

It was in 1902 or so that he really felt the clutch of England—
if not yet to the virtual exclusion of Imperial ideas—though
already by 1899 he was reading and degustating such books as
White's *Selborne*. Writing to Haggard at this time about the
latter's *Farmer's Year* he reports: "In our tiny way we have also
made experiments with land:" and on 2 December could say,
with evident delight, in spite of the 'alas!'

> I—alas!—hold land now. . . . An old house and a 25 acre farm
> of good hop land and fruit and a mill (water) that dates from 1196.
> The farm is let down and neglected: the tenant is a glib-tongued
> impostor and the buildings are disgraceful . . . I shall have to put
> up at least two decent cottages in the place . . . and I do want to
> make it possible to rear clean healthy men on my fraction of Eng-
> land.[1]

He was already prepared to act on Haggard's advice. Writing a
few days later, having previously said that hops "were a demora-
lizing gamble", he went on:

> Yours is advice of gold. Apples as you say, are likely to be the game.
> I have 335 trees bearing already mostly good sorts but grievously in
> need of oil and lime-wash & salt and soap & shaping which they will
> get this spring.
> But it's difficult about the tenant. [For a gloss on this see *Something
> of Myself*, Chapter VII.] You see there's that blessed mill which is a
> convenience for grinding pig food and any man who takes that wants
> a few acres of land. . . . Meanwhile I have to spend £239! (two
> thirty nine pounds!) on making neglected cottages habitable! Dog
> kennels aren't in it with their present state of filth.[2]

He was becoming part of the countryside, loving it not only
for its own sake, but also because of the sense of knowing how
things were done, and the joy of doing them. The technologist
in him was stimulated as was the humanitarian. He began to
feel that he really belonged, not to a somewhat abstract idea
such as the Empire, but to some particular solid thing, towards
which he had responsibilities. One of his best-known poems,
'Sussex', written in 1902 makes this plain. The first and penultimate stanzas state:

[1] *Cohen*, p. 195.
[2] ibid.

H

> God gave all men all earth to love,
>   But, since our hearts are small,
> Ordained for each one spot should prove
>   Belovèd over all;
> That, as He watched Creation's birth,
>   So we, in godlike mood,
> May of our love create our earth
>   And see that it is good. . . .
>
> So to the land our hearts we give
>   Till the sure magic strike,
> And Memory, Use, and Love make live
>   Us and our fields alike—
> That deeper than our speech and thought,
>   Beyond our reason's sway,
> Clay of the pit whence we were wrought
>   Yearns to its fellow-clay.

In the second stanza he had written:

> Each to his choice, and I rejoice
>   The lot has fallen to me
> In a fair ground—in a fair ground—
>   Yea, Sussex by the sea!

And, of course, being human, always a little schoolboyishly human, he expected others to agree with him about Sussex, whose earth and whose history were getting into his bones. Thus he wrote to Haggard about his *Rural England*, after generously praising it:

Sussex, Sir, has been badly treated by you. You have neglected the fattening grounds of the Ouse and the meetings of the curious old riverleet or whatever they call it, which apportions the rental of these pastures once a year I think.[1]

Evidently the strong tug of the earth was there, and by 1906 he could write in the 'Three-Part Song' attached to 'Dymchurch Flit':

> I'm just in love with all these three,
> The Weald and the Marsh and the Down countree,
> Nor I don't know which I love the most,
> The Weald or the Marsh or the white Chalk coast.

[1] *Cohen*, p. 196.

He had "buried his heart in a ferny hill", and "given (his) soul to the Southdown grass". This 'love-song', you might call it, is varied in the much later 'The Recall', which sets its seal on 'An Habitation Enforced'. In the poem he speaks happily of "the clinging magic" running under his feet in the grasses, and rapturously of

> Scent of the smoke in the evening,
> Smell of rain in the night,

feeling for himself what he had once attributed to the Australian soldier in the Boer War reminded of:

> The smell of the wattle by Lichtenberg,
> Riding in, in the rain.

Even the clay of the pit whence he was wrought had its magic properties, as he declared in the Introduction to *Rewards and Fairies*:

> Take of English earth as much
> As either hand may rightly clutch . . .
>
> It shall sweeten and make whole
> Fevered breath and festered soul.
> It shall mightily restrain
> Over-busied hand and brain.
> It shall ease thy mortal strife
> 'Gainst the immortal woe of life,
> Till thyself, restored, shall prove
> By what grace the Heavens do move.
>
> ('A Charm')

He could well say with Sir Richard Dalyngridge, "But now England hath taken me."

More significantly still he had fallen in love with the people of England. In the previously quoted letter to Haggard where he reproaches him for not having given Sussex its due, he adds: "Likewise you haven't made enough of our down shepherds, nor of our fruit; nor of our most primitive peasantry."

It was really the 'primitive peasantry' that he loved in England, certainly far more than the rulers, the bureaucrats, the politicians; nor did he like the authoritarian squires, two of whom figure in his revenge stories, 'The Village that Voted the Earth was Flat' and 'Beauty Spots'. He seems always to be saying, "Thy people, Lord, thy people, are good enough for me." His pleasure in them comes out particularly in three tales, of which we may take first 'My Son's Wife', in which Midmore, in London an adherent of the Immoderate Left, supporting the Wider Morality (what Henry James called the Larger Latitude) inherits a small house in the country, and meets the real country folk. We sense the relish with which Kipling described the genial old rascal Sidney, who could practice the Wider Morality without having recourse to polysyllables; we meet Rhoda, who kept house for Midmore—her story leaks out—and the idiot boy; Sperrit, the country solicitor with his Latin quotations, and his green-eyed daughter, who taught Midmore about riding to hounds, and whom he eventually married. And so on, including most of the characters in *Handley Cross* and other Surtees books. It is not the best constructed of Kipling's tales, but it is full of earthy life, and belly-laughter of a sort new to Midmore. On a central occasion, when Sidney had told him that he had refrained from taking advantage of him because " 'Twas too dam' like cheatin' a suckin' Baby",

For a few seconds the teachings of the Immoderate Left, whose humour is all their own, wrestled with those of Mother Earth, who has her own humours. Then Midmore laughed till he could hardly stand. In due time Mr. Sidney laughed too—crowing and wheezing crescendo till it broke from him in roars. They shook hands. . . .

The most England-loving of the stories is 'An Habitation Enforced', as early as 1905, summed up by the concluding poem, 'The Recall', a story in which two Americans, the Chapins, visiting England are captivated, not only by the countryside, but by the people, their whole life, the social structure. A brilliant little inset gives the whole sense of this. The Chapins have been to church on the first Sunday after buying a house, and are coming out with the congregation of local families, who are grouped at the lych-gate:

'Your people,' said the clear voice of Lady Conant in her ear.
'I suppose so,' said Sophie, blushing, for they were within two yards of her; but it was not a question.
'Then that child looks as if it were coming down with mumps.

You ought to tell the mother she shouldn't have brought it to church.'

'I can't leave 'er be'ind, my lady,' the woman said. 'She'd set the 'ouse afire in a minute, she's that forward with the matches. Ain't you, Maudie dear?'

'Has Dr. Dallas seen her?'

'Not yet, my lady.'

'He must. You can't get away, of course. M——m! My idiotic maid is coming in for her teeth to-morrow at twelve. She shall pick her up—at Gale Anstey, isn't it?—at eleven.'

'Yes. Thank you very much, my lady.'

'I oughtn't to have done it,' said Lady Conant apologetically, 'but there has been no one at Pardons for so long that you'll forgive my poaching. Now, can't you lunch with us?'

What appealed to Kipling was the way in which the Law was kept, the sense of responsibility holding the countryside together as one community. When Sophie Chapin says to her husband, "But it's our land. We can do what we like", he answers "It's *not* our land. We've only paid for it. We belong to it, and it belongs to the people—our people they call 'em." The people whom Kipling most loved are shown us too, old Iggulden who died, and his son; also the Clokes, farmers, the senior of whom is a sort of Hobden, not unlike the one the Kiplings employed at Burwash, of whom mention has already been made.

We meet him again in the Jabez and Jesse of 'Friendly Brook', a story in which there is no laughter, where the two hedge-cutters between them arrive at a solution of the death by drowning of the father of the girl who had been adopted by local folk, and had come, not so much to reclaim her, as to extract blackmail for leaving her alone.[1] The characters of the two men, of Wickenden who had adopted the girl, and of his dumb mother, are described so as to bring out their under-standing humanity, their wiliness and their wisdom. To this is appended the poem 'The Land', which traces the history of the Hobdens, the two final stanzas summing up the whole seventeen:

[1] One may compare Hardy's 'The Tragedy of Two Ambitions' in *Life's Little Ironies*, where two men let their father drown.

Not for any beast that burrows, not for any bird that flies,
Would I lose his large sound counsel, miss his keen amending eyes.
He is bailiff, woodman, wheelwright, field-surveyor, engineer,
And if flagrantly a poacher—'tain't for me to interfere.

'Hob, what about that River-bit?' I turn to him again,
With Fabricius and Ogier and William of Warenne.
'Hev it jest as you've a mind to, *but*'—and here he takes command.
For whoever pays the taxes old Mus' Hobden owns the land.

What counted was "the passion and the piety and prowess of his line". In numberless stories from his early middle period onwards there are touches about people and the way they live, light touches, perhaps, but often fundamental, as with the two old women in that great story 'The Wish House'. A passage in 'The Vortex' kaleidoscopically illustrates his pleasure in the whole active scene of English life along a road as full and as varied as the Grand Trunk Road we read of in *Kim*. In this tale Mr. Lingnam, everlastingly and boringly preaching Empire Federation—Kipling here allows himself a little humorous self-criticism, as he could afford to do by this time—is being driven in an open car "capable of some eighteen miles on the flat, with tetanic gears and a perpetual palsy".

Well settled on the back seat he did not once lift his eyes to the mellow landscape around him, or throw a word at the life of the English road which to me is one renewed and unreasoned orgy of delight. The mustard-coloured scouts of the Automobile Association; their natural enemies, the unjust police; our natural enemies, the deliberate market-day cattle, broadside-on at all corners, the bicycling butcher-boy a furlong behind: road-engines that pulled giddy-go-rounds, rifle galleries and swings, and sucked snortingly from wayside ponds in defiance of the notice-board: traction-engines, their trailers piled high with road metal; uniformed village nurses, one per seven statute miles, flitting by on their wheels; governess-carts full of pink children jogging unconcernedly past roaring, brazen touring-cars; the wayside rector with virgins in attendance, their faces screwed up against our dust; motor-bicycles of every shape charging down at every angle; red flags of rifle-ranges; detachments of dusty-putteed Territorials; coveys of flagrant children playing in mid-street, and the wise, educated English dog safe and quite silent on the pavement if his fool-mistress would but cease from trying to save him, passed and repassed us in sunlit or shaded settings.

Later, together with other allied delights, there was a Foresters Fête.

How did these people come to be like this, to live like this? That was a question that may have urged Kipling to the reading that made possible the tales in *Puck of Pook's Hill* and *Rewards and Fairies*. Professor Carrington suggests that he may have been asking "What should they know of England who only England know" as she is today? The meaning of all her thousand years, to echo the last stanza of 'The Recall', must be made plain. More and more he sensed the tradition that had gone to the building up of the English character as he plunged into history books of Roman, Medieval, and Elizabethan times, tracing the fusion of Saxon and Norman as in 'Young Men at the Manor', to take one example, all issuing in that strange mixture the Englishman, reticent, he liked to think, unboastful, as he stresses in his poem 'The English Way', written as late as 1929, where the Witch-wife decrees:

> "While there is fighting at the ford,
>   Or flood along the Tweed,
> That they shall choose the lesser word
>   To cloke the greater deed". . . .

> "Greater the deed, greater the need
>   Lightly to laugh it away,
> Shall be the mark of the English breed
>   Until the Judgment Day!"

He goes further in the poem 'The Puzzler' which belongs to the story of that name, where he decides that the English are "quite a race apart",

Being void of self-expression they confide their views to none;
But sometimes in a smoking-room, one learns why things were
  done. . . .

In telegraphic sentences, half nodded to their friends,
They hint a matter's inwardness—and there the matter ends.
And while the Celt is talking from Valencia to Kirkwall,
The English—ah, the English!—don't say anything at all.

He seems to have forgotten the strong Celtic strain in his own heredity, of which he had once been proud, and become absorbed in England.

It was not a sudden process, and the two sides of his head being always active, there are glaring contradictions. Sussex may have taken him, but it was at much the same time that he wrote the poem in which he delivered that devastating attack upon the character of the English, 'The Islanders'. Only gradually did he relinquish political activity; 'The City of Brass' appeared, after all, in 1909. There are still generalizations in poems, or inserted into stories, but they tend to be less frequent, though pungent enough.

But from 1918 onwards the tone grows more subdued. After the justifiably angry 'Mesopotamia', quoted in the previous section, his poems tend to be reproaches for forgetfulness. As head of the War Graves Commission he went to France with the King in 1922 to visit the War Cemeteries, and wrote 'The King's Pilgrimage', which ends, after a reference to "Five hundred thousand gentlemen of those that served their King":

> All that they had they gave—they gave—
>   In sure and single faith.
> There can no knowledge reach the grave
>   To make them grudge their death
> Save only if they understood
>   That, after all was done,
> We they redeemed denied their blood
>   And mocked the gains it won.

Ten years later his ire was stirred by the phrase "the eradication of memories of the Great War", which he culled from a 'Socialist Government Organ' and quotes at the head of his poem 'Memories'. The verses are sadly bitter—it is difficult to extract a quotation—as they describe by the use of "small, corroding words", how the We of the poem are going to destroy and tarnish not only the memory, but also the concept of "Faith, Obedience, Sacrifice, Honour and Fortitude", and the whole historical tradition, "the use and meaning of Their day". The Picts once more. It was his last political poem except for the warning he issued in 1932, 'The Storm Cone' much in his old manner, prophesying the war of 1939:

This is the midnight—let no star
Delude us—dawn is very far.
This is the tempest long foretold—
Slow to make head but sure to hold. . . .

The stories of his last period, and they are perhaps his best,
do not deal with contemporary affairs, though they have,
unavoidably, a metaphorical applicability to all times: 'The
Church that was at Antioch', 'The Eye of Allah', or those
dealing with people of the present day without any political
idea: 'The Wish House'; or dealing with compassion and
healing: 'Unprofessional', 'The Tender Achilles'; or, again
the Fables, 'The Enemies to Each Other' and 'Uncovenanted
Mercies', not denying himself the occasional release in the
cosmic laughter of such glorious farces as 'Aunt Ellen'. Politics
were out of his sphere, even when his cousin Baldwin became
Prime Minister, though the families continued on close friendly
terms; the Kiplings would dine at Downing Street or visit
Chequers, even though Ruddy regarded Stan as a bit too
'Socialist'.

There, then, is the curve, the perfectly normal curve—a
young man with aspirations and larger vision, his disillusion
in face of the unamenable facts of political life and the imperfect
nature of man, then resignation, and acceptance of things as
they are. After the vision the clouding, then the withdrawal,
and the interest in people simply for what they are against
the indecipherable background of existence. Optimism is the
spur to human endeavour, but in the end *il faut cultiver son
jardin*, and for Kipling this was the garden of England and its
people. It satisfied him; he found there infinite riches in a little
room—provided that he could ignore the surface look, and
really get down to the people. He might repeat what he had
written very early in the century:

> *If England was what England seems,*
> *An' not the England of our dreams,*
> *But only putty, brass an' paint*
> *'Ow quick we'd chuck 'er!—but she ain't.*
>
> ('The Return')

For Kipling, home was not where he started from, but where he
arrived.

CHAPTER V

The 'Reactionary'

If there be any among those common objects of hatred which I can safely say I doe contemne and laugh at, it is that great enemy of reason, the multitude; that numerous piece of monstrosity, which taken asunder seeme men, and the reasonable creatures of God; but confused together, make but one great beast, and a monstrosity more prodigious than Hydra: it is no breach of charity to call these fooles, it is the stile all holy writers have accorded them, set down by Solomon in canonicall Scripture, and a point of our faith to believe so.   *Religio Medici* II

Whether or not Kipling had read Sir Thomas Browne—and he probably had at school—there is no doubt but that he would have agreed heartily with the opinion quoted above. We know from 'On the City Wall' that he had experience of rioting mobs; and in 'His Chance in Life' he wrote of "the sound that a man never forgets all his life—the '*ah-yah*' of an angry crowd. [When that sound drops about three tones, and changes to a thick droning *ut*, the man who hears it had better go away if he is alone.]" He would have endorsed the 'Reflection' of the Marquess of Halifax that "The angry buzz of a multitude is one of the bloodiest Noises in the World." Halifax's previous 'Reflection' states one of the reasons for Kipling's dislikes, even fear of, democracy: "There is an accumulative Cruelty in a number of Men, though none in particular are ill-natured." That is a fact recognized by crowd-psychologists, Kipling's most emphatic statement of this being that "the People are tenfold more cruel than Kings".[1] It is rather more gently put in 'The Prophet and the Country', where the American, Tarworth, after some remarks about the Herd instinct and the Collective Outlook of Democracy, tells the narrator: "Those

---

[1] 'The Treasure and the Law.'

ancient prophets an' martyrs haven't got much on me in the
things a Democracy hands you if you don't see eye to eye with
it."

The thoughtlessness of mob-emotion, its tendency to panic,
was among the things that made Kipling detest crowds, and
in *Letters of Travel* ('Newspapers and Democracy') he wrote of:

. . . the blessed word 'Democracy' which means any crowd on the
move—that is to say, the helpless thing which breaks through floors
and falls into cellars; overturns pleasure-boats by rushing from port
to starboard; stamps men into pulp because it thinks it has lost six-
pence, and jams and grills in the doorways of blazing theatres . . .
all agreed that the only drawback to Democracy was Demos—a
jealous God of primitive tastes and despotic tendencies.

He varies the attack when in 'Judson and the Empire' he expa-
tiates a little on the theme of the beauties of a true democracy,
which has

. . . a large contempt for all other lands that are governed by Kings
and Queens and Emperors; and knows little and thinks less of their
internal affairs. All it regards is its own dignity, which is its King,
Queen, and Knave. So, sooner or later, its international differences
end in the common people, who have no dignity, shouting the common abuse of the street, which also has no dignity, across the seas
in order to vindicate their new dignity. The consequences may or
may not be war; but the chances do not favour peace.

In common with many thinkers since Aristotle, he believed
that democracy inevitably leads to tyranny or dictatorship as
did for instance Dr. Charles Burney: "There is no Tyrant so
cruel, nor no Sovereign so worthless, as that of the Mob."[1] He
would not have been surprised on reading that in 1957, Truong
Chinh, one of the leaders in South East Asia "was reported to
have denounced a tendency, which he said had appeared in
Vietnam to 'treat democracy and dictatorship as two dia-
metrically opposed things'".[2] To go back to 'Judson and the
Empire', there Kipling gives his opinion that Republics "glide
too quickly into military despotism", ending the story by telling
how the Governor "satisfied the love of a great and glorious

[1] To Mrs. Crewe, 19 September 1792. Roger Lonsdale, *Dr. Charles Burney*
(Oxford, 1963), p. 364.
[2] *The Times*, 19 April 1965. Letter from Michael Alison, M.P.

people, and saved a monarchy from the ill-considered despotism which is called a Republic". Speaking to the Rhodes Scholars in 1924,[1] he said:

And here, gentlemen, let me put before you the seductive possibility that some of you may end your days in refuges for the mentally afflicted—*not* because you will necessarily be more insane than you are at present, but because you will have preached democracy to democracies resolute that never again shall their peace be troubled by Demos.

Possibly this prophecy may be actuality, for in 1965 we read that in the hardly ten-year-old created republic of Ghana: "[the President] has taken all powers, silenced the opposition, made Parliament a rubber-stamp, and allowed himself to be extolled the fount of all wisdom".[2] It was only when profound peace brooded over the world that Kipling found that "republics rested content with their dictators".[3]

Democracies, then, were dangerous to peace, as they might well be, since their very basis was absurd. They settled affairs of state by the counting of noses, as the Socialist horse in 'A Walking Delegate' wished to do, being under the spell of abstract ideas. "It's this yer blamed abstrac' business that makes the young 'uns cut up in the Concord." Kipling seems to have thought what Arthur Young did when he visited France in the early 1790s: "I am inclined to think that the application of theory in matters of government, a surprising imbecility in the human mind," for surely to apply the idea of democracy was imbecile. In *From Sea to Sea* (XXIV) Kipling wrote:

Turn now to the august spectacle of a Government of the people, by the people, for the people, as it is understood in the city of San Francisco. Professor Bryce's book will tell you that every American citizen over twenty-one years of age possesses a vote. He may not know how to run his own business, control his wife, or instil reverence into his children, may be pauper, half-crazed with drink, bankrupt, dissolute, or merely a born fool: but he has a vote. If he likes, he can be voting most of his time—voting for his State Governor, his municipal officers, local option, sewage tracts, or anything else of which he has no special knowledge.

[1] *A Book of Words*, XXVI.
[2] *The Times*, 19 April 1965. Leading Article.
[3] 'The Devil and the Deep Sea.'

The whole thing becomes merely ludicrous.

As it was made to be in that major attack upon democracy, 'As Easy as A.B.C.' We may note that story as crucial, containing as it does Kipling's notion of the 'Utopia' which will exist in the world of 2065. Here, the Aerial Board of Control (whence the initials A.B.C.) is told that something is going wrong in Chicago: two of the greatest crimes are being committed there—namely Crowd-making and Invasion of Privacy. The town has cut itself off from aerial communication, thus compelling the intervention of the A.B.C., which—and this is the only government the world admits—is responsible for traffic "and all that that implies". The Board consists of four members; an Englishman (De Forest), an Italian (Pirolo), a Russian, and a Japanese, all of which might be considered a forecast, written in 1912, of the United Nations, except that it is effective, having no outsize committees. The Board has at its disposal an aerial fleet, armed with temporarily blinding lights, and a devastating noise which "touched the raw fibre of the brain", and which exists for "what used to be known as 'war' ". (War, incidentally, "as a paying concern, ceased in 1967" according to the preliminary story 'With the Night Mail'.)

Up to this time Illinois had been a thoroughly civilized state, abhorring crowds, careful not to invade privacy, and, with an average length of life of a hundred years, recognizing birth-control. Moreover, in common with the rest of this Planet, as Pirolo reassures himself and his colleagues, Chicago "has had her dose of popular government. She suffers from inherited agarophobia. She has no—ah—use for crowds." The people actually have a song, MacDonough's Song, which it is, however, forbidden to sing as it is apt to raise troublesome emotions; it has a slightly varied refrain to its stanzas:

> But Holy State (we have lived to learn)
> Endeth in Holy War. . . .

> For Holy People, however it runs,
> Endeth in wholly Slave. . . .

and has as finale:

Once there was The People—Terror gave it birth;
Once there was The People and it made a Hell of Earth.
Earth arose and crushed it. Listen, O ye slain!
Once there was The People—it shall never be again!

When the Board land in Chicago, De Forest asks the Mayor, "What was your silly trouble anyway?" "Too much dam' Democracy", the Mayor answers; and a little later his Medical Officer chimes in: "Transportation is Civilisation. Democracy is Disease." They told the Board that a group of people, whom they had come to call 'the Serviles', living in hotels and apartments because it saved them the trouble of looking after houses, had "got to talking . . . telling men and women how to manage their own affairs. (You can't teach a Servile not to finger his neighbour's soul.) That's invasion of privacy, of course, but in Chicago we'll suffer anything rather than make crowds." And later:

Would you believe me, they went on to talk of what they called "popular government"? They did! They wanted us to go back to the old Voodoo-business of voting with papers and wooden boxes, and word-drunk people, and printed formulas and news-sheets! They said they practised it among themselves about what they'd eat in their flats and hotels. Yes, sir! . . . Then they finished . . . by talking about "The People".

This so incensed the quiet, happy inhabitants of Chicago, used to living their lives in their own way, that they actually made crowds, though when they noticed this they were filled with horror, and shrank away when they found that they were touching each other. And here the danger of MacDonough's Song became apparent, since the last stanza runs:

> Whatsoever, for any cause,
>   Seeketh to take or give
> Power above or beyond the Laws,
>   Suffer it not to live!
> Holy State or Holy King—
>   Or Holy People's Will—
> Have no truck with the senseless thing.
>   Order the guns and kill!

for they threatened to murder the Serviles, the women being foremost in this, "For the female of the species is more deadly

than the male." Thus the officials of Chicago called upon the
A.B.C. to help them protect the Serviles, or carry them away.

The latter solution was found to be the practical one. But
what to do with the Serviles when they were got back to
England? Why, obviously, lend them to the manager of the
most successfully entertaining variety show, where, to the
immense delight of the audience, they would be exhibited as
an untouched primitive community, going through all the old
rigmarole of voting, counting noses, making crosses on bits of
paper and stuffing these into boxes. Moreover, they would talk
for hours about how to "raise the Planet to loftier levels". All
this the Board arranged by wireless while on their way back,
describing the Serviles to the delighted manager panting for
an original comic turn.

During the talk on the way back, the members of the Board
"all marvelled how [the Serviles] had contrived to extract and
secrete so much bitter poison and unrest out of the good life
God gives us" on this by now normally "tolerant, humorous,
lazy little Planet". For Kipling, as for Gide, "Politics is the
organisation of hatreds." And as a gloss upon this, also an
illustration of the baleful effect of abstract ideas, there is a
curious snippet of conversation between the Serviles and Pirolo:

'But can't you understand,' said Pirolo pathetically to a shrieking
woman, 'that if we'd left you in Chicago you'd have been killed?'

'No, we shouldn't. You were bound to save us from being mur-
dered.'

'Then we should have had to kill a lot of other people.'

'That doesn't matter. We were preaching the Truth.'

Truth must prevail, though man's limited heavens fall.

A further objection to democracy allies Kipling once more
with Nietzsche as being among the "we who regard the democratic movement, not only as a degenerating form of political
organisation, but as equivalent to a degenerating, a waning
type of man, as involving his mediocritising and depreciation".[1]

"In an enlightened and democratic age like ours" [he wrote], "it
is possible to say that, if a man's skill has not found favour with the
public, the blame must lie with the man, not with the skill. This is
a pretty doctrine. I wish I could subscribe to it myself. There are,

[1] *Beyond Good and Evil*, p. 203.

however, men who devote their skill to producing things and expressing ideas for which the public has no present need."[1]

And, beyond this he deplored its effects upon education.

For Kipling, education was a severe training, as we see from 'The Centaurs', the poem that goes with 'The United Idolators'. But beyond that, he believed that a man's action in a crisis was determined by what he had built himself up to be in his early years. This is clearly expressed in 'The Hour of the Angel', one of Kipling's rare sonnets:

> Sooner or late—in earnest or in jest—
> (But the stakes are no jest) Ithuriel's Hour[2]
> Will spring on us, for the first time, the test
> Of our sole unbacked competence and power
> Up to the limit of our years and dower
> Of judgment—or beyond. But here we have
> Prepared long since our garland or our grave.
> For, at that hour, the sum of all our past,
> Act, habit, thought, and passion, shall be cast
> In one addition, be it more or less,
> And as that reading runs so shall we do;
> Meeting, astounded, victory at the last,
> Or, first and last, our own unworthiness.
> And none can change us though they die to save!

That this should be added to the chapter 'Stalky' in *Land and Sea Tales* makes it clear that this is a poem about education. And here Kipling would seem to fall in line with Jeremy Taylor (it may be worth noting how much Kipling fell in line with seventeenth-century thought), who wrote in *Holy Dying*:

Softness is for slaves and beasts, for minstrels and useless persons, for such as cannot ascend higher than the state of a fair ox, or a servant entertained for vainer offices: but the man that designs his son for noble employments, to honours and to triumphs, to consular dignities and presidencies of councils, loves to see him pale with study, or panting with labour, hardened with sufferance, or eminent by dangers. And so God dresses us for heaven.

[1] *A Book of Words*, II.

[2] "Ithuriel was that Archangel whose spear had the magic property of showing everyone exactly and truthfully what he was." Note to the poem in *Land and Sea Tales*.

Kipling, we may be sure, would have deplored the 'softness' in
the upbringing of our young at the present day, where nothing
is denied, and all is padded. For him, education was, or should
be, aimed at developing individuality of person and outlook—
how else should there be the glorious diversity of God's creature?
—but the whole trend of education, as he not without some
reason assessed it, was to produce a dull, tutored uniformity.
Twice in *A Book of Words* he makes this point. In 'England and
the English' we read: "We are further promised an unparalleled
outbreak of education guaranteed to produce a State-aided
mind." In 'Independence' he speaks of "our derivatively
educated minds or our induced emotions": and we can imagine
his reaction to the present-day Socialist-conceived notion of
universal comprehensive schools. He had the gloomiest fore-
bodings of its effects upon literature, and 'Dayspring Mishandled' opens with:

In the days beyond compare and before the Judgments, a genius
called Grayson foresaw that the advance of education and the standard of living would submerge all mind-marks in one mudrush of
standardised reading-matter, and so created the Fictional Supply
Syndicate to meet the demand.

This is where Progress leads to: "A rich Democracy inevitably
rots." In this instance, however, individuality decisively broke
through.

Then there was the matter of progress married to the idea of
democracy and the vote, and he might have smiled at the
phrases used by the Archbishop of York in his Minster sermon
at Easter 1965:

We may have a vote, but what does it avail? The system grinds
on like a huge monster of a machine—and what can one man or
woman do to alter its inexorable progress, if progress it can be
called?[1]

For Kipling the idea of the progress of humanity was meaningless: there could be no such thing. His Rectorial Address at
St. Andrews[2] contains the already quoted passage:

Remember always that, except for the appliances we make, the
rates at which we move ourselves and our possessions through space,
and the words we use, nothing in life changes.

[1] *The Times*, 19 April 1965.   [2] *A Book of Words*, XXIV.

I

There are, of course, changes of a sort, "when the just hour shall strike", and over milleniums; and if the gods change, it is only in their names—the words we use. But he could not concede that there had been any change for the better in humanity, having always present to his mind the atrocities committed by the Germans in the First World War, which to some extent he described in 'Swept and Garnished'; he could hardly have conceived of the horrors of the next World War, of Belsen and Auschwitz. Certainly he welcomed any betterment in the lives of poorer people, as the improvements he made on his own small estate bear witness; but the disgust he felt for the kind of 'social reform' he heard talked about is made plain in 'The Gods of the Copy-Book Headings'. For him, as we have seen, social reform was no more than the pastime of the idle rich, patronage without understanding. He associated it with intellectuals, with whom he did not feel himself at all allied, describing them all by implication in 'The Conversion of Aurelian McGoggin'—he names only Comte and Spencer— as men who "deal with people's insides from the point of view of men who have no stomachs".

For the 'arty' intellectual he had a special dislike, as he proclaimed very soon after he came to London, in a not very good poem[1] expressing his home-sickness for India, and the people whom he met there:

> But I consort with long-haired things
>   In velvet collar-rolls,
> Who talk about the Aims of Art,
>   And 'theories' and 'goals',
> And moo and coo with women-folk
>   About their blessed souls.
>
> But that they call 'psychology'
>   Is lack of liver pill,
> And all that blights their tender souls
>   Is eating till they're ill,
> And their chief way of winning goals
>   Consists of sitting still.

[1] 'In Partibus', which appeared in the *Civil and Military Gazette*, 23 December 1889. It was reprinted in *Abaft the Funnel*, but was not included in the Definitive Edition of his poems.

He had not yet been initiated in the Savile Club, where he met Lang, Gosse, Hardy, and others, above all Rider Haggard; these were men whom he by no means despised, for they were not among those who "spout hashed libraries" or "think the next man's thought". It was not till a good deal later that he seemed to think that such people as he described in the stanzas quoted above could be redeemed, as was Midmore in 'My Son's Wife'.

It was in his two final Fables that he had his humorous parting shots. " 'What always impresses me most', said Death to St. Peter," in 'On the Gate', " 'is the sheep-like simplicity of the intellectual mind.' " In 'Uncovenanted Mercies', one of the deepest reaching and most compassionate of his Fables, he finds time to have enormous fun with the Archangel of the English, so happy to rely on training and environment to counteract ideas of destiny, which he refers to as auto-suggestion. 'Rightly or wrongly,' the Archangel declares:

'I'm an optimist, I *do* believe in the upward trend of life. It connotes, of course, a certain restlessness among my people—the English you know.'

'The English I know,' said Satan.

'But in my humble judgment, they are developing on new planes. They must be met and guided by new methods. Surely in your dealings with the—er—more temperamental among them, you must have noticed this sense of a larger outlook?'

'. . . I am giving them each full advantages for self-expression and realisation. These will include impeccable surroundings, wealth, culture, health, felicity (unhappy people can't make others happy, can they?) and—everything else commensurate with the greatness of the destiny for which I—er—destine them.'

The Archangel of the English rubbed his soft hands and beamed on his colleagues.

'I hope you're justified,' said Satan. 'But are you quite sure that your method of—er—may I call it cossetting people, gets the best out of them?'

'Rather what I was thinking,' said Azrael.

And they instance the case of Job, who "didn't reach the top of his form" Satan points out, "as your people say, till I had handled him a little—did he?"

His complaint against administrators, democratically appointed, besides their ignorance, was their application of abstract ideas or ideals, which, as has been shown, he disliked. In *Something of Myself* ('Seven Years Hard'), he wrote with indignation of

... the bare horrors of the private's life, and the unnecessary torments he endured on account of the Christian doctrine which lays down that 'the wages of sin is death'. It was counted impious that bazaar prostitutes should be inspected; or that the men should be taught elementary precautions in their dealings with them. This official virtue cost our Army in India nine thousand expensive white men a year always laid up from venereal disease.[1]

But principle is principle, though the streets swim.

So, of course, with the notion that Democracy can provide the solution of all ills; and he comments on many occasions on the attitude of M.P.s. We have seen it in 'Little Foxes', but there the inhabitants of 'Ethiopia' realized that the Member "was driven out of his own land by Demah-Kerazi, which is a devil inhabiting crowds and assemblies": we meet this point of view not only in 'The Enlightenments of Pagett, M.P.' but also in the poem on Pagett, where he spoke too soon of "the Asian solar myth" while innocent of the tortures of the hot season. So also in 'Without Benefit of Clergy', where

... the Member for Lower Tooting, wandering about India in top-hat and frock-coat, talked largely of the benefits of British rule and suggested as the one thing needful the establishment of a duly qualified electoral system and a general bestowal of the franchise. His long-suffering hosts smiled and made him welcome.

He had yet to experience the delights of "the Asian solar myth".

Given his expression of these views, it is easy to see how readily Kipling was dubbed 'reactionary'. How far he may have been right, especially in the creation of democracies in Africa, only time will show, as it will as regards the new 'advances' in education. What he saw did not inspire confidence, and it is certain that if he read the Epistle Dedicatory that Shaw wrote to preface his *Man and Superman* he would have applauded the remark concerning "our political experiment of democracy,

[1] See also 'One view of the Question'.

the last refuge of cheap misgovernment, [which] will ruin us if our citizens are ill-bred". Kipling is no isolated figure in this period, witness Norman Douglas, who in *South Wind*, 1917, wrote:

What I mean by progress is the welding together of society for whatever ends. Progress is a centripetal movement, obliterating man in the mass. Civilization is centrifugal; it permits, it postulates, the assertion of personality. The terms are, therefore, not synonymous. They stand for hostile and divergent movements. Progress subordinates. Civilization co-ordinates. The individual emerges in civilization. He is submerged in progress.

Or, to take something written after Kipling's death, in 1953, by Miss Kathleen Nott in *The Emperor's Clothes*, where we read "When we build intellectual structures, we all drive more and more to the crudely mechanical and away from the life of imagination and experience."

Whatever Kipling's attitude may seem to have been in respect of current ideologies—a word he would have detested— it must be clear that he was always strongly bent towards manifestations of individuality, not of self-expression in the commonly accepted sense of the term, but in the doing of things, in the carrying out of work, or in the making of objects. Though no democrat, he was clearly opposed to any form of tyranny, and democracy was one such form. The person, the common person, God's people who were good enough for him, not The People, was what concerned him. It is likely that he would have stood by Coleridge when he said in *Table Talk*, 19 September 1830:

It has never yet been seen, or clearly announced, that democracy, as such, is no proper element in the constitution of a state. The idea of a state is undoubtedly a government ἐκ τῶν ἀρίστων—an aristocracy. Democracy is the healthful life-blood which circulates through the veins and arteries, which supports the system, but which ought never to appear externally, and as the mere blood itself.

His three soldiers, his Carnehans and Dravots, his Sidneys, and all who are supposed to belong to the subsidiary levels of society, as many in the Puck stories, must have freedom to live as they wish, even quietly to themselves, as did the people

in the Chicago of 2065. Whether they are the equals of the
Stalkys of this life, or of the Milners and the Rhodes, is of no
account. Men are not equal, as he would have supported
T. H. Huxley in arguing, but they all have their natural
rights—within the Law—allowing them to act and be in
whatever circumstances their birth may have provided. So
far as that goes, Kipling was a democrat.

There are certain contradictions to be met with in much of
what has been sketched out here, as one might expect from
the 'two-sided man'. Even crowds—but this is an extreme case
—may act beneficially. At the end of the poem 'The Benefactors'—which exists also as a story—each benefactor having
provided man with a more efficient weapon—when it came
to the invention of what might be described as a prevision of
the nuclear bomb:

> Man, schooled in bulk by fear and pain
>   Grew weary of the thing;
>
> And, at the very hour designed
>   To enslave him past recall,
> His tooth-stone-arrow-gun-shy mind
>   Turned and abolished all.

Again, his Chicagoan Utopia lacks spirit: "Easy communica-
tions nowadays, and lack of privacy in the past, have killed
all curiosity among mankind." When one of the members
of the A.B.C. asks the Mayor of Chicago what the Serviles
talked about, he answered:

First, how badly things were managed in the city. That pleased us
Four—we were on the platform—because we hoped to catch one or
two good men for City work. You know how rare executive capacity
is.

Further, we may ask, by what means did the officials of the
A.B.C. become such? Who chose them? Were they elected?
Again we may ask ourselves how the Mayor of Chicago ob-
tained his position. Was there some form of election, if not by
popular choice, some Voodoo-business of vote-counting, then
by whose choice? Perhaps the heads named their own succes-
sors, as seems to be indicated by the Mayor's remarks quoted
above.

Most strange of all the contradictions appears in a curious passage in that story, quite logical in its context, but surprising in Kipling, however much it may be justified by experiences at the present day:

There had, for instance, been no printed news-sheet in Illinois for twenty-seven years. Chicago argued that engines for printed news sooner or later developed into engines for invasion of privacy, which in turn might bring the old terror of crowds and blackmail back to the Planet. So news-sheets were not.

The same sentiments are expressed in 'Newspapers and Democracy' (*Letters of Travel*) where we read such phrases as ". . . newspapers in new countries seem so outrageously personal": however "there is very little of the brutal domestic terrorism of the Press in Canada, and not much blackmailing." All of which seems strange in a man whose first, delighted work had been on newspapers. He sang that

> We've only one virginity to lose,
> And where we lost it there our hearts will be!
>
> ('The Virginity')

"the little Civil and Military Gazette" being his "first mistress and most true love".[1] And in 'The Press' he wrote:

> Who once hath dealt in the widest game
>   That all of a man can play,
> No later love, no larger fame
>   Will lure him long away.
> As the war-horse snuffeth the battle afar,
>   The entered Soul, no less,
> He saith: "Ha! Ha!" where the trumpets are
>   And the thunders of the Press!

But the 'game' for him there was "News! News!", not the invasion of privacy.

[1] *Something of Myself*, III.

CHAPTER VI
The Story Teller

§1. THE REALIST

And only the Master shall praise us, and only the Master shall blame;
And no one shall work for money, and no one shall work for fame,
But each for the joy of the working, and each, in his separate star,
Shall draw the Thing as he sees It for the God of Things as They
are!

L'Envoi to The Seven Seas

Not so much "the Thing as he sees It"—unless it be the thing
that happens—as the Man—and the Woman. Kipling, born
into one of the ages when 'the perfectibility of man' was
canvassed, reacted against it, as did D. H. Lawrence who
remarked, "The Perfectibility of Man! Ah heaven, What a
dreary theme!"[1] He would readily have agreed with Pharaoh
Ahkenaton, who, when he met him,[2] told him:

The raw fact of life is that mankind is just a little lower than the
angels, and the conventions are based on that fact in order that men
may become angels. But if you begin . . . by the convention that
men are angels they will assuredly become bigger beasts than ever.

Kipling having experienced the House of Desolation, did not
begin with that convention. But the literary groups of his own
'perfectibility of man' age could not tolerate what he revealed—
those were matters best kept hid. Thus Harold Laski could
declare that he would symbolize the literature of hate, of
malignant grandiosity; and others have stressed his 'brutality'.
And still do, which seems a strange anomaly in this age of
violence, when most 'entertainments', on television, film, and
even in the theatre, offer brutal violence and cruelty as an

[1] *Studies in Classical American Literature* (Martin Secker, 1924), p. 58.
[2] *Letters of Travel*, 'Dead Kings'.

attraction. And Kipling knew, from common sense and sense of himself, as well as from experience, that men were not altogether lovely, that there are brutal, primitive passions in us all. These were part of the being even of that admirable person Learoyd. When, for instance, in 'On Greenhow Hill' he was telling how he was tempted to murder Barraclough, his rival for the love of 'Liza Roantree', "The thick lips curled back over the yellow teeth, and that flushed face was not pretty to look upon." Men could be filled with the lust to kill, and in the same story we read that the three soldiers "were talking in whispers, for the stillness of the wood and the desire of slaughter lay heavy upon them". In 'The Drums of the Fore and Aft' we learn that "a young man may be worked up to a blind passion of fighting, which is, contrary to general belief, controlled by a chilly Devil and shakes men like an ague". And in 'The Ballad of Boh da Thone' we are told that:

> As the shape of a corpse dimmers up through deep water,
> In his eye lit the passionless passion of slaughter.

Kipling, then, realized that these emotions existed, but this does not mean that he applauded them. That he wrote a satirical poem 'Loot' from the point of view of the looter does not mean that he approved of the practice—though he could understand the impulse prompting it—any more than he approved of Little Tobrah, in the pitying story of that name, pushing his sister down a well—though one may well think that a quick death is better than the long misery of slow starvation.

It was his business to serve the God of Things as They are—as, of course, he saw them—with a brilliantly understanding eye. He was vividly aware of the complex nature of man. Soldiers could be murderous and callous; they could be generous and brave; they could also be subject to funk, as detailed in 'The Drums of the Fore and Aft', in the comic story 'The Rout of the White Hussars', or in the piercing poem 'That Day':

> I 'eard the knives be'ind me, but I dursn't face my man,
>   Nor I don't know where I went to, 'cause I didn't 'alt to see,
> Till I 'eard a beggar squealin' out for quarter as 'e ran,
>   An' I thought I knew the voice an'—it was me!

There are other instances.

Apart from the passion of killing, which lies dormant in most men, there is also the lust for cruelty, beyond the impulse to shoot, or cut, or stab, tales of which alone sickened Kipling.[1] This was an emotion which, in common with other emotions, he had to explore, to try to understand. He had suffered from cruelty in the 'Baa, Baa, Black Sheep' period of his childhood, upon which Dr. Tompkins comments, and it is hard to disagree, that as a result of these experiences "Kipling was left, not, as has been loosely said, a cruel man, but certainly with an emotional comprehension of cruelty and an intellectual interest in it."[2] The story above mentioned gives us something of this, but the one which comes closest to describing, realistically, as well as comprehendingly, the urge to cruelty is 'The Moral Reformers'. There, Study No. 5, as suggested by that excellent man, the Rev. John Gillett who did not envisage the details, stop two bullies, Campbell and Sefton, from making a misery of the life of young Clewer. By a trick, Beetle being made to pretend that he is being bullied, the two real bullies are attracted, since "the bleatin' of the kid excites the tiger", and then trapped. They are then 'put through it', as we would say, having various tortures applied to them till they abjectly surrender, and the unfortunate Clewer is for ever freed from their attentions. That is plain enough; it is a moral tale, in a sense didactic. It is in its details that it is so curious; the realist as to man's emotions investigating them inevitably to some extent sensing his own.

It begins calmly enough; but as the tortures are applied—we are told what they are called, but the description is mercifully witheld—the excitement rises. Beetle himself seems to be the worst infected. " 'What a bait you're in!' said Stalky. 'Keep your hair on, Beetle.' 'I've had it done to me,' said Beetle." The whole thing fatigues both the bullies and the reformers. Sefton goes into a deep sleep. As to Study No. 5: "There should have been a war-dance, but that all three were so utterly tired that they almost went to sleep above their tea-cups in their study, and slept till prep."

The other notorious story where deliberate cruelty is em-

[1] *From Sea to Sea*, XXVIII.
[2] *Tompkins*, p. 28.

ployed is 'The Mark of the Beast'. There again the purpose is
the saving of a human soul. A number of lonely men from out-
stations have met to celebrate the New Year, with due feasting.
It was a very 'wet' night. One of the party, Fleete, on going
home grinds "the ashes of his cigar-butt into the forehead of the
red, stone image of Hanuman". There is no fuss in the temple,
though crowds gather, much to Strickland's dread, but—a
naked leper as white as snow, "ran in under our arms, making a
noise exactly like the mewing of an otter, caught Fleete round
the body, and dropped his head on Fleete's breast before we
could wrench him away". As a result, Fleete becomes ever
more bestially animal, demanding raw flesh to eat, becoming
in himself so shocking that he terrifies any horse he comes near.
Strickland, after, without any hope, calling in the doctor, sees
only one remedy. The leper must be caught, and tortured till
he lifts the spell off Fleete: ropes and red-hot gun-barrels are
prepared, and the leper subjected to tortures. But, "This part
is not to be described." The leper is compelled to do as he is
told, and take away the evil spirit from Fleete; and at last the
watchers see "the soul of Fleete coming back into his eyes".
When the process begins, the narrator says: "I understood
then how men and women and little children can endure to
see a witch burnt alive . . ." with details that need not be repeated. It is an earlier story than 'The Moral Reformers'.

Kipling, we see, could understand cruelty; possibly he could
be aware of tendencies towards it in himself, as he seems to
confess: but the man or woman who can honestly say that he
has not at some time or other felt this when sufficiently provoked by some horror must be rare indeed. The witness to the
God of Things as They are did not shirk showing this. The
earlier story to be sure was written when Kipling was in
the stage of most young people, attracted to horror, even
the horror story, and he gives more than one of these, as the
mysterious 'Bubbling Well Road', or again the terrible tale
of 'Bertran and Bimi', where the half-human ape, out of
jealousy, hideously kills the owner's young wife. That tale,
also, has a moral, a variant of "If you begin by the convention
that men are angels," substituting 'beasts' for 'men'. These
three stories were all written between 1887 and 1889, to be

collected in *Life's Handicap*. Kipling did not later write any story in which cruelty itself is the subject, though there are others in which it occurs incidentally, the most severely criticized being 'Mary Postgate' and 'Sea Constables'. They are considered by the unthinking or prejudiced as exhibiting his approval of cruelty, or even his sadistic relish in it, an accusation which is, to put it gently, wildly absurd.

'Mary Postgate', moreover, is said to illustrate his irrational hatred of the Germans. That he did hate the Germans is true—which does not necessarily mean that he hated every individual German; we need think only of Muller of 'In the Rukh': the House of Desolation, he tells us, had "drained (him) of any capacity for any real personal hate".[1] But to state that his hatred was irrational will not convince any who remember the horror with which the outrages committed by the German soldiery in 1914—already referred to—overwhelmed the English people. It was not merely that the Germans relied on "No Law except the sword . . .", but that

> Coldly they went about to raise
> To life and make more dread
> Abominations of old days,
> That men believed were dead.
>
> ('The Outlaws')

The former might be understandable enough; but then there were besides the barbaric sack of Louvain, the hideous massacres of women and children in French villages, as brought out in 'Swept and Garnished', the tale that immediately precedes 'Mary Postgate'. Again the crucifixion of prisoners of war, the rape and mutilation of women, as described in the Argument preceding Sir Herbert Read's poem 'The End of a War', and which Kipling deals with in two of his 'Epitaphs of the War'. In *France at War*[2] he tells how a French woman said to him:

This is not war. It is against wild beasts that we fight. There is no arrangement possible with wild beasts:

upon which he commented:

[1] *Something of Myself*, I.
[2] 1915, p. 28.

This is the one vital point which we in England must realise. We are dealing with animals who have scientifically and philosophically removed themselves inconceivably outside civilisation.

In a speech at Southport in June 1915, he said: "However the world pretends to divide itself, there are only two divisions in the world to-day—human beings and Germans."[1] That is not a sadistic utterance, nor one prompted by 'irrational' hatred: it expresses the outraged feelings of a man deeply believing in the value of civilization, "the ages' slow-bought gain", and in the Law by means of which life is made comely. It might be said that he harboured these feelings too long; but as Bevin said in 'A Friend of the Family': "What *I* say is, there *must* be a right and a wrong to things. It can't all be kiss-an'-make-friends, no matter what you do."

'Mary Postgate', however, is not a story embodying hatred of the Germans. Written in the autumn of 1915, it is a realistic tale about the reactions of a middle-aged spinster employed as companion to a slightly older woman, Miss Fowler, who has the care of a not very pleasant nephew, Wynn. Mary, a somewhat repressed character, gives all her frustrated tenderness and love to Wynn, whom she looks after on the practical side during his school days. He joins the Royal Flying Corps, as it was then called, at the outbreak of war, and is killed in a trial flight. In due course Mary and Miss Fowler go through his things, which, except for two symbolic objects, are consigned to the incinerator at the bottom of the garden. To get these to burn properly, Mary goes down to the village to get some paraffin. While she is there, a German airman drops a bomb, killing a small girl. Mary sees "the ripped and shredded body", and, terribly shocked, but controlled, goes back to the incinerator. Nearby she finds the German airman who has crashed from his plane, is badly injured, and begs to be helped. In utter revulsion she refuses all aid, saying in bad German to the man who is appealing to her, "Nein! Ich haben der todt Kinder gesehn"—I have seen the dead child. She goes on with her bonfire, and waits till she is sure that the German is dead.

Kipling, of course, is not suggesting, as he has been accused

[1] See 'Kipling's opinion of the Germans', by Basil M. Bazley in *The Kipling Journal*, July 1945.

of doing, that this is how people should behave; he is merely telling us 'this is what happens'. He is the realist; and this particular story gets some support—though the case is not so extreme—by what is recorded by Lady Glenavy in some reminiscences of the war years. She had been engaged in some war work on the land, and tells us that:

> I was interested how all my fellow workers condemned a woman who had given food to German prisoners working on her land. She had given them cocoa and sandwiches, and said half of them were 'mere children'. They arrived very early in charge of a sergeant and got nothing to eat all day. The sergeant was glad to see them fed, but the practice was stopped because it was against the law.[1]

Terrible as Kipling's story is, one may wonder whether, if people would look into themselves, realize Mary's feelings about the dead Wynn, especially just then, when she is, so to speak, burying him; and imagine the shock she felt at seeing the mangled child, and then finding the man who had dropped the bomb, they could with certainty say that they would have acted otherwise? Especially a woman. As Mary says to herself:

> A man at such a crisis, would be what Wynn called a 'sportsman'; would leave everything to fetch help, and would certainly bring It into the house. Now a woman's business was to make a happy home for—for a husband and children. Failing these—it was not a thing one should allow one's mind to dwell upon—but—
>
> 'Stop it!' Mary cried once more across the shadows. 'Nein, I tell you! Ich haben der todt Kinder gesehn.'

A woman could not afford to be a 'sportswoman': woman wasn't given man for that:

> But the Woman that God gave him, every fibre of her
>   frame
> Proves her launched for one sole issue, armed and engined
>   for the same:
> And to serve that single issue, lest the generations fail,
> The female of the species must be deadlier than the male.
>
> ('The Female of the Species')

She had seen the ripped and mangled child—that was enough; she did not consider that, after all, Wynn was equipped to do

[1] Beatrice, Lady Glenavy, *To-day we will only gossip* (Constable, 1964), p. 108.

the same thing; and Kipling could have pointed out to her that the German was only obeying *his* Law. A further note of shocking realism is given at the very end of the story. When Mary came in,

she scandalised the whole routine by taking a luxurious bath before tea, and came down looking, as Miss Fowler said when she saw her lying all relaxed on the other sofa, 'quite handsome!'

It is a little horrifying; but for once, at last, she had been able to release her suppressed emotions towards Wynn, and as Thackeray said in the Preface to *Pendennis*, "If truth is not always pleasant, at any rate truth is best." And Kipling, to repeat, was serving the God of Things as They are.

It is the poem, 'The Beginnings' which follows the story, that, as so often, reveals the deeper theme, which was born of realistic acceptance of the fact that the spirit of hate should have been engendered by the actions of the Germans, and records Kipling's sorrow at the outcome:

> It was not part of their blood,
>   It came to them very late
> With long arrears to make good,
>   When the English began to hate. . . .
>
> It was not suddenly bred,
>   It will not swiftly abate,
> Through the chill years ahead,
>   When Time shall count from the date
>   That the English began to hate.

For the English "were not easily moved", "there was neither sign nor show", and "No man spoke it aloud", unless it were some muted muttering in a smoking-room.

Another story of the same sort as 'Mary Postgate', which, though not so horrifying has nevertheless called forth some opprobrium, is 'Sea Constables', sub-titled 'A Tale of 1915', and was first published in October of that year. Just as in 'Mary Postgate' Kipling gives rein to his anger against people who could do such things as the German airman had done, so here he expresses his anger against neutrals, who, regardless of the lives of other people, extracted profit from the war. The

story is told at a dinner party of four, three of them owners of
small craft just large enough to be lightly armed and used as
patrols, and are employed as temporary naval officers as
indicated by the prefatory verses 'The Changelings' written
after the war:

> Or ever the battered liners sank
>   With their passengers to the dark,
> I was head of a Walworth Bank,
>   And you were a grocer's clerk. . . .
>
> Now there is nothing—not even our rank—
>   To witness what we have been;
> And I am returned to my Walworth Bank,
>   And you to your margarine!

The fourth man is Tegg, "of the Royal Navy afloat, and,
occasionally, of the Admiralty ashore". They all had "the
coarse-grained complexions of men who habitually did themselves well, and an air, too, of recent, red-eyed dissipation",
the result, actually, of being dead-tired "weather-beaten
mariners". Henri, the head-waiter, ushers them to a special
table, and announces a very special menu. This inspires the
comment of a foreign music-hall entertainer, "the latest thing
in imported patriotic piece-goods. She sings 'Sons of the
Empire, Go Forward!' at the Palemseum. It makes the aunties
weep." Disappointed of her table, she says to her companion,
"the most recent foreign millionaire":

'*That's* what I mean. . . . They ain't *alive* to the war yet. Now
what's the matter with those four dubs yonder joining the British
Army or—*doing* something?'

And when, knowing the head-waiter, Portson, the host, a peace-
time stockbroker, says about choosing the menu, "I left it all
to Henri," she comments: "My Gord! . . . Get on to that! Ain't
it typical? They leave everything to Henri in this country."

The main figure in this story is the middle-aged Maddingham
—we don't learn till the end of the tale that he is 'Sir Francis'—
who has spent a harassing time dogging the ship of a neutral
who is trying to deliver oil to German submarines somewhere
in the Irish Sea; the other two temporary sailors have also had

dealings with this neutral, young Winchmore in the North Sea, and Portson in the English Channel. At length, after dangerous and wearisome clinging to the 'Newt', a season broken by a Court of Inquiry where Maddingham has to answer charges of lack of tact and endangering foreign political relations—this is where Tegg comes in—the 'Newt' gives up, goes to port in Ireland, and sells his oil to the Admiralty. Maddingham goes to see him. The Neutral tells him that he is "all in", and will die unless Maddingham runs him across to England so that he can see his doctor in town. Maddingham says that this is out of the question, since his boat is "a man-of-war in commission", and when told that he is as good as condemning the neutral to death, the latter having given himself away by saying that he had 'surrendered', Maddingham said:

'there wasn't any question of surrender. If he'd been a wounded belligerent, I might have taken him aboard, though I certainly shouldn't have gone a yard out of my course to land him anywhere: but as it was he was a neutral—altogether outside the game. . . .
    'I was perfectly polite. I said to him: "Try to be reasonable, sir. If you had got rid of your oil where it was wanted, you'd have condemned lots of people to death just as surely as if you'd drown'd 'em."'

The 'Newt' died the next day.
    It is complained that this is a 'brutal' story. Maddingham should have taken the man across to England—it would no doubt have been 'sporting' of him. But, as he said, his boat was in Admiralty commission: why should he risk it, or waste its time, in doing so? Besides, Maddingham was tired to death. And Kipling expresses the contemptuous anger most people felt at this neutral behaviour in a poem, 'The Neutral', printed at the end of *Sea Warfare* (it is called 'The Question' in the Definitive Edition of the Poems). The same feeling was expressed by Conrad in 'The Tale' (*Tales of Hearsay*), where the Commanding Officer (no name is given), on the suspicion, not the certainty, that a stray ship, apparently Scandinavian, is supplying the German submarines with oil, gives it sailing directions which will ensure it being wrecked with the loss of all hands. He confesses that he did not know whether he had done stern retribution or murder. He is far more 'brutal'

K

than Maddingham, who was at least surprised at his having acted as he did, but now came to see how the pressure of events often invites, sometimes forces people to do what they would normally revolt from doing, as Kipling illustrated also in 'Mary Postgate', and gruesomely in 'The Mark of the Beast'. No one accuses Conrad of 'malignity'; he too was a realist.

It cannot perhaps be said that Kipling's frequent descriptions of violence, which faded out as he grew older, are entirely due to his worship of the God of Things as They Are. One is aware of a certain zest in many of them, as though, in common with many men built for physical action to whom this is denied—in his case by defective eyesight—he could relieve his frustration by imagining an extreme of violence. Some do so by a certain amount of destructiveness, but this, in Kipling, is largely a form of imagined schoolboy ragging, like the smashing up of form-rooms in *Stalky & Co*; for together with his precociousness, he long retained a modicum of the schoolboy in him. One feels that he sympathizes with Ortheris—if he doesn't approve he at least understands—when he bully-rags the unfortunate Samuelson and throws his things about the barrack-room.[1] The unutterable Jevon in 'A Friend's Friend' is treated, royally treated we might say, much as a boy who had earned unpopularity would be treated by schoolboys. Certainly there is an unnecessary degree of violence at the end of 'The Bronckhorst Divorce Case'; Bronckhorst deserves a thrashing, and we can understand Biel's fury: but it is a little too much to read:

> Biel came out of the Court, and Strickland dropped a gut trainer's whip in the verandah. Ten minutes later, Biel was cutting Bronckhorst into ribbons behind the old court cells, quietly and without scandal. What was left of Bronckhorst was sent home in a carriage: and his wife wept over it and nursed it into a man again.

Realism, we feel, might have been achieved without so much detail.

There are, to a considerable number, stories of men shooting each other, the Danny Deevers of the Army. They are always cases of jealousy, of a husband shooting a man for making love to his wife. Kipling was intent to show the sort of strain under

[1] 'His Private Honour.'

which the soldier lived in India, the intolerably harsh conditions of his life in an oppressive climate. We get it in 'Black Jack', where Mulvaney saves Vulmea from actually committing murder; we get it in 'In the Matter of a Private', which begins bitterly enough with the epigraph:

> Hurrah! Hurrah! a soldier's life for me!
> Shout, boys, shout! for it makes you jolly and free.
>
> ('The Ramrod Corps')

and the first paragraph reads:

Now, the Mother superior of a Convent, and the Colonel of a British Infantry Regiment would be justly shocked at any comparison being made between their respective charges. But it is a fact that, under certain circumstances, Thomas in bulk can be worked up into dithering, rippling hysteria.

The 'prologue' goes on tellingly—a plea for the understanding of the Tommy. Sometimes, as in 'The Solid Muldoon', which is partly a 'supernatural' story, a fight with fists is the answer. Here this is described horribly enough, with a jaw smashed out, and then, with another blow, 'jammed straight'. All this is sheer realism; it does not necessarily connote Kipling's relish in it. People enjoy fighting, as did the soldiers in 'The Brushwood Boy':

We tried it with the gloves, sir, for twenty minutes, and *that* done us no good, sir. Then we took off the gloves and tried it that way for another twenty minutes . . . an' that done us a world of good.

Ortheris, again, thoroughly enjoyed his contest with Ouless, although he was beaten. After all, men—and women—gather in crowds to watch a fight: men—and women—go to see animals slaughtered, as Kipling had witnessed.[1] He enjoyed neither, but he knew that other people did, and said so.

Similarly with revenge. It is curious, a sign of prejudice, how many critics of Kipling have made a crime of his interest in revenge, as though this had not always been a subject for treatment by literary creators. We find it in Greek tragedy, in the Œdipus plays; it was a prominent theme in Elizabethan drama —*The Revenger's Tragedy*, for instance. *Hamlet* is a revenge play.

[1] *From Sea to Sea*, XXXV.

It is a sentiment most people are aware of in themselves. It may be quite light, as in Kipling's 'The Sending of Dana Da': "Look out! You laughed at me once, and now I am going to make you sit up." The result was not very devastating, the story being, as already noted, mainly an attack upon the silliest form of 'spiritualism'. Kipling was early attracted to the theme; and if *Stalky & Co.* is any guide to his thoughts as a schoolboy, it might be noted that a good many of the stories are in a sense 'little revenges' as Stalky calls them, upon King for his sarcastic remarks. Study No. 5 did not exactly make King 'sit up', but what they did was largely because he had mocked them. Nearly all the revenge stories involve laughter, sometimes of the genial variety, at others of the deeply searing kind. One notable exception is 'The Broken Link Handicap', in which an unlucky jockey is badly smashed. The tale, a very early one (1887) may have been meant in the first instance to express Kipling's dislike of horse-racing as practised in India; but it is also the story of the retribution which overtook a man for dishonest dealing. All Kipling's revenge stories are moral fables, even the genially humorous 'His Wedded Wife'—some two months earlier than 'The Broken Link Handicap'—where a junior subaltern, 'the Worm', gets his own back on 'the senior subaltern' who had made his life a burden. An admirable actor, who can make up convincingly as a woman, he suddenly presents himself publicly as the senior subaltern's deserted wife. The joke is hugely appreciated by everyone, except the senior subaltern. The laughter here is pointed, but not shattering.

"Revenge", Bacon remarked, "is a kind of wild justice", and Kipling's revenge stories are those of a moralist illustrating retributive justice. All his victims have erred, and are brought to book, except in the last, rather baffling tale of that nature, 'Dayspring Mishandled'. In none of his cases would Bacon's strictures against revenge be applicable, for the offences committed were not such as the law might right. True, it is more noble to ignore offences than to counter them; a sensible man might prefer to ignore them: but then the mass of men are not noble, a great many are not sensible, and here again Kipling was a realist.

Besides, most people think it rather fun to get their own back amiably, and with Kipling the punishment is often beautifully proportioned to the crime, as in 'Pig'. Here Pinecoffin was guilty of selling to Nafferton, his departmental superior, a horse "with a twist in his temper", which he did not mention. So the latter pursues Pinecoffin with endless departmental demands for information about pigs: the Indian Pig, the Primitive Pig, the Dravidian Pig—even the Mythology of the Pig, and limitless other queries, such as "the food supply of the indigenous Pig", and the quality of the bristles in various breeds. For a time Pinecoffin quite enjoys this; it is 'up his street'; but ultimately it becomes an unbearable chare, and one day he sends back a short-tempered, inaccurate answer to a request for reiterated information. Pinecoffin—and this was playing rather a dirty trick—publishes this reply. The story, however, ends by Nafferton saying when they meet:

'Have you ever been stuck with a horse? It isn't the money I mind, though that is bad enough; but what I resent is the chaff that follows, especially from the boy that stuck me. But I think we'll cry quits now.'

Pinecoffin found nothing to say save bad words; and Nafferton smiled ever so sweetly, and asked him to dinner.

It is rather different in 'Watches of the Night', where an evil-speaking woman, who has caused much domestic unhappiness has her own domestic happiness ruined.

The stories mentioned so far are very early ones. The next of any importance in this context is 'Bread Upon the Waters' of 1896, and is more complex. Here we meet the engineer McPhee, a man of great integrity, and of supreme loyalty to the ships' engines that he serves (as he might put it), and who has been stupidly dismissed by a new and not very upright board of directors of the firm Holdock, Steiner and Chase that employed him, and whose interests he had too much at heart. His next employer is old McRimmon, who hates the firm of Holdock, Steiner and Chase, especially Steiner. They discover that McPhee's old ship, the *Grotkau*, is to put to sea with a crack in the propeller shaft that is almost certain to break in any sea. So Bell, the captain of McPhee's new ship is ordered to dog the

Grotkau on her way across the Atlantic to await her almost certain breakdown, and get the reward for towing her in. They are lucky beyond their expectations, for the crew of the *Grotkau* desert her, and Messrs. Holdock & Co., have to pay a vast sum of money for salvage. McRimmon gives McPhee a handsome rake-off. It is a story full of entertaining side-details, and is not exactly a revenge story, for the actors who bring the dishonest ship-owners to book do not themselves engineer the result; they merely seize an opportunity. It is a revenge story in that it preaches the same sort of moral.

We can now take three tales in which revenge will have the most dire consequences for the offenders. They are pitiless stories, if you like, but retributive justice is dealt—with satisfaction—on people guilty of unutterable conduct. 'The Village that Voted the Earth was Flat' and 'Beauty Spots' have much in common, being in the first place gay stories full of humour, 'The Village' becoming sheer farce. In either case men who pretend to be gentlemen, but are largely snobs, behave like cads towards people whom they think below them, and are destroyed by the laughter that has been plotted for this purpose. Brutal perhaps, but no more brutal than the revenge Sir Toby Belch and Sir Andrew Aguecheek exercised upon the unfortunate Malvolio, in fact more just, since Malvolio had committed no very evil act. Laughter, of course, has traditionally been the method by which pretenders of various kinds are brought to book; one thinks of Tartuffe or Sir Willoughby Patterne. It may not be the business of comedy *parcere subjectis*, but in the greatest type of pure comedy it is certainly *debellare superbos*.

In 'The Village that Voted the Earth was Flat', Sir Thomas Ingell, Bart., M.P., is guilty of tempting motorists into speed-limit traps, and, as a self-inflated little authoritarian, feudally respected by his village of Huckley, is abominably insulting to people brought up to the magistrates' court. The particular group in this story who are subjected to his rudeness are journalists, an M.P., and later a famous music-hall impresario, whom the clever young journalist of the party describes as "the Absolutely Amoral Soul". A campaign on several fronts —newspapers of various levels, the music-hall with a wildly catching song, the invention of a Geoplanarian Society which induces the Village of Huckley to vote unanimously (no vote, no dinner) that the earth *is* flat; questions in the House and so on, finally crushes Sir Thomas, who, we gather, is forced by the laughter of the House, to retire from public life. The whole thing is an elaborate farce, fascinatingly worked out, worked up, one might say; as readers we cannot help following the whole development with amused gusto; we almost sing the popular song, as did the House of Commons on its feet, and dance the Gubby Dance. The laughter admittedly is barbed; the outraged victims of Ingell's inexcusable behaviour are relentless in their pursuit; yet, we feel, they forget their own victim in the ardour of playing their fantastic game, though deriving ultimate satisfaction from the result of their destructive laughter. The story is wonderfully improbable; the realism lies, not only in certain details, but in the picturing of men's emotions under certain conditions. Man can be ruthless in dealing out what he may consider this kind of wild justice.

The same holds for 'Beauty Spots', in which a certain Major Kniveat, pronounced 'Kniveed', snobbishly reacts against new-comers to his part of the country, and whom he thinks are up-starts trying to worm an upward way into the society of country gentry. As a matter of fact, all they want is to be left alone, Mr. Gravell desiring merely to follow out some theories about the effect of certain chemicals on vegetation, so as to produce first-rate chemical manure. His son Jemmy, his complexion some-what blotchy as the result of a gas attack in the war, manages all the practical affairs. He and his god-brother, you might call him, Kit Birtle, a doctor with psycho-analytical interests, now and then come down to stay with Gravell.

Kniveat is abominable from the start. He refers to the Gravells as 'the manure people', and suggests that Jemmy's complexion is the result of Mr. Gravell's 'co-habitation' with a person of colour. Jem cannot make him out.

'We came down here to be quiet, but this sword-merchant seems to take it as a personal insult. What's the complex, Kit?'

'We've something like it in our hamlet—a retired officer bungfull of public spirit and simian malignity. Idleness explains a lot, but

I've a theory that it's glands at bottom. 'Rather noisome for you, though.'

Where Kniveat's behaviour is outrageously unforgivable is when, deliberately seizing the chance of an absence abroad of the Gravells to visit a French specialist in the results of war-gas poisoning, he tells the men ordered by the parish council to trim a few branches that overhang a road (the notice having been sent to Gravell two days after he had left for France) to get the trees mangled and lopped, and a wall broken down, so that a beautiful rhododendron dell is laid open to trippers to defile with litter. Unfortunately, the bit of land above the dell is used by Gravell for experimenting with various chemicals which he injects into the soil, with the result that many of the visitors undergo a short spell of blotches on their skin, an epidemic known as 'Bloody Measles'.

And here comes in one of the most charming and entertaining of the characters of the story, an enormous white sow named Angelique, who lives in the one time home farm of the little estate, and is the pivot of the narrative. She is much liked by Jemmy and Kit, by the Enochs at the farm, and indeed by most people except 'Major Knivea*d*', who asserts that she is in danger to those using the right-of-way paths, of which he considers himself the especial public-spirited guardian. Angelique, through grubbing about in the gas-leaking dell is herself infected with 'Bloody Measles', and must be kept from Kniveat's sight. Therefore for a few days she becomes an inmate of the farm ("Mrs. Enoch said she was company when one knitted"). This gives Jem and Kit an idea; in due course they paint Angelique with horrifying effect, and allow the Major to see her as he goes his customary beneficent Sunday-after-church round of the rights of way. Here is his chance! He reports the matter, goes to the Gravell's house, where he sees Mr. Gravell and Kit's father (Sir Harry Birtle, the famous lawyer), invites them to come and see Angelique, an appalling sight to which he had already invited many villagers. But by the time they get there Angelique has been scrubbed "pure as a lily"; there is no sign of any blotch or spot. The inference is that either Kniveat was drunk when he paid his visit after church, or that he has lost his reason. The last scene is beautifully done; the just retribution is presented as comedy, finally as harsh, unforgiving comedy:

The generation that tolerates but does not pity went away. They did not even turn round when they heard the first dry sob of one from whom all hope of office, influence, and authority was stripped for ever—drowned by the laughter in the lane.

The moral is stated in the prefatory poem, 'Neighbours':

> The man that is open of heart to his neighbour,
> And stops to consider his likes and dislikes,
> His blood shall be wholesome whatever his labour,
> His luck shall be with him whatever he strikes. . . .

and with him is contrasted "he that is costive of soul toward his fellow", whose life and fate are very different.

Human beings do feel a desire for revenge, and, as a realist, Kipling portrayed them as enjoying their revenge. 'Dayspring Mishandled', however, has a different ethos; there is very little laughter in the story, though there is a modicum of humour, and the revenge, though carefully, laboriously prepared over a number of years, is never carried out. Manallace, the revenger, though immensely enjoying the plotting, and all its skilful detail, stays his hand. Castorley, the designated victim, though certainly an unpleasant person, is not a cad in quite the same way as Sir Thomas Ingell or Major Kniveat. He is a snob, hankering after the knighthood which he gets; he is self-considering, not a bully, but his chief crime is that he makes an unforgivable remark about, and exhibits a callous lack of feeling towards, a woman to whom he has proposed, and to whom Manallace is devoted, spending most of his small earnings on supporting her in due comfort when she grows paralysed and blind.

Castorley had at one time been, together with Manallace, member of a syndicate that turned out popular literature, but when he came into a little money stated that he was giving up 'hack-work' in favour of 'literature'. In due course he becomes the outstanding authority on Chaucer. Manallace sits in as his coadjutor, and learns so much from him about writing in Chaucer's day that he is able to produce a most convincing fake of a 'discovered' Chaucer fragment (we are given this haunting poem, 'Gertrude's Prayer' at the end of the story). He has learnt all about the inks used in the period, and meticulously manufactures some; about the pens used by certain copy-scribes, the parchment of the period. He engineers the 'discovery', and everybody is taken in, including Castorley who is going to earn immense credit by certifying the piece to be genuine. Then, at long last, Manallace is going to expose the fraud, and subject Castorley to scornful ridicule.

Something prevents him. It has been suggested that Kipling was changing his mind about the wild justice of revenge, but this seems unlikely since this tale appeared some four years before 'Beauty Spots', so was probably written earlier. It is a complex story, and really hinges on the character of Manallace, "a darkish, slow northerner of the type that does not ignite, but must be detonated". He has worked with Castorley, who wants to inscribe his great book to him, and though he cannot forgive him for his behaviour as regards the woman he adores, rather likes him, and can appreciate his virtues as a thorough scholar. Moreover Lady Castorley is an evil woman, who, in love with her husband's doctor, desires the death of her husband that she may marry the doctor; he, however, will not hasten the death of Castorley, at any rate due to die soon from kidney trouble, and behaves honourably as a doctor should towards his patient. Manallace has a shrewd suspicion that Lady Castorley knows all about the fake; she is eager for the publication of her husband's book, to be followed by the exposure which she is sure will kill him. Manallace will not go so far as that; he would not kill a man for revenge, and he intensely dislikes Lady Castorley as a mean, unscrupulous woman. So he induces Castorley to delay publication. It is as though Kipling were saying that revenge is no simple matter; his realism again stands him in good stead—that, and his capacity for empathy, even into the people whom he has himself created. He has put himself into Manallace's position. The story is among the most remarkable of his triumphs.

Kipling wrote little in the way of realistic fiction in the common use of the word, as depicting the grimier sides of living, of the Arthur Morrison *Tales of Mean Streets* kind. Though there is something of this in *The Light that Failed*, his one example is 'The Record of Badalia Herodsfoot', where the subject is not the grime and the brutality of Gunnison Street, but the loyal, almost heroic behaviour of Badalia herself, her touching devotion. But I have used the word as is commonly done, so excluding the better qualities of mankind, such as are pictured in those tales exhibiting self-abnegation, loyalty to an idea as well as to people, and the many virtues and higher endeavours of human beings, which he treats of in just as 'real' a manner as their failings or vices. What I have tried to bring out is his capacity for assessing the 'reality' of human charac-ters reacting not always too prettily to the events in which they are caught up, a side most writers avoid, or, where murder is committed, investing it with a halo of romance. He was con-cerned to explore the plausible reasons for their actions, and they are not always likeable. It may be that, as he said at the end of 'A Matter of Fact' that:

Truth is a naked lady, and if by accident she is drawn up from the bottom of the sea, it behoves a gentleman either to give her a print petticoat or to turn his face to the wall and vow that he did not see,

but he was not concerned to be a gentleman, rather a creative artist faithful to life as he saw it. It would be hard to contest that he saw it wrong.

§2. THE FABULIST

When all the world would keep a matter hid,
   Since Truth is seldom friend to any crowd,
Men write in fable, as old Æsop did,
   Jesting at that which none will name aloud.
And this they needs must do, or it will fall
Unless they please they are not heard at all.
               'The Fabulists'

Kipling did not resort to the fable because the truths he wished to emphasize would be elbowed off by the crowd if more directly stated. As a realist he shirked no unpalatable truth. From the beginning—perhaps from an early reading of Stevenson—he seems to have been attracted by the medium, witness 'The Strange Ride of Morrowbie Jukes', a near-fable, which appeared before he was twenty years old; moreover fable-writing appealed to him to the end, the final tale in *Limits and Renewals* being 'Uncovenanted Mercies', while the last story he ever wrote was 'Teem; A Treasure Hunter'.

Fables are necessarily stories—or they would not please at all; they would merely be tedious sermons. All stories worthy of the name are partly fables, in that they contain an idea—otherwise they are no more than anecdotes. The 'point' of a story is its revelation of, or singling out of, some characteristic of human nature or behaviour; its moral is applicable to our daily doings. The 'idea' of a fable goes beyond the local or immediate; its theme is universal. But it is impossible to draw a clear line between the two. In any event, the word 'fable' is very vague, more so than 'parable' or 'allegory', in themselves constituting elements in a fable, which, according to common usage, is an impossible, or at least highly unlikely story, though improbability is not in itself a criterion.

Fiction is often a better way than plain statement of impressing actuality upon the imagination. Thus Kipling related that Truth, confronted with the unbelievable events of the war, the handling of which Fiction had resigned to her,

> . . . faced herself at last, the story runs,
> And telegraphed her sister: "Come at once.
> Facts out of hand. Unable overtake
> Without your aid. Come back for Truth's own sake!
> Co-equal rank and powers if you agree.
> *They need us both, but you far more than me!*"

('A Legend of Truth')

But fiction also has its limitations. Hardy went so far as to declare that "one of the first rules of a writer of fiction is that it must not be made so strange as fact",[1] an idea echoed by Meredith at the opening of *The Tragic Comedians*. Kipling did not find it a simple matter to resolve. In 'A Fallen Idol' he tells of a club, the members of which compete in telling lying stories; one of them lost his reputation because, having told a superbly impossible story about himself which was awarded the prize, it turned out to be true! He puts the case against fiction most plainly at the head of 'The Benefactors', itself a prophetic fable:

---

[1] To Sidney Cockerell. See *Cockerell*, by Wilfrid Blunt (Hamish Hamilton, 1964), p. 215.

Ah! What avails the classic bent
And what the cultured word,
Against the undoctored incident
That actually occurred?

And what is Art whereto we press
Through paint and prose and rhyme—
When Nature in her nakedness
Defeats us every time?

The fable attempts to go deeper than the nakedness of Nature; after all, nakedness is only skin-deep.

Of Kipling's 'supernatural' Fables—distinguished throughout as Fables with a capital F—much will not be said here, as they have already been liberally drawn upon to illustrate his 'religion' or his 'basic intuitions'. As he wrote these, he more and more integrated the realistic with the fabular: it is only in the very early Fable at the end of 'The Bridge-Builders', where we meet the Hindu pantheon, that supernatural figures are separated from humanity. Even in 'The Legend of Mirth', where mankind does not appear, the four Archangels, humanly filled, as we have seen, with the doubt that sickens, in utter mirth forgot both Zeal and Pride, so that

> . . . e'en Gehenna's bondsmen understood
> They were not damned from human brotherhood.

The first evident Fable, 'The Children of the Zodiac', tells of how the six Children stepped down upon earth, gradually to become human beings, understanding the value of work and song, the meaning of tears and laughter, and learnt that, though the death decreed them by the Six Houses was their unavoidable end, they must not be afraid. In becoming human beings they ceased to be largely meaningless, starry half-gods. And when Kipling here quotes from Emerson, "When the half-Gods go The Gods arrive", it is as though he were already going back to his Westward Ho! days with their lesson *Dis te minorem quod geris imperas*, the Children coming almost to rule because they held themselves lower than the Gods—had, in fact, become men and women. As regards the fear of death, the half-fable 'The Wandering Jew' written some two years earlier, may be considered as a preface to 'The Children of the Zodiac'. There, John Hay, whose fear of death was driving him mad, tried to cheat death, first by travelling as fast as he could Westerly round the world, then by living

> sitting in a chair swung from the roof, over a sheet of thin steel which he knows so well destroys the attraction of the earth . . . racing against eternity.

Yet doubt crept in, and he asked, "Why does not the sun always remain over my head?" The story lacks the force of the Fable.

The two most significant Fables, linked together by virtually the same opening phrase suggesting that the Order Above is but a reflection of the Order Below, are 'On the Gate. A Tale of 16', of 1926 (though apparently written by May 1918); and 'Uncovenanted Mercies' of 1929, of which Kipling stressed its value to him by placing it where he did, at the end of the book. In both of these the main theme is the importance of love, the need for forgiveness, and the salve of compassion; but in both the grace of humour which engenders a sense of proportion is given by social criticism, and by making the Archangels very human, even all too human. In between these, in 1924, there appeared 'The Enemies to Each Other', which though it opens as a Fable of Divine compassion, becomes largely a story describing the adjustment of Adam and Eve to the condition of human beings living together, an amusing comedy of sex-antagonism. Here the fusion of story and Fable is not so complete.

It would seem more clarifying to group Kipling's fables under what he wished to accomplish by them rather than under the headings Archangelical, animal, mechanical. Up to a point they can be classified as moral, political, mysterious, philosophical; but then, as always with Kipling, dovetailing is apt to occur. In all of them one feels that he experienced the craftsman's delight in making just that thing, in ordering the material handled, not always too much minding if the Truth that was to emerge was somewhat trite. This delight seems to have been the main impulse in the machine fables, in which also we find the further delight Kipling loved to indulge in, of personification. It had always amused him to regard engines as sentient, intelligent beings; as early as 1888, when 'Among the Railway Folk'[1] he judged that "Engines are the 'livest' things that man ever made. They glare through their spectacle-plates, they tilt their noses contemptuously." He came across "a sleek white and brindled pariah . . . a horrible machine, which chews red-hot iron bars and spits them out perfect bolts. Its manners are disgusting, and it gobbles over its food." The fun of personification is especially evident in '.007', the nomenclature of a new, small locomotive engine, a locomotive being "next to a marine engine, the most sensitive thing man ever made". All the machines are humanized, made into individuals, each with a distinct character, their interchange being amusing enough, in the way that one may find club chatter amusing, and men's vanities and petty jealousies. This fable, which one may put among the 'moral', figures the introduction of a boy or youth into the affairs and duties of life; he is told, he is taught, he suffers, and soon becomes adult; the moral, in fact, is that of *Captains Courageous*. As a side issue is the illustration of how small things, accidents, can upset great matters, little men bring down great ones, as when a little eight-pound wild piglet derails a monarch of express-train engines, worth "all of a hundred thousand pound".

Preceding this by two years, in 'The Ship that Found Herself'—which might be grouped with the political fables—personification is not quite so apparent; yet we listen to the skipper of the newly-launched *Dimbula*, the ship that had yet to find herself, explaining to the owner's daughter:

For a ship, ye'll obsairve . . . is in no sense a reegid body closed at both ends. She's a highly complex structure o' various an' conflictin' strains, wi' tissues that must give an' tak' accordin' to her personal modulus of elasteecity.

To feel this seems to have given Kipling the same deep pleasure as McAndrew felt when he rejoiced in the sound of his 'purrin' dynamoes', quite apart from the moral of the fable, which is simple enough. All parts must work together to make a valid, viable whole, here a ship which emerges with its own distinctive

[1] *From Sea to Sea*, II.

voice, a character that other ships recognize: thus in any definite society all individuals must give and take, and resolve
conflicting strains so that an influential nation may exist. But
the application of the fable does not intrude while we read.
Kipling carries us along with his eagerness to show what a
wonderful thing a ship is, the various parts talking, quarrelling,
complaining; and occasionally he stimulates attention, always
with an application in view, by a holding description of what
a ship, or a nation, has to encounter:

As soon as she had cleared the Irish coast a sullen, gray-headed
old wave of the Atlantic climbed leisurely over her straight bows,
and sat down on her steam capstan used for hauling up the
anchor.

It must be confessed, however, that neither this story, nor
'.007' is one to which the reader will often return.

In this category—of doing the thing for the fun of it—we can
put 'With the Night Mail', set in the year A.D. 2000, where, also,
he rejoices in the romance that brings up the 9.15. It is an
amazing prophetic vision of the conquest of the air, Kipling
evidently enjoying his realistic inventiveness, especially in the
matter of machines. He pictures for us, with superbly imagined
detail, on the basis of dirigible airship, the planes of the then
future, so vividly that without a knowledge of engineering we can
see the drift. Although he did not foresee the supersonic jet plane,
it is an astonishing flower of the imagination, written, it may
be noted, some four years before Blériot performed the daring
feat of flying the Channel. In texture it has all the richness of
present-day actuality, with sketches of personalities and implications of stories. It has no fabular theme in the sense of
conveying a universal truth, abounding, rather, in 'points' such
as we expect from a story, as when we read of Magniac who
had devised a

rudder that assured us the dominion of the unstable air and left its
inventor penniless and half-blind. . . . Magniac invented the rudder
to help war-boats ram each other; and war went out of fashion and
Magniac he went out of his mind because he said he couldn't serve
his country any more. I wonder if any of us ever knows what we're
really doing.

Nor did Kipling here delight only in drawing the characters and devising machinery; he envisaged what the world would look like from 'up there'. We are transported half a mile above the dappled level of Atlantic clouds, and occasionally get a glimpse of things seen, as when "Tim slides open the aft colloid and reveals the curve of the world—the ocean's deepest purple—edged with fuming and intolerable gold."

That fable—if fable may be defined as something which has never happened—has no moral, nor can one be discerned in what we may think a most unlikely story, the amusing 'The Janeites', in which a battery on the front in France becomes, so to speak, 'possessed' by Jane Austen, skilfully allotting to guns and humans the names and characters of people in her novels. Maybe it illustrates how men, of whatever class or calling or rank, can become unified by one interest, so that all distinctions disappear. C. S. Lewis dubbed this story hateful, presumably on account of its incredibility. Yet it is an oddly prophetic fable, or shall we say that here Nature in her nakedness, if she did not defeat Kipling, caught up on him. Not long since a visitor to an Antarctic station "was at a loss to account for the quaint mid-Victorian quality of the men's everyday dialogue and the old-world courtesy of their behaviour". It turned out that they had been seeing a film of *Pride and Prejudice* again and again, preferring in the end to have it silent so that they could together chant the familiar dialogue.[1]

We can turn to the clearly moral fables, such as 'The Maltese Cat', an account of a polo-match so brilliantly told that even those with no experience of the game can feel the excitement, understand what is going on, and appreciate the tactics the Cat orders his fellow-ponies to pursue. He is the hero of the tale, bought as a pony when pulling a vegetable cart in Malta. For he belongs to the Skidars, a regiment far from rich, who defeat the Archangels, men able to buy ponies from especially bred stock. There are two subsidiary, anti-snob morals there, money is not a 'value', birth is not a 'value'. The main theme, however, comes from the mouth of the Maltese Cat himself, captain of the team more than is his owner, Lutyens, as he adjures his fellow-ponies:

[1] Philip Law in *The Medical Journal of Australia*. See *The Times*, 17 March 1964.

L

Play the game, don't talk. . . . Keep yourselves to yourselves . . . we don't want to rub noses with those goose-rumped half-breed of Upper India. . . . Don't take it out of yourselves. Let them do the lathering. . . . For pity's sake, don't run away with the notion that the game is half-won because we happen to be in luck now. . . . Follow the ball. . . . And now . . . remember that this is the last quarter, and follow the ball.

The tale ends—a little sentimentally—with the Cat coming into the Officers' Mess after the dinner where the match is celebrated; he has incurably strained a sinew by swerving against a goal-post to save Lutyens from banging fatally against it after driving the ball that makes the winning goal. He can be used afterwards only as an umpire's mount,

a flea-bitten gray with a neat polo-tail, lame all round, but desperately quick on his feet, and, as everybody knew, Past Pluperfect Prestissimo Player of the Game.

"Player of the Game"; that is the moral of the fable; but that the Game is worth more than the Player of the Game was a truth the Archangels had not learnt; each player was too keen on his own prowess to forego any exhibition of personal skill for the sake of the side.

When in 1897 Kipling wrote 'An English School',[1] and began to dwell on 'memories of his frolic youth', incidents grew into stories; and it would seem that as he continued to muse he found a thread of meaning connecting them; so the series of 'tracts or parables', as he called *Stalky & Co.*, became a sustained moral fable. Each amusing tale has its 'point' of immediate applicability, but a universal significance emerges from the total collection. To gird at the book because it does not give an accurate picture is manifestly to misunderstand it: Kipling's remark to his cousin "What shall we make them do next?" is clear enough indication that it was not meant to be 'true'. Much we know to be fact, but much is invention.[2] Many of the events are, to say the least of it, unlikely, and no doubt many of the more violent episodes represent what schoolboys would

[1] *Land and Sea Tales.*

[2] *See Something of Myself*; L. C. Dunsterville, *Stalky's Reminiscences* (Cape, 1928), G. C. Beresford, *Schooldays with Kipling* (Gollancz, 1936).

like to happen, fantasies "true to the imaginative life of many a boy".[1] There is more truth in the quieter background, with Beetle roaming through the Head's library, M'Turk reading Ruskin and De Quincey, Stalky revelling in Surtees, and King throwing Browning's *Men and Women* at Beetle's head (as a gift) that he might know where the name Gigadibs came from.

The characters are to some extent fabulized. King is a rather tiresome puffed-up pedant, but in actual life the Beetle–King campaign was a conflict of individuals who had great respect, even admiration for each other. It was to King (that is Crofts) that Kipling sent the first literary articles that he wrote in India. Facts are adjusted to make a story. In 'An English School' it is recorded that "The Head . . . saved a boy's life from diphtheria once at much greater risk than being shot at, and nobody knew about it till years afterwards." But in 'A Little Prep' the boy who had been ill tells Stalky that "they stuck a tube or somethin' in my throat, and the Head sucked out the stuff'", whence followed the demonstration by the whole school and the old boys, organized by Stalky; after which the Head caned the whole Upper School, itself a fabulous enough feat, and quite contrary to what we know of 'Uncle Crom'.

The book is, beneath the surface, a tractate upon education, to some extent summed up in the poem 'The Centaurs' attached to 'The United Idolators'. Education is a hardening, self-disciplining process, as well as an enlargement. There are minor morals in that story, conducing to the same theme, as that "youth is its own prophylactic", and that, as the Rev. John Gillett puts it, "in our loathsome calling, more things are done by judicious letting alone than by any other", a belief more than once stated, and not intended by Kipling to be applied merely to school-mastering. As shown by the treatment of the prefects, a little brief authority is no substitute for individuality. But the main theme of the fable would seem to be the stressing of the value of the in-group, as pictured by Study No. 5 in its life of communal sharing, and which, "so far as its code allowed friendship with outsiders, it was polite and open-hearted to its neighbours on the same landing",[2] a sound

---

[1] *Carrington*, p. 29.
[2] *Slaves of the Lamp*, I.

basis for international politics. Moreover, justice is not to be expected in life, as 'the Prooshian Bates' does not fail to point out when he 'unjustly' canes Study No. 5—an episode which made Stalky laugh immoderately as he considered "the flagrant injustice of it all".[1]

From fairly early, Kipling it would seem, felt that the fable had more to say than the story: it runs as an under-current through the tales. This is particularly so where the moral shades into the political through the road of social behaviour. Not very explicit, as one or the other, is the main fable running through four of the stories in *Puck of Pook's Hill*. The theme, gold and its power, is faintly touched upon in 'Weland's Sword' (though we do not realize this till the end of the book) by the mere mention of the runes. It comes in at the end of 'The Joyous Venture', when Sir Richard Dalyngridge, after his terrific fight with the gorillas, receives the ingots and the gold-dust; then it occurs, more plainly, in 'Old Men at Pevensey', a story of the Saxon–Norman conflict, when the ingots and the gold-dust are relegated to the well of the castle (a well that Kipling invented, and was later found to exist), the end-poem being 'The Runes on Weland's Sword'; it comes to its conclusion in 'The Treasure and the Law', when Kadmiel loads the bulk of the treasure into a boat, and casts it into the sea. Gold is the hidden Fifth River of which Israel is the master, alone knowing the secret of its flow, and where it will be needed. Or where it should not flow, for here it is its absence that forces King John to sign Magna Carta.

It is in his political fables that Kipling is most nakedly fabulous, in that he employs the animal, Æsopian method, since much of the world at the time they were written would have the matter hid. There is, for instance, 'A Walking Delegate', the story of the untrustworthy agitator horse, trying to get his fellow horses, who appreciate the nature of society and the integration of its parts, to rebel against the human 'oppressors' who prevent them from freely enjoying the air of the great plains. A not very exciting and rather savage story, with a trite moral, a little enlivened by the fun of personification. Better directed, and interesting in itself and in its bee-lore

[1] 'The Impressionists.'

(whether accurate or not), is 'The Mother Hive'. (Both have been referred to on incidental points.) There, thanks to a moment's bad temper, due to fatigue, on the part of the Guard of the hive, a wax-moth is able to seize the opportunity she has been waiting for to get in. She is a charming, soft creature, who raises up in the bees the vision of that happy Socialist state where, in the words of 'The Gods of the Copy-Book Headings', "all men are paid for existing, and no man shall pay for his sins". She lays eggs promiscuously, and when told that to do so is the privilege of the Queen Bee protests that they are not eggs that she lays, but principles, a lie she later justifies. She and her brood eat into and destroy all the wax essential to the structure of the hive, which becomes useless; malformed and morally uninspired bees are produced, no honey is gathered, and the call to swarm is ignored. Worst of all, the scrap-wax pillars which should guard against the entry of Death's Head Moths fail to be built. Scrap-wax pillars?

'That's nonsense', a downy day-old bee answered. 'In the first place I've never heard of a Death's Header coming into a hive. People don't *do* such things. In the second, building pillars to keep 'em out is purely a Cypriote trick, unworthy of British bees. In the third, if you trust a Death's Head, he will trust you. Pillar-building shows a lack of confidence. Our dear sister in grey says so.

In the end the hive is destroyed by the human owners in a grand holocaust, and all the bees are killed, save for a group of sensible, disciplined ones, who create a Queen, and swarm. The implications are obvious when it is noted that this was written in 1908, during the period when 'The City of Brass' and 'The Dykes' (itself a fable) were published. It is the old lesson, the old warning, that Kipling at that time was urgent to impress on his countrymen. Stop this self-regarding Socialist nonsense, think of the Germans, and look to your Army and Navy!

It was the writing of 'With the Night Mail' that gave Kipling the idea for his political fable, 'As Easy as A.B.C.', as is shown by the notes of the earlier story. The later one had already been sufficiently quoted from to need no further mention here. It is a piece of wishful thinking as is the double story 'The Army of a Dream', where Kipling let his imagination roam on devising a perfect citizen army—or, rather, defence force since the Navy is included—the 'dream' being carried through with Kipling's usual humanly realistic touches: it hums with personalities. Written in 1904 it is a prophecy of the Territorial Army, in actuality partly realized, and is a lively criticism of the military set-up of the time, being prefaced by 'The Song of the Old Guard'. Prophetic also we may hope, are the poem and story 'The Benefactors', already referred to and quoted.

Whether, as has been argued, 'The Man Who Would be King' is a fable of Empire is not so sure.[1] We are first held by the extravagant, brilliantly realized story of Peachey Carnehan and Daniel Dravot, the two out-at-heel vagabonds who make a kingdom out of Kafiristan. The two adventurers, partly by using weapons of a quality unknown to the natives, partly by a queer link with Freemasonry, weld together the warring tribes and introduce some sort of order. They persuade the village priests and chiefs to become magistrates, and by stern action mitigated by understanding friendship, attain the status of kings. As story it has a plain 'point'; you cannot be a god *and* a sensuous human being, the men losing their divine stature when Dravot insists upon acquiring a wife. Its parallel with the British Empire is the setting of warring tribes to productive work, making some of them into an army, and establishing a central government administering laws. The parallel certainly seems to be in Dravot's mind: "there is only one place now in the world", he says, "that two strong men can Sar-a-*whack*. They call it Kafiristan." And later, "Rajah Brooke will be a suckling to us", and he is going to hand over the crown he is then wearing to "Queen Victoria on my knees, and she'd say: 'Rise up, Sir Daniel Dravot!'" It is not to be suggested that the disastrous end of the story in any way prefigured what Kipling thought would be the final withdrawal of the British from India.

As Kipling developed, always doing different things ("never repeat yourself!"), attempting new ways of saying things, the fable and the tale became ever more closely integrated. He is fabulist together with being realist, many of the stories where

[1] As is well done by Professor Louis L. Cornell in *Kipling in India* (Macmillan, 1966), p. 162–4.

he develops his most fundamental intuitions having in them a strong element of the fabular. These might be called 'concealed fables', of which *Stalky & Co.* is an early example. He progressively made his stories become immensely packed and complex, and moreover they go further than most novels, as does *Wuthering Heights.* The fable emerges gradually, perhaps only after several readings—with one startling exception, 'The Gardener'. This one takes as a straightforward touching tale until the last sentence, which forces a sudden readjustment in the reader's apprehension; a story has become a fable. Kipling resorts to the concealed method more especially where his philosophical thinking is concerned. There is something of this in the *Puck of Pook's Hill* stories already discussed; but in *Rewards and Fairies* there are two stories which go beyond any immediately applicable moral, stimulating a pondering on the basis of living.

First 'The Knife and the Naked Chalk', where a primitive man, anxious to save from the wolves the sheep by which his tribe lives—and, moreover, "the sheep are the people"—obtains a knife, superior to any of the flint instruments which are all that his tribe knows of, from the Children of the Night. For this he has to sacrifice one of his eyes, and more, all human relationships, since his tribe now regard him as a god. There are two things developed here; the gods will let you have anything you ask for—at a price (a favourite idea of Kipling's); and, here again, you cannot be both a god and a man. The theme of 'Cold Iron' would seem to be that of necessity, the impossibility of escaping Fate. The Boy, for all his fairy powers, and his strong poetic imagination, comes across the slave-ring that Thor had made, and thrown so that some day the Boy should find it. He puts the strange iron object round his neck, and fastens it permanently with its clip. Therefore he

. . . must go among folk in housen henceforward, doing what they want done, or what he knows they need, all Old England over. Never will he be his own master, nor yet any man's.

Necessity, the necessity of the Law that makes society possible, is the slave-ring that binds us all. The concluding poem strengthens the theme with its reference to the Crucifixion, ending:

'But Iron—Cold Iron—is master of man all!
Iron, out of Calvary, is master of man all!'

Those stories approach the mystery of existence; and it may be that these varied inventions, the method of the concealed fable, were developed from an earlier story where Kipling had used a more evident form, feeling perhaps the value of the fabulous element *in* a story, as, possibly, redeeming the painful elements of actuality, enlarging experience to fit sorrow into the scheme. In 'They', written in 1904, life is closely mingled with, rather than integrated with, the mystery which constitutes the fabular. We begin with a sun-spangled realistic description of the English countryside—already quoted from—and such recur throughout as a setting; the narrator drives into the garden of the lovely old house, and then—here the fable begins—he is stayed by the topiary horseman's green spear laid at his breast, because he must not know.[1] A child appears at an upper window, seemingly waving a friendly hand. And here one must interpolate to reveal the emotional drive that made Kipling need to write it. Soon after the Kiplings' return from America, where their elder daughter had died, Lockwood Kipling wrote in a letter:[2]

The house and garden are full of the lost child, and poor Rud told his mother how he saw her when a door opened, when a space was vacant at table, coming out of every dark corner of the garden, radiant—and heart-breaking.

His sense, or hope, that dead children want to come back is poignantly phrased in the prefatory poem 'The Return of the Children', which ends with Christ asking: "Shall I that have suffered the children to come to me hold them against their will?"

All through the realistic blends with the 'other world' element. The blind owner of the house is immensely aware of the intangible world—the children, cold iron, the mystic Egg; but she is no mere sentimentalist, being as practical as her butler, who, having himself lost a child, is sensitive to the presence of the child-ghosts. She manages her property very

---

[1] I owe the elucidation of this symbol to Dr. Tompkins.
[2] *Carrington*, p. 372.

shrewdly, as is shown by the way she handles a bad tenant-farmer who comes to beg for a new shed for young stock. She refuses his plea:

You are overstocked already. Dunnett's Farm never carried more than fifty bullocks—even in Mr. Wright's time. And *he* used cake. You've sixty-seven and you don't cake. You've broken the lease in that respect.

It isn't that which she minds so much about: what angers her comes out in the next sentence: "You're dragging the heart out of the farm." Realistic touches are mingled with the fabular ones. The blind woman uses tallies because "Since I can't read or write I'm driven to the early English tally for my accounts." As a setting to the house is the near-by, earthy village, with the unmarried woman whose natural child is dangerously ill; and we get sketches, largely humorous, of the village characters, and learn something of the busied, varied, and responsible life of the local doctor. The tale is one of Kipling's early experiments towards his later manner; a main story, with layer upon layer of others implied. Possibly 'A Madonna of the Trenches' comes into this 'mystery' group, as do 'The Brushwood Boy', 'The Dog Hervey', and some others.

Kipling's last two volumes contain many concealed fables. 'The Eye of Allah', for example, is a wonderfully detailed realistic tale; we clearly see the medieval monastery in its characteristically English setting; we are close to the textual copyists and illuminators, to the infirmarian, and we hear the echoes of the boys at choir practice; we glimpse, or more than glimpse, the story of John of Burgos smitten with sorrow for the death in childbirth of his Spanish-Jewish mistress; there is a sketch of the Abbot and his consumptive love, Anne of Norton. We meet the two scientists, Roger of Salerno and Roger Bacon, and, as the main holding-together theme, the early microscope, the Eye of Allah. Some of the 'aphorisms', we might call them, on art and the artist, and on the anodyne of work have already been quoted, as has the main 'fabular' meaning of 'Untimely'. Besides this we get the age-long struggle between orthodox faith and scientific enlightenment, bluntly stated by the two Rogers—early illustrations of what in due course would happen with Galileo, Newton, and Darwin. Nowadays we are accustomed to what the microscope reveals, but the kind of shock it originally was Kipling tells us in another place,[1] when he speaks of

the attitude of Swammerdam, half-crazed at the sight of the marvels his microscope showed him in a drop of water, shutting his notebook and vowing such revelations were not to be communicated to mankind.

That story does not, however, contradict Kipling's sense of age-long growth, brought out in the clear fable 'Below the Mill Dam', mixed as regards characters; the wheel, the mill-stones, and the waters talk as well as the rat and the cat, not to mention the humans. It tells of political developments since Domesday Book, the wheel tending to quote it automatically as it dwells on the past, but quickly adapting itself to changed conditions, such as the introduction of electricity, finally deriving pride from being converted into a turbine. The moral would seem to be, "Joyfully accept what is happening: don't forget the past, but welcome the future"; all the same, like one of the humans in the story, you may be allowed to regret the disappearance of the black rat.

Fable, perhaps, peeps only rather dimly through 'The Church that was at Antioch', again a complex story, made alive through various characters; the Gallio-like Prefect of Antioch in the first century A.D.; the story of his excellent nephew—the perfect British subaltern—his intelligence, his efficiency, his love; and finally his murder, and dying Christian plea, "Forgive them; they knew not what they did!" The conflicting character of St. Peter and St. Paul are splendidly indicated. (Why, we may ask parenthetically, was Kipling so repeatedly moved by St. Peter's denial of his Lord?) It is all actual, immediate, vividly conveyed; we take part. The themes, beyond the story itself are those of the wise, humane government of an empire, racial conflicts, the basic likeness of religions (here of Mithraism and Christianity), and the forging together of ideas before a religion can be established. Three more stories in his last volume could come under the heading of 'concealed fables', namely 'Fairy-Kist', 'Unprofessional', and

[1] *A Book of Words*, XXV. Some two years after 'The Eye of Allah'.

'The Tender Achilles', the two latter dealing with stages of scientific progress at present undreamt of, certainly unrealized, and perhaps always to remain so. 'Influences' were part of the Fable by which Kipling lived.

To many readers, Kipling's fables about art, the artist, and his relation to the public are the most intriguing, since they are the most personal. Perhaps the earliest of all can hardly be called a fable, namely 'The Last of the Stories' (1888), in which Kipling, prey to the Devil of Discontent, dreams that he is swept into a limbo where authors meet the characters they have created. He is horrified at Mrs. Hauksbee, "a limp-jointed, staring-eyed doll was hirpling towards me. . . . 'Keep her off, Devil!' I cried. . . . 'I never made *that*!' " Mrs. Mallowe describes him as the man "who thinks he understands"; he meets his three soldiers, but Mulvaney, after Ortheris has thanked their visitor for all the beers, concludes, "On my sowl an' honour, Sorr, you did not onderstand." A strong note of humility there! But humility was not Kipling's strong point in his early days, and in his next fables, of the early 'nineties, all of them in verse, mostly maintain his own point of view as a practising writer.

'The Conundrum of the Workshops', of 13 September 1890, reflects the literary world he encountered when he came to London, where "each man talked of the aims of art, and each in an alien tongue", all, moreover, haunted by the doubt Satan continually insinuates, saying, it's pretty, it's human, it's clever, "But is it art?" The resolution of the artist's doubt is, however, made in 'The Story of Ung', in the MS.[1] described as 'A Fable for the Criticized'. After all, the artist, here a dweller in the ice-age, 'sees' in a way a man of action never can. Defiance of critics who want to reduce everything to pattern is declared in 'In the Neolithic Age', of December 1893, which roundly states, in a now well-worn phrase, that

There are nine and sixty ways of constructing tribal lays,
And—every—single—one—of—them—is—right.

Another fable of December 1890 might be attached to these, 'The Rhyme of the Three Captains', a too long poem in

[1] Add. MSS. 44841.

boisterous sixteeners (approximately) in which he upbraids Walter Besant, Thomas Hardy, and William Black—happy acquaintances at the Savile—for defending Messrs. Harper & Bros., in the matter of copyright, where Kipling thought they had behaved piratically. Near the end we get a couplet containing the most atrocious pun Kipling ever perpetrated:

Then fore-sheet home as she lifts to the foam—we stand on the outward tack.
We are paid in the coin of the white man's trade—the bezant is hard, ay, and black.

His victims took it in good part.

A more puzzling one is 'Evarra and His Gods', the best of his rare exercises in unrhymed verse, published on the same day as 'The Conundrum of the Workshops'. Evarra was a "man—Maker of Gods in lands beyond the sea". First he was held in high esteem by a rich monarch, and he made

> An image of his God in gold and pearl,
> With turquoise diadem and human eyes.

In his next existence, a despised member of a poor community,

> He hewed the living rock, with sweat and tears,
> And reared a God against the morning-gold,
> A terror in the sunshine.

In his succeeding incarnation, as a villager, "He cut an idol from a fallen pine", duly making a very primitive image. Lastly, a half-wit, living among cattle, he made a monstrous God out of dung and horns. In each case his patrons were immensely pleased, praised him loudly, brought him rewards; and if the cattle could do no more than low at twilight-time, "He dreamed it was the clamour of lost crowds". On each occasion, too, he was smitten with pride, and wrote or carved or scratched or howled:

> Thus Gods are made
> And whoso makes them otherwise shall die.

Finally he came to Paradise, where he found his own four Gods, and was ashamed, marvelling "What oaf on earth had made his toil God's law". But God mocked him kindly, telling Evarra that but for him he would be

". . . the poorer by four wondrous Gods,
And thy more wondrous law, Evarra. Thine,
Servant of shouting crowds and lowing kine!"
Thereat, with laughing mouth, but tear-wet eyes,
Evarra cast his Gods from Paradise.

The implications of that fable, and they are many, need no gloss.

In the Definitive Edition of his verse, Kipling grouped all these verse-fables together, and included with them a poem written some twenty years later, 'The Craftsman', in which Shakespeare, after a long revel at The Mermaid, tells Ben Jonson how his ideas came to him, and 'opened his heart till the sunrise/Entered to hear him'. The poem goes on:

London waked and he, imperturbable,
Passed from waking to hurry after shadows . . .
Busied upon shows of no earthly importance?
    Yes, but he knew it!

Here, at this date, we get, possibly, the note of real humility: there is, however, the other meaning that might be given to the phrase "no earthly importance".

Kipling's great triumph in the genre of concealed fable, about art, the artist, and the public, is 'The Bull that Thought', a story very much in Kipling's most complex late manner, with a number of subjects, and layer upon layer of meaning.[1] It begins deceivingly with an account of how Kipling was indulging his love of speed and a perfect engine by testing his car on a road in the Crau and Camargue regions of France, in which he is joined by an old proprietor of the district, Voiron, who tells the tale of the bull. We guess early that the story is to be fabular, since the wine they drank at dinner was "composed of the whispers of angels' wings, the breath of Eden, and the foam and pulse of Youth renewed". The art theme is soon introduced. The dictum that no artist will tolerate being asked to repeat himself has already been noted; the bull even resents being asked for an encore of a performance he gave at Arles, where bloodless bull-fights take place. He had learnt "a breadth of technique that comes of reasoned art, and, above all, the passion that arrives after experience". His was "the detachment of

---

[1] For possible autobiographical implications see *Bodelsen*, Chapter IV.

the true artist who knows he is but the vessel of an emotion whence others, not he, must drink". And near the end Voiron suggests to Kipling that "Life is sweet to us all; to the artist who lives many lives in one, sweetest."

Apis, the bull, named after the Egyptian bull-god, is not the only artist in the story when it comes to the real bull-fight in Spain. There is Villamarti, a rather flashy matador, not a true artist, too much playing for effect, whose reputation Apis destroys for ever. The third artist is the matador Christo, "a laborious middle-aged professional who had never risen beyond a certain dull competence" in whom also there may be something of self portraiture. The show was going very dangerously, with the prospect of the Civil Guards having to fire. But then Fate sent in "none other than Christo, the eldest, and I should have said (but never again will I judge!) the least inspired of all; mediocrity itself, but at heart—and it is the heart that conquers always, my friend—at heart an artist". Apis appreciates him, responds to his invitation to put on a real display. "It was the Master, wearied after a strenuous hour in the atelier, unbuttoned and at ease with some not inexpert but limited disciple." They put on a superb pantomime—Villamarti tries to join in, but is chased off—and the bull-fight ends, not with the death of the bull, but with Christo casting his cape and his arm round the bull's neck, taking him to the gate where so many bulls enter but none go out alive, throwing up his hand and crying: "Gentlemen, open to me and my honourable little donkey." The concluding poem, 'Alnaschar and the Oxen' somewhat cryptically implies that the story might be about Kipling the artist.

But there is more than one theme running through. The Egyptian idea is stressed (the eternal likeness of things!), and there are several references to the war—before the war, after the war. This links up with the violence and brutality that had so long been absent from Kipling's work, the reappearance of which has puzzled some commentators. But these killings and murderous side-kicks represent the great battles France had fought; Voiron calls Apis "this Foch among bulls". Thus it is a fable also in praise of France, her valour, her art. At the end of the story Voiron and Apis's owner drink to 'her'.

There is one other fable of 1935, 'Teem; A Treasure Hunter', a purely animal fable in which a dog recounts his own experiences: it was the last story Kipling wrote, and it has a personal implication, as was early recognized.[1] The theme throughout is art, and we meet such phrases as "At all hazards follow your Art. That can never lead to a false scent," and, twice, "Outside his Art an Artist must never dream." But it also concerns the relation of the artist to the public, and is, rather sadly, autobiographical.[2] As such it is fascinating and revealing: as a dog-story it has all the sentimentality of Kipling's dog stories. It is fairly simple—unlike most of Kipling's later tales—its only complication being the consumptive girl, whose presence adds a little to the dog's perplexities. His saving her from intruders is part of his reward, and perhaps makes the tale a little more three-dimensional, but it is, it would seem, unnecessary to the theme. It is best to follow the story as an autobiography, which is most easily done by allowing oneself to pick up the thread of the tale as it develops. It is told by a small French dog, in Frenchified English—Teem is the French pronunciation of Tim—a dog with a great talent for story-telling!

We may prelude the account by saying that Teem's art consisted in the discovery of truffles:

From my father I inherit my nose, and, perhaps, a touch of genius. From my mother a practical philosophy without which even Genius is but a bird of one wing.

His adored Mother, we are told at the beginning, used to demand immediate reward for every truffle that she found, whereas his Father, once their Master had been told of the find, moved on to fresh triumphs. At all events his parents came from a

---

[1] Professor J. C. Griffin, *The Kipling Journal*, September 1937.

[2] For full analysis see *Bodelsen*, Chapter V and for support *Tompkins*, p. 113.

It should be said that Kipling's daughter, Mrs. Elsie Bambridge, firmly rejects the view that these fables are in any degree autobiographical. She writes:

'My father read the story to me ('The Bull that Thought') and we discussed it often, and I promise you that it is a straight tale and nothing more.

'The same goes for 'Teem'. R.K. had always been interested in the hunting of truffles, and at the time they had been found in a wood at Bateman's.

'Again R.K. and I discussed the tale, and I can assure you that it is a story and nothing more.'

gifted stock; they stood apart from the generality, but not for that would Teem make light of worthy artisans who had not their gift. Teem was an artist born, and does not recall that he was ever trained by anybody; he watched, imitated, and at need improved upon the technique of his parents. He had friends—Pluton and Dis, identifiable as Stalky and M'Turk, and "my preceptor, my protector, my life-long admiration", a Marshall of Bulls, who though he did not understand what Teem was after, nor understand his art, "Yet always, unweariedly, he gave me the fruits of his experience and philosophy." Here we see Crofts, 'Mr. King' of Westward Ho!, or possibly, Cormell Price. Teem was, then, born in France, but he was bought by some English, who, however, lost him in a motor crash, and he became owned by a charcoal burner, who smelt good, and whose daughter, the Girl, was a bed-ridden consumptive.

From his parents he had inherited his Nose—"that gift which is incommunicable"; but when he put it to use his genius was misunderstood. His Master, for whom he had great regard, set him to watch and do all the duties of a guardian dog; but when Teem proudly brought back some "Truffles of the best", and laid them before him as a gift and a tribute,

He and the Girl thought that I amused myself, and would throw—throw!—them for me to retrieve, as though they had been stones, and I a puppy! What more could I do? The scent over the ground was lost.

Nor did he get much help from his 'Aunt', a sheep-dog, who explained to him that until he had a collar, he lived by favour and accidents.

'But, ma Tante,' I cried, 'I have the secret of an Art beyond all others.'

'That is not understood in these parts,' she replied. 'You have told it me many times, but I do not believe. What a pity it is not rabbits! You are small enough to creep down their burrows. But these precious things of yours under the ground which no one but you can find—it is absurd!'

He tried to get away. He fled to the edge of the woods where he had wandered so often with his Master, but found that they were bounded by a stone wall through which he could find no opening. The situation seemed hopeless. But at last there came a woman, a Born One, who inhabited the château of the district. She knew what truffles were, and paid a high price for them. So Teem got due regard, and the Girl got the treatment appropriate for consumptives.

The whole fable is clear enough. Kipling, in his mature period, coming from abroad, brought his treasures of story-telling to an unappreciative public who had not the faintest idea what he was getting at. His old admirers did not follow him. Why didn't he stick to rabbits? He used to be very good at catching them, as in *Plain Tales*, *Life's Handicap* and so on. The Wall one guesses to be the great obstacle of current criticism and reviewing, the then 'establishment' in our jargon today, a barrier almost impossible to climb or break through: but at last the Born One, that is the small group of perceptive and intelligent people, were made aware of, and appreciated his truffles, meaningless to the crass multitude, even to the charcoal burner, excellent as he was in himself, with the smell of Hobden about him. So at the end he received the reward of recognition for the Nose of genius that could find such delicious things. The Girl is something of a puzzle; she may be Literature itself, rescued from being captured by the two people representing the law (not with a capital L), medical officers of health who threatened to take her off to a sanatorium, placing her in academic confines. The details are a little obscure, but the main point of the fable is abundantly plain. It was a fitting last story.

It would seem then that Kipling, as his broodings on life became deeper as a result of his family disasters and his later increasing physical pain, and his mastery of the short-story form increased, became always more inclined to introduce an element of fable, adding a fourth dimension to the pictures he presented of human beings, their actions and reactions. It was no doubt partly this that brought about the period of 'the Kipling that nobody read'. Great realist as he was, it is impossible to see what he was really saying unless the fabular element is at least glimpsed. Even so, he remains the Kipling it is impossible *wholly* to understand, but to realize him as a fabulist makes him less difficult to appreciate.

M

PART II

THE POET

Introduction

> Now a polo-pony is like a poet. If he is born with a love of
> the game he can be made.
>
> 'The Maltese Cat'

One day, when Beetle was browsing in the Head's library,
rather idly conning through D'Israeli's *Curiosities of Literature*,
suddenly

. . . at the foot of a left-hand page [there] leaped out on him a
verse of—incommunicable splendour, opening doors into inexplic-
able worlds—from a song which Tom-a-Bedlams were supposed
to sing. It ran:

> With a heart of furious fancies
> Whereof I am commander,
> With a burning spear and a horse of air,
> To a wilderness I wander.
> With a knight of ghosts and shadows
> I summoned am to tourney,
> Ten leagues beyond the wide world's end—
> Methinks it is no journey.

He sat mouthing and staring before him, till the prep-bell rang.
('Propagation of Knowledge')

What doors that would open to a boy—he was then about
fifteen—poetically endowed! It would suggest that poetry
works, not so much through reason, as through the intuitions,
guiding our existence by awakening us to the basic, though in
our daily commerce, unrecognized assumptions by which we
live at all, and stirring unaccustomed levels of consciousness.
Furious fancies, a burning spear, and a horse of air.

Born with the love of the game, Kipling was responsible for
the verse which enlivened the amateur theatricals at Westward
Ho!, japes on the masters, and so on.[1] Most of his other verses

---

[1] *Stalky & Co., passim.*

are of the imitative kind to be found in *Schoolboy Verses*, which, unknown to him, his parents had printed in India before he returned there, though he did write one poem, 'Ave Imperatrix' thought by T. S. Eliot worthy of inclusion in his selection: and on one occasion he was paid a whole guinea for some verses, untraced, which he sent up to a paper, so that "the Study caroused on chocolate and condensed milk and pilchards and Devonshire Cream". Rhyme throughout his life was an essential part of verse, and he very rarely wrote anything without it. Having to 'do' Horace at school, he rebelled against him; and pretending not to understand classical quantities, declared that "he could do better if Latin verse rhymed as decent verse should". When as an imposition he was told to send up a translation of Ode III. ix, "he turned 'Donec gratus eram' into pure Devonshire dialect",[1] the first example of a manner he could later use so effectively. The first two stanzas read:

> *He.*   Ez long as 'twuz me alone
> An' there wasn't no other chaps,
> I was praoud as a King on 'is throne—
> Happier tu, per'aps.

> *She.*   Ez long as 'twuz only I
> An' there wasn't no other she
> Yeou cared for so much—surely
> I was glad as glad could be.

He did, however, make a by no means despicable attempt at blank verse before his sixteenth birthday.[2]

How important verse was to Kipling for expressing the whole range of his ideas and emotions from the lightest to the most profound is evident from the extent to which it has been appropriate to quote it in the process of trying to elucidate his thought or emotion. It would seem that he turned for expression to verse as readily as to prose, the one medium being as natural to him as the other. As Eliot stressed, he did not try to write 'poetry'. When the thought lent itself to what we call poetry,

---

[1] 'An English School.' *Land and Sea Tales.*

[2] Neither is included in Definitive Edition. Printed *Carrington* p. 39 and Chapter XV.

or the emotion was deep enough, the 'verse' became 'poetry'.

Thus whether he wrote in prose, or, to invert Dryden's phrase, "in the other harmony of verse", seems to have been with him not so much a matter of indifference as of the mood of the moment, sometimes, of course, of subject-matter. States of mind are not always susceptible of being conveyed in story form, except too clumsily. What could be made of, say, 'The Two-Sided Man'? But often, with his thirst to formulate, even project what he had to say in different ways, he came to accompany his tales with a poem, either as preface or as conclusion, sometimes both. These to some degree elucidate the tale, or the tale explains the poem. Eliot went so far as to say that he invented a kind of dual form, story and poem making one whole, each being incomplete without the other: but this is rare. Occasionally there seems to be little connexion. How, for instance, does 'Akbar's Bridge' throw a light on 'The Debt'? One may well feel that the former, good as it is, would be better as a prose story, perhaps after the manner of 'The Amir's Homily'.

At all events he laboured at his verse as indefatigably as he did at his prose; the briefest study of the manuscripts will show this with their drafts, corrections, scribblings over and re-writing. One extended example will illustrate the point, 'A Song in Storm', already partly quoted. The MS. version[1] has for first stanza:

> Be well assured that from our side
>   Good luck has taken flight—
> And nosing wind and raging tide
>   Make us their prey to-night.
> Our past so nearly, clearly won
>   Alas! is far removèd:
> Then welcome Fate's discourtesy
>   Whereby it shall be provèd
>   How in all time of our distress
>   (Whatever Fate shall do)
>   The game is more than the player of the game,
>   As Fame is more than the seeker after fame,
>   And the ship is more than the crew.

[1] British Museum. Add. MSS. 44841.

In the Definitive Edition this has become:

> Be well assured that on our side
>   The abiding oceans fight,
> Though headlong wind and heaping tide
>   Make us their sport to-night.
> By force of weather, not of war,
>   In jeopardy we steer:
> Then welcome Fate's discourtesy
>   Whereby it shall appear
>   How in all time of our distress
>   And our deliverance too,
>   The game is more than the player of the game
>   And the ship is more than the crew!

That was not merely correcting: the change of idea in the first four lines is radical. Nor did he cease revising. Just as in collecting his stories he would make alterations of the magazine versions, so he did when collecting his poems, even from one garnering to another—as has been marginally exampled earlier.

Whatever opinion may be held of him as a poet, it is agreed that he was brilliant in versification. Some of his verse admittedly is jingle, but of set purpose, and always disciplined, prosodically controlled. He could handle all sorts of metres, while his rhythms are complex, sometimes indeed subtle, as quotations already made will have illustrated. He was at home in the heroic couplet, common measure, ballad forms; the iambic or the rollicking anapaest, as well as more difficult prosodic units; the octosyllable or the sixteener; literally 'free' verse, though rhymed; a variation of the *terza rima*, the varied seventeenth-century stanza, or something too readily regarded as Swinburnian, though dating from much earlier. If, however, he excelled in metre, forms beyond that of the stanza did not much attract him. His ballades are poor, his few sonnets, although one or two are good poems, are unimpressive as sonnets, lacking the structural movement, his one triumphant success in an exacting form being 'Sestina of the Tramp Royal'. His long poems tend to be too protracted, though exception must be made of the great monologues, 'McAndrew's Hymn' and 'The "Mary Gloster"', to which may be added the semi-dialogue, 'Tomlinson'.

There is little point in considering influences. After his *Schoolboy Lyrics* and *Echoes*, not collected, there is no trace of the pre-Raphaelite note, except perhaps in 'The Love Song of Har Dyal'. It appeared in 1884 as part of 'Beyond the Pale', and purports to be a rendering of an Indian poem, very moving in the original: "In English you miss the wail of it. It runs something like this—

> Alone upon the housetops to the North
>   I turn and watch the lightning in the sky,—
> The glamour of thy footsteps in the North,
>   *Come back to me, Beloved, or I die!*
>
> Below my feet the still bazar is laid—
>   Far, far below the weary camels lie,—
> The camels and the captives of thy raid.
>   *Come back to me, Beloved, or I die!*
>
> My father's wife is old and harsh with years,
>   And drudge of all my father's house am I.—
> My bread is sorrow and my drink is tears,
>   *Come back to me, Beloved, or I die!*
>
>   (*Def. Ed.* differs slightly)

That is clearly influenced by the Rossetti ear; we meet the vaguely evocative phrase, "the glamour of thy footsteps in the North", absent from Kipling's more characteristic verse.

The monologues may have been suggested by Browning, but the attack and versification are different. Only the very early 'One Viceroy Resigns' (1888) is obviously after the manner of Browning. Parodies there are: the early one of Swinburne, where he puts the first chorus from *Atalanta in Calydon* to more mundane uses; and those in 'A Muse Among the Motors'. All that can usefully be said is that, widely read in English poetry, he used, or dropped into, whatever form of rhythm either came to him, or that he felt to be appropriate. When he smote 'is bloomin' lyre he winked at all the Homers down the road of history.

More general considerations present themselves before embarking on any detailed study. Most readers will be aware of the crucial difficulty Eliot laid finger on when he said in the Introduction to his *A Selection of Kipling's Verse*:

While I speak of Kipling's work as verse and not as poetry, I am still able to speak of individual compositions as poetry, and also to maintain that there is 'poetry' in the 'verse'.

Admittedly Kipling was a dazzlingly able versifier in the matter of rhythm and metre, as already said; but it will be claimed here that he was a poet in the full sense of the term. Notoriously, to try to define poetry is to rush in where angels fear to tread; it may, finally, depend upon what each person expects poetry to do for him. One may begin, however, by what Moneta said in *The Fall of Hyperion*:

> The poet and the dreamer are distinct,
> Diverse, sheer opposites, antipodes.
> The one pours out a balm upon the world,
> The other vexes it.   (I. 199–202)

Much of what Kipling wrote vexed the world, sometimes by direct attack upon its complacency, but more importantly, and more in Keats's meaning, by forcing the individual to face himself, the conditions of living, or the abyss of darkness which he sometimes feels may engulf him. But before he spoke with those ends in view, he vexed the secluded, self-conscious literary world of his time in a more superficial way, by using the colloquial idiom of the people. His sin was to act on Wordsworth's precept—which is more than Wordsworth did— of writing poetry in the language men (ordinary men) use in speaking to men; or, as Ben Jonson put it, animated by the same cyclical desire to purify the dialect of the tribe, to write poetry in words "such as men doe use". 'Tommy' Kipling wrote in plain vernacular, then decried but now seen as contributing to that freedom of 'poetic' diction which has been one of the feathers in the cap of present-century metrical writing. His was better than most, for, as Robert Bridges declared, "nothing in [his] diction is common or unclean". We get such pieces as 'For to Admire', which opens:

> The Injian Ocean sets an' smiles
> So sof', so bright, so bloomin' blue:

verses in which there may not be much 'poetry', except perhaps for the striking

> Old Aden, like a barrick-stove
> That no one's lit for years an' years . . .

But there was certainly poetry in the later 'Sestina of the Tramp Royal', as there was in 'Chant-Pagan':

> Me that 'ave been what I've been—
> Me that 'ave gone where I've gone—
> Me that 'ave seen what I've seen—
> 'Ow can I ever take on
> With awful old England again,
> An' 'ouses both sides of the street,
> An' 'edges two sides of the lane,
> And the parson an' gentry between,
> An' touchin' my 'at when we meet—
> Me that 'ave been what I've been.

'Danny Deever' which appeared first in February 1890, to be included in *Barrack-Room Ballads* later in the year, is now recognized as a poem proper, and a very powerful one.

But he 'vexed' more deeply than that. As R. G. Collingwood noted, he "burst into the stuffy atmosphere of the aesthetes' china-shop not only by his diction, but by writing 'magical' poetry, poetry that is, that 'evokes and canalises the emotions that are to men as the steam in the engine of their daily work, and discharges them into the affairs of practical life'."[1] That would, naturally, be repugnant in an 'art for art's sake' period. There is a deal of this sort of work at a certain period of Kipling's career, 'The Islanders' for instance, which vexed more than the aesthetes; 'The Dykes', 'The Truce of the Bear', and, though this gained considerable support to the tune of many thousands of pounds, 'The Absent-Minded Beggar'. There is not very much poetry to be found in these pieces, which were mainly the result of irritated impatience rising sometimes to indignation, for if in his case it was true that *facit indignatio versum*, the verse was hardly poetry. The political poems have plenty of 'punch', as Mr. Hilton Brown remarks, but one cannot altogether agree with him that they make dull reading now, and would seem to have only an historical interest. Read in the context of their time, as one reads, say, *Absalom and Achitophel*, they take on life, while some, for example 'The City of Brass', are startlingly

---

[1] *The Principles of Art* (Oxford, 1938).

prophetic of today. Yet it is where the 'magical' fuses with the philosophic, as, to give an early, and possibly best-known example, 'Recessional', that our minds become receptive in the way that poetry induces.

A major difficulty in treating of Kipling's poetry is that he adventured along so many of the nine-and-sixty ways. He is as varied in the subject-matter of his verse as he is in his story-telling, as also in his manner. To try to simplify the discussion (though this is to be more than a little arbitrary) it might be suggested that in the main, apart from his 'magical' verse, he wrote three kinds of poetry. The edges of such things are, how-ever, always *con*fused, Kipling sometimes *fusing* the kinds. These I would call the 'lyric-romantic' or dreamer's poems: poems of thought and experience; and, to coin a word to be explained in its due place, 'actuality' poems. It is not possible to separate these into periods. 'Romantic' poetry Kipling wrote all through his life; the next group soon appeared and continued to the end; the outstanding 'actuality' poems, though mainly related to his later development, are embryonically present at a fairly early date. It is only 'magical' poetry that belongs to a period, that during which he was emotionally involved in politics, and it disappeared when he had reached the stage of acceptance.

CHAPTER I

Lyrical and Romantic

Lyrical poetry . . . is designed to express . . . some one
mood, some single sentiment, some isolated longing in
human nature.

Walter Bagehot, 'Hartley Coleridge'

Romantic poetry may be described as that meant to evoke
memories, to express and communicate the universal common
emotions, "the weeping and the laughter, love and desire and
hate", to awaken yearning, to induce meditation based on
the sentiments. It communicates, not logical thought, but
feeling; and if it teaches it does so, in De Quincey's phrase,
"by deep impulse and hieroglyphic suggestion". It depends
largely upon its musical effect, rhythm, and the play of vowel-
sound. As often as not it can be imagined set to music. With
Kipling, as with many poets, verse often had its origin in a tune
running in his head, and he would walk about his study while
composing poetry humming a hymn, a nursery rhyme, a
music-hall song, a song sometimes that even music-halls
refrained from disseminating.

There are all manner of lyrical or romantic poems throughout
Kipling's career, though few are sheer songs without much
meaning beyond the obvious emotion. The one which springs
most readily to mind is the marching song, which, as the Roman
centurion explains in 'On the Great Wall' was:

one of the tunes that are always being born somewhere in the Empire. They run like a pestilence for six months or a year, till another
one pleases the Legion, and then they march to *that*.

It goes:

When I left Rome for Lalage's sake
By the Legion's Road to Rimini,

> She vowed her heart was mine to take—
> With me and my shield to Rimini—
> (Till the Eagles flew from Rimini!)
>   And I've tramped Britain and I've tramped Gaul
>   And the Pontic shore where the snow-flakes fall
> As white as the neck of Lalage—
> As cold as the heart of Lalage!
>   And I've lost Britain and I've lost Gaul
>   And I've lost Rome, and worst of all,
>   I've lost Lalage!

That is light-hearted enough, and the voice of Parnesius who sang it "seemed very cheerful about it". The poem was later 'enlarged' as 'Rimini' in the Definitive Edition.

There is tremendous vigour in Kipling's song-lyrics, especially in his early days, the note being somewhat muted later. There is, for instance, the exuberance of 'To the True Romance' of 1891. The first stanza, in italics, is partly repeated at the end, after the tenth: It opens:

> Thy face is far from this our war,
>   Our call and counter-cry,
> I shall not find Thee quick and kind
>   Nor know Thee till I die.
> Enough for me in dreams to see
>   And touch Thy garments' hem:
> Thy feet have trod so near to God
>   I may not follow them! . . .

The fourth stanza is, one might say, typical of the rest:

> Who holds by Thee hath Heaven in fee
>   To gild his dross thereby,
> And knowledge sure that he endure
>   A child until he die—
> For to make plain that man's disdain
>   Is but new Beauty's birth—
> For to possess in singleness
>   The joy of all the earth.

Only once does a slightly different note intrude, with the already quoted couplet stating Romance to be:

> A veil to draw 'twixt God His Law
>   And man's infirmity.

But throughout, its speed, aided by the internal rhyme in the alternate eight-syllable lines, makes it cling to the memory. Not a great poem, no; but verse so ringing that we forgive the slight archaism, more tolerated when Kipling was a young man of twenty-five than it is today. Romance, of course, for him resided in the practical creative imagination of men: it was Romance that brought up the 9.15, we remember. And in a poem of some three years later we find the 'Viscount loon' saying:

Mister McAndrew, don't you think steam spoils romance at sea?

to get the stout comment:

Damned ijjit! I'd been doon that morn to see what ailed the throws,
Manholin', on my back—the cranks three inches off my nose.
Romance! Those first-class passengers they like it very well,
Printed an' bound in little books; but why don't poets tell?
I'm sick of all their quirks an' turns—the loves and doves they
    dream—
Lord, send a man like Robbie Burns to sing the Song o' Steam!

He then proceeds with high lyric intensity himself to sing that song:

To match wi' Scotia's noblest speech yon orchestra sublime
Whaurto—uplifted like the Just—the tail-rods mark the time.
The crank-throws give the double-bass, the feed-pump sobs an'
    heaves,
An' now the main eccentrics start their quarrel on the sheaves:
Her time, her own appointed time, the rocking link-head bides,
Till—hear that note?—the rod's return whings glimmerin' through
    the guides.
They're all awa'! true beat, full power, the clangin' chorus goes
Clear to the tunnel where they sit, my purrin' dynamoes.
Interdependence absolute, foreseen, ordained, decreed,
To work, Ye'll note, at ony tilt an' every rate o' speed.
Fra' skylight-lift to furnace-bars, backed, bolted, braced an' stayed,
An' singin' like the Mornin' Stars for joy that they are made. . . .

It is an extraordinary poem—a sympathetic biography, a psychological study, and a paean in praise of man's creative imagination. Kipling was the first to make machinery the matter of a poem.

As a contrast, in another two years, we get such a song-poem as 'The Flowers', in a sense an Imperial poem, in which men scattered about the Empire feel a nostalgia for their own part of it. I give here the South African passage, the richest in vowel-sound, as though expressing the love that Kipling had for that part of the world, visiting it every year for some time at the beginning of the century, hoping vainly for a non-racial integration to heal the wounds of the war.

> Buy my English posies!
>   Here's to match your need—
> Buy a tuft of royal heath,
>   Buy a bunch of weed
> White as sand of Muizenberg
>   Spun before the gale—
> Buy my heath and lilies
>   And I'll tell you whence you hail!
> Under hot Constantia broad the vineyards lie—
> Throned and thorned the aching berg props the speckless sky—
> Slow below the Wynberg firs trails the tilted wain—
> Take the flower and turn the hour, and kiss your love again!

The prosody is remarkable, compelling, with the pause imposed after 'Constantia' to bring the emphasis on the heavily vowelled 'broad'; the long movement of 'slow below', bringing the very sense of slowness; and the sharp 'tilted' awakening the visual image.

Then, in the same year, as a complete contrast, Kipling writes 'Sestina of the Tramp Royal':

> Speakin' in general, I 'ave tried 'em all—
> The 'appy roads that take you o'er the world.
> Speakin' in general, I 'ave found them good
> For such as cannot use one bed too long,
> But must get 'ence, the same as I 'ave done
> An' go observin' matters till they die.
>
> What do it matter where or 'ow we die,
> So long as we've our 'ealth to watch it all—
> The different ways that different things are done.
> An' men an' women lovin' in this world;
> Takin' our chances as they come along,
> An' when they ain't, pretendin' they are good?

So it goes on in conformity with the rigorously demanding form, each stanza taking up the final word of the preceding one, till we come to the three-line conclusion:

> Gawd bless this world! Whatever she 'ath done—
> Excep' when awful long—I've found it good.
> So write, before I die, " 'E liked it all!"

Thus quieter lyrics gradually take the place of the more vociferous ones, though ever and anon we meet some in the old manner with rather too much insistence on rhythmic stress, though devoid of the 'magical' element. We have 'Poor Honest Men':

> Your jar of Virginny
> Will cost you a guinea. . . .

or the more imagination-compelling 'A Smuggler's Song':

> If you awake at midnight, and hear a horse's feet,
> Don't go drawing back the blind, or looking in the street,
> Them that asks no questions isn't told a lie.
> Watch the wall, my darling, while the Gentlemen go by!
>   Five and twenty ponies
>   Trotting through the dark—
>   Brandy for the Parson,
>   'Baccy for the Clerk;
>   Laces for a lady, letters for a spy,
> And watch the wall, my darling, while the Gentlemen go by!

But the change took place gradually; the quieter voice occurs early, and we hear the loud voice fairly plainly in the verses 'The Song of Seventy Horses' at the end of 'The Miracle of Saint Jubanus', nominally a poem vaunting a powerful car, actually one in praise of France.

The variations in mood, in degree of songfulness, can be seen as perhaps is already plain, in the *Puck of Pook's Hill* and *Rewards and Fairies* period. We have, for example, 'A Song to Mithras' at the end of 'On the Great Wall', a hymn with the lyrical quality to be found in many hymns:

Mithras, God of the Morning, our trumpets waken the Wall!
'Rome is above the Nations, but Thou art over all!'
Now as the names are answered, and the guards are marched away,
Mithras, also a soldier, give us strength for the day!

N

It has also a near refrain, for Kipling did not avoid the lyrical refrain even in his hymns, such as 'Recessional'. In this poem each last line begins "Mithras, also a soldier", who is asked successively to keep the worshippers true to their vows, pure till dawn, and finally asked "teach us to die aright". The two poems belonging to 'A Centurion of the Thirtieth' are also varied in tone, the preface being the great poem with hymn-like quality, 'Cities and Thrones and Powers', which, however, belongs to a different category, while the concluding verses, 'A British-Roman Song. (A.D. 406)' should go, one feels, to the tune of a traditional folk-ballad, and in movement resembles Kipling's Horatian 'translations':

> My father's father saw it not,
>   And I, belike, shall never come,
> To look on that so-holy spot—
>   The very Rome—

And then there are those poems which have a depth that is not immediately apparent.

Such is 'The Looking-Glass'; and here one may quote, at some length, from what Robert Bridges said about it.[1] But it may be as well first to give some of it from *Rewards and Fairies* where it first appeared, and not from the Definitive Edition which Bridges had not seen, where it was 'enlarged' and made into 'A Country Dance'.

Queen Bess was Harry's daughter!

> The Queen was in her chamber, and she was middling old,
> Her petticoat was satin and her stomacher was gold.
> Backwards and forwards and sideways did she pass,
> Making up her mind to face the cruel looking-glass.
>   The cruel looking-glass that will never show a lass
>   As comely or as kindly or as young as once she was!

and it ends:

> And she faced the looking-glass (and whatever else there was),
> And she saw her day was over and she saw her beauty pass
> In the cruel looking-glass that can always hurt a lass
> More hard than any ghost there is or any man there was!

---

[1] 'Wordsworth and Kipling.' *Collected Essays of Robert Bridges*, XIII (Oxford, 1933). The spelling has been normalized.

Bridges comments:

In this masterly poem the motive is heroic and almost tragic. Great Queen Bess is portray'd with the vain woman's vanity and the tyrant's bad conscience, and with a vast pride, sufficient to drown them both; and the picture is done with such force that many readers will have the four stanzas by heart when they have read them twice. Now observe the diction; the first line runs thus:—

The Queen was in her chamber, and she was middling old.

This is of course founded on

The Queen was in her parlour eating bread and honey,

and the key of the emotion is thus deliberately pitched at the level of the nonsensical nursery rhyme. Observe, too, the expression 'middling old'. This sets the Queen down among the homeliest of her subjects; but in so doing it may humanize and provoke common sympathy. Later on Lord Leicester's ghost comes 'scratching and singing' at the door, which degrades the ghost; and yet, in spite of those things, the whole has an irresistible force, so that our dislike of the incongruities, if we feel any, is overpower'd; and this force, though it may not be due to the apparent obstacles, may seem the greater for its victory over them. . . . Mr. Kipling's method . . . at its best refuses the foolish inversions and bad rhymes that lower the standard of so many of Wordsworth's scholastic stanzas. . . .

Now suppose that we had never heard the rhyme of the Queen and her bread and honey, and did not know English well enough to understand the true values of 'middling' and 'scratching', would the poem affect us less or more powerfully than it does with this knowledge? What would it be without the queer quality that it actually has? . . . we may be content with the surer ground that Kipling is Kipling, and that without Kipling we should never have had the poem; and we are glad to have got it.

And later:

He has so true a feeling for the value of words, and for the right cadences of idiomatic speech, and so vast a vocabulary, that his example is generally useful to a generation whose cultured speech-rhythms are so slovenly and uncertain.

He adds, a criticism supported by others:

It is . . . to be regretted that out of his abundance he is sometimes tempted to overload his lines with the weight either of sound or meaning, or of both at once.

This is a point easy to illustrate from poems of almost any date where he uses the long line; but he is remarkably economical when he uses any metre up to and including the decasyllabic.

The song-like quality, then, tends to disappear from Kipling's verse, though it is never entirely absent. His final phase in the 'lyric' of this kind is best represented by the haunting 'Gertrude's Prayer' which is essential to the whole understanding of the tale 'Dayspring Mishandled'. It opens:

> That which is marred at birth Time shall not mend,
> Nor water out of bitter well make clean:
> All evil thing returneth at the end,
> Or elseway walketh in our blood unseen.
> Whereby the more is sorrow in certaine—
> Dayspring mishandled cometh not againe . . .

the sense being so strong that we ignore the deliberate Chaucerian pastiche. It is unmistakable Kipling.

If in this sort of poem Kipling did not add to the tradition of English verse-writing, he contributed some examples which haunt the memory, perhaps a sufficient indication of their poetic quality (though this is no sure guide) by the images of sight or touch or smell that they evoke, as in 'Alnaschar and the Oxen', which glosses 'The Bull that Thought', with its refrain, "My Sussex cattle feeding in the dew"; or 'The Recall'; or, most famous of all, perhaps, 'The Way Through the Woods' which rounds off 'Marklake Witches', where the rhyme, often near-rhyme, does not impose itself, and the unstressed almost faltering end achieves one of the objects of romantic poetry, the release of the imagination. If you enter the woods

> You will hear the beat of a horse's feet,
> And the swish of a skirt in the dew,
> Steadily cantering through
> The misty solitudes,
> As though they perfectly knew
> The old lost road through the woods . . .
> But there is no road through the woods.

Where he did, however, widen the scope of English romantic poetry was, it may be thought, in the ballad. Here, perhaps, a little clarification is necessary. 'Ballad' is a very vague term; it may or may not be a communal production; it usually contains a story, perhaps traditional; up to the eighteenth century it was anonymous. There have been many collections since Pepys began to gather them: those of Allan Ramsay, of Percy in his *Reliques*, Scott, Child, and in the present century those of Quiller-Couch (*The Oxford Book of Ballads*) and Mr. Robert Graves. Many modern poets, for example Mr. W. H. Auden and Mr. Charles Causley, have written ballads. They all have one thing in common; they can be imagined sung to a rather sad folk-tune, such as we know in the case of 'The Lyke-Wake Dirge', and most of them involve more than one voice, as in the well-known 'Lord Randall'. A few communal ones may yet occasionally appear—we think of:

> Oh my, I don't want to die,
> I want to go 'ome,

of the First World War; or

> Oh, oh, oh what a lovely war!
> What d'you want with eggs an' 'am
> When you've got your plum and apple jam?
> Oh, oh, oh, I never was 'appy before,
> Oh, oh, oh what a lovely war!

of the same period. But in the main they are written by poets, with a muted half-heard, melancholy melody. There is, however, a considerable amount of folk-poetry written in Australia.[1]

Many of Kipling's most moving poems are in this form. Here are not meant the poems that he specifically called ballads, such as 'The Ballad of East and West', or 'The Ballad of Boh da Thone', or of 'Bolivar', 'Clampherdown', or 'The Rhyme of the Three Captains', the blank verse 'Er-Heb', all early, and, we may well think, too long and elaborate, though 'The Ballad of Minepit Shaw', to be quoted from later, may justly fall into the category. Here he uses the traditional story, as he does in the far better 'Old Mother Laidinwool', who emerges from her grave on the anniversary of her burial, which is also hopping-time, so she is sure to meet some of the lads she picked with when she was young and fair, toddles round—that is not an inappropriate word—to see them and her relatives

---

[1] See *A Review of English Studies*, October 1965.

going to church, and finding all well, returns happily to her coffin. Kipling, in his best ballad-poems resorts to the duologue, or dialogue method, sometimes using or implying a story, sometimes simply expressing a humble state of being; nearly always using a refrain, as many of the old ballads do.

He seems to have needed no apprenticeship, the famous 'Danny Deever' appearing in February 1890. It is, maybe, too well known to need quotation, but it is relevant to repeat the first stanza to revive memories of the whole, which becomes ever closer to horrified feelings as it progresses:

"What are the bugles blowin' for?" said Files-on-Parade.
"To turn you out, to turn you out," the Colour-Sergeant said.
"What makes you look so white, so white?" said Files-on-Parade.
"I'm dreadin' what I've got to watch," the Colour-Sergeant said.
 For they're hangin' Danny Deever, you can hear the Dead
  March play,
 The Regiment's in 'ollow square—they're hangin' him to-day;
 They've taken of his buttons off an' cut his stripes away,
 An' they're hangin' Danny Deever in the mornin'.

That has the communal sense in the phrase 'Files-on-Parade', as representing the mass of the rank and file; it has the refrain; it is a great poem of its kind. It is not 'romantic' in the ordinary sense; it is too close to actuality. Nor has it the sad reminiscent sense of the true ballad; the refrain would seem to go with a rousing tune rather than to the subdued tones of a folk-song. His most perfect poem in that form—and it also is a great poem —is 'Bridge-Guard in the Karroo' of the Boer War period. It has not the dialogue element, but is entirely communal, and one can imagine it sung to a slow, melancholy tune. It is an example of the deep sympathy Kipling felt for the common soldier, felt to a degree which would today be called empathy, an intimate 'feeling with'. It is a reverie, subconscious, because the 'speaker' of the poem would not have clearly felt what is expressed, and would certainly not have said it. It records the feelings of a man—among many—without glamour or hope of glory, not a combatant, only a detail guarding the line. He vaguely feels the splendour of the scenery by which he is surrounded:

Sudden the desert changes,
   The red glare softens and clings,
Till the aching Oudtshoorn ranges
   Stand up like the thrones of Kings—

Ramparts of slaughter and peril—
   Blazing, amazing, aglow—
'Twixt the sky-line's belting beryl
   And the wine-dark flats below.

Royal the pageant closes,
   Lit by the last of the sun—
Opal and ash-of-roses
   Cinnamon, umber and dun.

The twilight swallows the thicket,
   The starlight reveals the ridge,
The whistle shrills to the picket—
   We are changing guard on the bridge.

Then, after this perhaps not very ballad-like opening, the
more poignant individual element emerges, and for twelve
stanzas we have a true ballad, reinforced by the occasional
refrain:

(Few, forgotten and lonely,
   Where the empty metals shine—
No, not combatants—only
   Details guarding the line.)

Isolation, loneliness—a recurrent theme in Kipling—becomes
more and more stressed, a loneliness broken only by the pas-
sing of a train, its white car-windows shining, as the guard
reaches

For a handful of week-old papers
   And a mouthful of human speech,

and catch voices "Of women talking with men":

So we return to our places,
   As out on the bridge she rolls;
And the darkness covers our faces,
   And the darkness re-enters our souls.

> More than a little lonely
> Where the lessening tail-lights shine,
> No—not combatants—only
> Details guarding the line!

A commonplace experience, no doubt, but felt to a depth where it becomes universal, that is, poetry. Equally deep, but more general, since one can imagine it intoned by a group, is 'Harp Song of the Dane Women':

> What is a woman that you forsake her,
> And the hearth-fire and the home-acre
> To go with the old grey Widow-maker?

lamenting the lure that the sea has for the male.

It may be thought, however, that Kipling's greatest ballads are those where a story is told—though not, to repeat, in the long ones. 'The Ballad of Minepit Shaw', for instance deftly tells of when

> Two lads went up to the keepers' hut
> To steal Lord Pelham's deer.

After they have had some success, the keepers put a bloodhound on to them; they run, and meet a man with a green lantern "That called and bade 'em stand". They carry out his instructions, are precipitated into a pit, into which the bloodhound follows them, breaking his neck as he falls. They are therefore saved:

> But whether the man was a poacher too
> Or a Pharisee[1] so bold—
> I reckon there's more things told than are true
> And more things true than are told!

His triumph in this form is where the story is implied, not told, namely 'Heriot's Ford'. It gains from being wholly in dialogue form, with phrases at the end of each stanza that have the effect of a refrain. It has extraordinary force. Only a few stanzas are to be quoted here, enough it is hoped to suggest the terror that pervades it.

[1] A fairy.

St. 1   "What's that that hirples at my side?"
    The foe that you must fight, my lord.
    "That rides as fast as I can ride?"
    The shadow of your might, my lord.

St. 4.   "Oh, do not slay me in my sins!"
    You're safe awhile with us, my lord.
    "Nay, kill me ere my fear begins!"
    We would not serve you thus, my lord.

St. 7.   "You would not kill the soul alive?"
    'Twas thus our sister cried, my lord.
    "I dare not die with none to shrive."
    But so our sister died, my lord.

St. 8.   "Then wipe the sweat from brow and cheek."
    It runnels forth afresh, my lord.
    "Uphold me—for the flesh is weak."
    You've finished with the Flesh, my lord!

    (the last line to be said quietly.)

It is a terrifying vision of doom, deserved it would seem, and inescapable. Pondered, the poem may have a more universal meaning, especially for those who have some work they want to accomplish before they die, aware that doom is always hirpling at their side.

Where Kipling is most poignant is in his ballad-like personal poems, the earliest of which is 'Merrow Down', at first sight a meditative poem, an historical evocation of the down by Guildford and the River Wey. The second part is a disguised lament for his elder daughter, Josephine. Taffy is, of course, his daughter, Tegumai is himself. We read:

    But as the faithful years return
      And hearts unwounded sing again,
    Comes Taffy dancing through the fern
      To lead the Surrey spring again. . . .

    For far—oh, very far behind
      So far she cannot call to him,
    Comes Tegumai alone to find
      The daughter that was all to him!

The connexion with 'They' is evident.

Or again there is a poem written in the 1914–18 period[1] which is an expression of his grief at the loss of his son, reported 'missing' at the battle of Loos, namely 'A Nativity'. Each eight-line stanza has a different 'refrain' after the fourth line.

The first stanza runs:

> *The Babe was laid in the Manger*
> *Between the gentle kine—*
> *All safe from cold and danger—*
> "But it was not so with mine,"
>   (With mine! With mine!)
> "Is it well with the child, is it well?"
> The waiting mother prayed.
> "For I know not how he fell,
> And I know not where he is laid."

It ends, however, with a reassurance:

> *The Star stands forth in Heaven.*
> *The watchers watch in vain*
> *For Sign of the Promise given*
> *Of peace on Earth again—*
>   (Again! Again!)
> "But I know for Whom he fell"—
> The steadfast mother smiled,
> "Is it well with the child—is it well?
> It is well—it is well with the child!"

This perhaps, is not in the usual ballad form, though there is an undercurrent of the tune. Closer to that form, with its constant refrain is the more general lament of 'London Stone', a poem written for Armistice Day, 11 November 1923:

> When you come to London Town,
>   (Grieving—grieving!)
> Bring your flowers and lay them down
>   At the place of grieving.

It ends with some comfort in the sense of community:

[1] Dates of composition or publication are irrelevant.

What is the tie betwixt us two
(Grieving—grieving!)
That must last our whole lives through?
"As I suffer, so do you."
That may ease the grieving.

His most moving poem, however, with its personal reference, is 'My Boy Jack', which first appeared in *Sea Warfare*, and has the same stoical ending as 'A Nativity'. The first speaker is the mother of a boy serving in a destroyer at Jutland:

"Have you news of my boy Jack?"
Not this tide.
"When d'you think that he'll come back?"
Not with this wind blowing, and this tide.

"Has anyone else had word of him?"
Not this tide.
For what is sunk will hardly swim,
Not with this wind blowing and this tide.

"Oh, dear, what comfort can I find?"
None this tide,
Nor any tide,
Except he did not shame his kind
Not even with that wind blowing and that tide.

Then hold your head up all the more,
This tide,
And every tide,
Because he was the son you bore,
And gave to that wind blowing and that tide!

By that poem alone one might establish Kipling's right to a high place among 'romantic' poets, using the dialogue ballad form, with a refrain, to its most deeply imaginative effect.

One might, in this category, add the near-carol 'Eddi's Service', again from the *Rewards and Fairies* period. There Eddi, 'priest of St. Wilfrid',

Ordered a midnight service
For such as cared to attend.

> But the Saxons were keeping Christmas,
>   And the night was stormy as well.
> Nobody came to the service,
>   Though Eddi rang the bell.

In due course, however, there appeared "an old marsh-donkey" and "a wet, yoke-weary bullock". That was enough for Eddi; three were gathered together—here again we get Kipling's Biblical and Prayer-book upbringing—and he preached them the Word "just as though they were Bishops":

> And he told the Ox of a Manger
>   And a Stall in Bethlehem,
> And he spoke to the Ass of a Rider
>   That rode to Jerusalem.

It has all the moving simplicity Kipling could achieve when he wanted to, reinforced by his use of the common word. After Eddi's sermon, the animals "wheeled and clattered away".

CHAPTER II

Poetry of Thought and Experience

"The figure a poem makes. It begins in delight and ends
in wisdom."

Robert Frost, Prelude to *Complete Poems*

Many poems which would come under this head have already
been quoted from in earlier parts of this book (as might be expected) to illustrate Kipling's thought. Some express what might
be called his 'mysticism', such as 'The Astrologer's Song', with its
superb lyrical vigour; or his 'religion', for example 'The Rabbi's
Song', a clutching in despair, or 'Buddha at Kamakura', quiet
contemplation: many deal with his sense of the infinity of
time, and the smallness of man's duration—'Cities and Thrones
and Powers', to mention only one: and other aspects of his
thought. Here I would wish to treat, rather, of poems which
either show the process of his thinking, or are the result of his
experience of life, of "men an' women lovin' in this world". Yet,
as one reads, it becomes increasingly difficult to see how any
kind of division, however arbitrary, can be made between his
various 'kinds'. For just as the 'lyrical' enlivens the poems
mentioned above, so does thought colour even such a song as
'Philadelphia', which we inevitably connect with 'I'm off to
Philadelphia in the morning'. It opens with a warning of
change:

> If you're off to Philadelphia in the morning,
>   You mustn't take my stories for a guide.
> There's little left indeed of the city you will read of,
>   And all the folk I wrote about have died.

And it ends with a reminder that whatever is done leaves its
mark:

> They are there, there, there with Earth immortal
> (Citizens, I give you friendly warning).

The things that truly last when men and times have passed,
They are all in Pennsylvania this morning.

And where is one to 'place' 'A St. Helena Lullaby', that remarkable flash-back of Napoleon's career? The first stanza is sheer balladry:

'How far is St. Helena from a little child at play?'
What makes you want to wander there with all the world between?
Oh, mother, call your son again or else he'll run away.
(*No one thinks of winter when the grass is green!*)

But, as the poem goes on, more and more generalizations suggest themselves. Take, for instance, the penultimate stanza:

'How far is St. Helena from the field of Waterloo?'
A near way—a clear way—the ship will take you soon.
A pleasant place for gentlemen with little left to do.
(*Morning never tries you till the afternoon!*)

Though clearly meant to have a background of song, as the name 'lullaby' implies, it follows a progressive line of thought: it is not 'lyrical' in Bagehot's sense of the word.

In his earlier days Kipling's 'thoughtful' poems have none of the economy which in the main—one must always make reservations where he is concerned—characterize his more mature work. They have all the exuberance of a young man revelling in the fertility of his imagination. There is no denying that he could, in this manner, be extremely effective, as in 'Tomlinson' (1891), which can be called a fable. Tomlinson "gave up the ghost at his house in Berkeley Square", no doubt duly respected, as befits a solid householder. When this happened, first

A Spirit gripped him by the hair and carried him far away,
Till he heard as the roar of a rain-fed ford the roar of the Milky Way:
Till he heard the roar of the Milky Way die down and drone and cease,
And they came to the Gate within the Wall where Peter holds the keys. . . .

This decorative elaboration is maintained throughout the long poem (this was the period of his narrative ballads), but the thought, or the moral, is soon apparent. When St. Peter asks him what good he ever did, "the naked soul of Tomlinson grew white as a rain-washed bone". He says he can bring a friend to vouch for him, but is told that "the race is run by one and one and never by two and two". And soon a further moral is brought forward, that of independence. When Tomlinson defends himself by saying that he has read this, been told that, and heard the other,

> . . . Peter twirled the jangling Keys in weariness and wrath.
> "Ye have read, ye have heard, ye have thought," he said, "and the tale is yet to run:
> "By the worth of the body that once ye had, give answer—what ha' ye done?"

Much the same occurs when he applies to Satan, who asks him what harm he has ever been responsible for: but we do not get an immediate answer, for first

> . . . Tomlinson looked up and up, and saw against the night
> The belly of a tortured star blood-red in Hell-Mouth light;
> And Tomlinson looked down and down, and saw beneath his feet
> The frontlet of a tortured star milk-white in Hell-Mouth heat.

He offers a mild love-affair with his neighbour's wife, but that is of no help, "For the sin ye do by two and two ye must pay for one by one", almost echoing St. Peter's dictum. Again the responsibility for self and for society. Finally, denied admittance both to Heaven and Hell, he is sent back to earth to acquire a soul of his own, to become somebody, not a pale replica of what he has read and heard, Satan's final remark being, "And . . . the God that you took from a printed book be with you, Tomlinson!", and we can imagine with what utter contempt the name is pronounced. The poem is a dazzling cinematograph vision, behind which the thought is evident; but the rich imagery, the forward-compelling rhythm, the enthralling story, a vision full of colour, obscures the thinking which inspired it.

Two years later we have the far more controlled and prosodically brilliant 'Anchor Song':

Heh! Walk her round. Heave, ah, heave her short again!
 Over, snatch her over, there, and hold her on the pawl.
Loose all sail, and brace your yards aback and full—
 Ready jib to pay her off and heave short all!

Well, ah, fare you well; we can stay no more with you, my love—
 Down, set down your liquor and your girl from off your knee;
   For the wind has come to say:
    "You must take me while you may,
   If you'd go to Mother Carey
   (Walk her down to Mother Carey!)
 Oh, we're bound to Mother Carey where she feeds her chicks
  at sea!"

One must pause to note the extraordinary skill of the versification, the vigour of the first four lines expressing effort, the
purposefulness of which is stressed by the three heavy 'longs'
of "Loose all sail" at the beginning of the third line, and the
similar use of 'longs' at the end of the fourth—"heave short all",
a structure kept up through the four stanzas of the poem. It is,
however, the more lyrical second half of the stanzas which
conveys the meaning. We have to bear in mind that the chicks
that Mother Carey feeds at sea are drowned sailors, and then
we must remember that the poem succeeds the fable 'The
Children of the Zodiac', in which the Children learnt, among
other human realities, that death is inevitable and must not be
feared. That is the thought behind the poem, which seems at
first sight to be one of Kipling's characteristic lyrics.

 Kipling did not normally make use of strong rhythmic
effects in his later poems of thought or experience, but often a
strong lyrical element is noticeable, as in 'Butterflies', originally
named 'Kaspar's Song in "Varda" (from the Swedish of
Stagnelius)'[1] which follows 'Wireless'. The story, as Dr.
Tompkins elucidates it, is largely about poetic inspiration; the
poem would seem to be, rather, about the earthy basis of all
spiritual growth, telling us that we must be able, in Meredith's
phrase, to "see the rose in mould unfold"; or, as put differently
by Yeats, that

 [1] For the probable origins of this strange title see Bodelsen: 'Wireless and
Kaspar's Song'. *Orbis Litterarium*. Copenhagen.

> all the ladders start
> In the foul rag-and-bone shop of the heart.

'Butterflies' is a similar statement:

> Eyes aloft, over dangerous places,
> The children follow the butterflies,
> And, in the sweat of their upturned faces,
> Slash with a net at the empty skies.

They scratch themselves on brambles, sting toes on the nettle-tops, till their father comes to "still the riot of pain and grief",

> Saying, "Little ones, go and gather
> Out of my garden a cabbage-leaf."

for it is from the "whorls and clots of /Dull grey eggs" found on the cabbage-leaf, and turning to worms, that butterflies will come. Beauty is not to be gathered ready-made, however ardently pursued; it must be distilled from the drab; we must not listen to highfalutin nonsense:

> "Heaven is beautiful, Earth is ugly,"
> The three-dimensioned preacher saith;
> So we must not look where the snail and the slug lie
> For Psyche's birth. . . . And that is our death!

It is our death because the man who gives the advice is three-dimensioned—of material solidity, and three dimensions are not enough. There are 'influences', Hertzian waves, perhaps, as in 'Wireless'; and it is, above all, the creative imagination that brings Psyche to birth. But such indeterminacy is foreign to Kipling, who later did not much employ the lyrical mode for ideas of that kind, though 'Gertrude's Prayer' might seem to be an exception.

There is, however, a kind of 'thought' poetry which could better, perhaps, be considered as a pondering upon a particular event, thought which is also deeply emotional. In the following poem Kipling is brooding about the irrevocable, in this case about the 1914–18 war, which transformed the whole outlook of man upon himself, making impossible a return to the old conception of living. This is 'Rebirth' of 1917, which follows 'The Edge of the Evening', that story foretelling the war:

o

> If any God should say
>   "I will restore
> The world her yesterday
>   Whole as before
> My Judgment blasted it"—who would not lift
> Heart, eye, and hand in passion o'er the gift?

But no God can make this gift; and at all events, as the second stanza tells us, we must face these present deaths, the poem going on:

> For we are what we are—
>   So broke to blood
> And the strict works of war—
>   So long subdued
> To sacrifice, that threadbare Death commands
> Hardly observance at our busier hands.

But it concludes:

> Yet we were what we were,
>   And, fashioned so,
> It pleases us to stare
>   At the far show
> Of unbelievable years and shapes that flit
> In our own likeness, on the edge of it.

It is an agonizing emotion, which those old enough may be able to share, an emotion disciplined by thinking.

To turn without apology, as a reader of Kipling is almost forced to do, one may draw attention to a comment upon the, broadly speaking, two classes of human beings, those who reap the fruits of the labour of others, and those who "do the work for which they draw the wage", we meet the more 'romantic'—in the sense that it employs more imagery—'The Sons of Martha', first printed in 1907:

The Sons of Mary seldom bother, for they have inherited that good part:
But the Sons of Martha favour their Mother of the careful soul and the troubled heart.
And because she lost her temper once, and because she was rude to the Lord her Guest,
Her Sons must wait upon Mary's Sons, world without end, reprieve, or rest.

It goes on to describe the work of the world, its perils, its sacrifices, the devotion of the Sons of Martha to the bettering of the world, to providing graces which others enjoy and take for granted:

And the Sons of Mary smile and are blessèd—they know the Angels are on their side.
They know in them is the Grace confessèd, and for them are the Mercies multiplied.
They sit at the Feet—they hear the Word—they see how truly the Promise runs.
They have cast their burden upon the Lord, and—the Lord He lays it on Martha's Sons!

The tone of contempt which this Son of Martha adopts towards the Sons of Mary is pungent enough.

There are some pieces which convey thought which has little emotional background, as, for instance, the 'verses' (they hardly constitute anything that could be called a 'poem') in which he expresses the relation of man to machinery, which is not the excited worship once attributed to him. In 'The Secret of the Machines' (1911), the latter, after boasting of their power, their inexorable judgement on a man who makes a mistake with them, end by saying:

> *Though our smoke may hide the Heavens from your eyes,*
> *It will vanish and the stars will shine again,*
> *Because, for all our power and weight and size,*
> *We are nothing more than children of your brain!*

But it is to one of the Horatian Odes that we must turn for a 'poem' on the subject. These 'translations' are triumphs of Kipling's quieter, more meditative, art; many have already been quoted. He was steeped in Horace. We have seen how, in his earlier years, he had thought little of Latin verse, owing to its innocence of rhyme: but, as he tells us,[1] "C— taught me to loathe Horace for two years; to forget him for twenty, and then to love him for the rest of my days and through many sleepless nights." We here turn to one named simply 'A Translation'. After three stanzas, enumerating the activities

[1] *Something of Myself*, II.

of scientists of various kinds, the trains, motors and aeroplanes
of technologists, he goes on:

> Me, much incurious if the hour
> Present, or to be paid for, brings
> Me to Brundusium by the power
> Of wheels or wings:
>
> Me, in whose breast no flame hath burned
> Life-long, save that by Pindar lit,
> Such lore leaves cold. I am not turned
> Aside to it.
>
> More than when, sunk in thought profound
> Of what the unaltering Gods require,
> My steward (friend but slave) brings round
> Logs for my fire.

It is self-revelation. At this date (1916), he was detaching himself from affairs, becoming, in the vulgar phrase, more 'philosophic', his ultimate values are becoming clear—poetry, and
submission to what the unaltering Gods require.

In that sort of poetry there is necessarily something of the
dreamer. After all, Keats himself was very much a dreamer,
pouring out a balm upon the world, and it was only in his last
(unfinished) work that he wrote the lines quoted earlier. Like
all romantic poets he invited you to enter unexplored realms,
whether within yourself or outside. The poet who vexes, asks
you, rather, to assess experience, to face the reality within
yourself. He refuses to employ the strongly stressed or swinging
rhythms, and his poems are poems of statement rather than of
winged imagination, and have a touch of the didactic, forbidden
the romantic poet, whose work, to quote De Quincey again,
"can teach only as nature teaches, as forests teach, as the sea
teaches, viz. by deep impulses, by hieroglyphic suggestion".

The most impressive, and deliberately least musical of
Kipling's 'thought' poems are in regular sustained metre, to be
said, or read aloud, quietly, as we find in 'Seven Watchmen'
(1918) and 'The Hour of the Angel' (1923), both quoted
earlier. There, the bareness of utterance, the denial of all
'poetic aids', brings us close to the poems of 'actuality'.

CHAPTER III
Actuality' Poetry

"Not ideas about the Thing, but the Thing itself."
Wallace Stevens

The poems belonging to this third suggested division are
written in a style, a language, which, rather than inviting the
imagination to roam, concentrates it on our half-apprehended
intuitions, "exciting", as Coleridge put it, "a more continuous
and equal attention than the language of prose aims at". We
meet that sort of poetry more recently written in the work of
Wallace Stevens, who, at least in some of his poems was trying
to make the actuality of the emotions more vivid, more strikingly
real, writing

> For the listener, who listens in the snow,
> And, nothing but himself, beholds
> Nothing that is not there and the nothing that is;

who could say:

> After the leaves have fallen we return
> To a plain sense of things. It is as if
> We have come to an end of the imagination,

and the title of whose last poem in the 1955 Collected Edition
provides the epigraph for this chapter. This is the kind of
poetry I venture to call 'actuality' poetry, which Kipling came
to write, from time to time, in his later and final phases.

Came to write; for though he very early touched upon
matter appropriate to this kind of poetry, it was not till late
that he evolved the scrupulously winnowed technique, the
telling form. And there are not many examples of this form.
The matter consists of disastrous, ineluctable facts, or searing
thoughts against which there is no defence, such as are fleetingly
referred to in 'The Song of the Banjo':

I am Memory and Torment—I am Town!

or the line which tells of "the thoughts that burn like iron if you think". But a song of that sort, with its "Tinka-tinka-tinka-tinka-tink!" or whichever variant Kipling made play with, may do for the somewhat sentimental nostalgia that the verses express, but will not compel any grim facing of facts: and one may well answer 'Yes' to the query put before us near the end:

> ". . . the Song of Lost Endeavour that I make
> Is it hidden in the twanging of the strings?"

The young man who wrote this in 1894 had by no means got his bearings. Yet he had shown something of the starkness of his latest method in verses written at the age of twenty, 'Arithmetic on the Frontier', of which the third stanza runs:

> A scrimmage in a Border Station—
>   A canter down some dark defile—
> Two thousand pounds of education
>   Drops to a ten-rupee jezail—[1]
> The Crammer's boast, the Squadron's pride,
> Shot like a rabbit in a ride!

That is no more than verse; it is memorable, certainly, as poetry usually is, but it makes no great impact. Yet in the same year as 'The Song of the Banjo' Kipling could compose 'Mary, Pity Women!' which, without being very striking has the strength of economy:

> You call yourself a man,
>   For all you used to swear,
> An' leave me, as you can,
>   My certain shame to bear?
> I 'ear! You do not care—
> You done the worst you know.
> I 'ate you grinnin' there. . . .
> Ah, Gawd, I love you so!

The force of the stanzas, such as it may be, is somewhat impaired by the varied 'refrain' lines that follow each, the first one reading:

[1] A cheap native rifle.

Nice while it lasted, an' now it is over—
Tear out your 'eart an' good-bye to your lover!
What's the use o' grievin', when the mother that bore you
(Mary, pity women!) knew it all before you?

It was not until the 1914–18 war, with the ghastly re-appraisal of 'civilized' man that it necessitated, that Kipling approached something of his final manner, notably in the great acceptant yet despairing poem 'Gethsemane', already quoted in full; and there is the lesser, somewhat bitter poem 'The Hyænas', which preluding "After the burial parties leave . . ." goes on to describe how hyenas tug up and devour the corpses of men, and concludes:

And the pitiful face is shewn again
    For an instant ere they close;
But it is not discovered to living men—
    Only to God and to those

Who, being soulless, are free from shame,
    Whatever meat they may find.
Nor do they defile the dead man's name—
    That is reserved for his kind.

He is at his barest in 'Epitaphs of the War'—again showing his mastery in another form, as the quotation of a few will show:

AN ONLY SON
I have slain none except my Mother. She
(Blessing her slayer) died of grief for me.

THE COWARD
I could not look on Death, which being known,
Men led me to him, blindfold and alone.

Sometimes his hatred of bungling, evasive politicians intrudes:

COMMON FORM
If any question why we died,
Tell them, because our fathers lied.

It is, of course, experience of living, a knowledge of how things come about, that lies at the back of these poems, a knowledge of men's behaviour which appeared to make humanity less praiseworthy than it had seemed when he wrote his earlier

pieces. One not so bitter as 'The Hyænas', in rather lighter
mood, but 'actual' nevertheless, is 'The Disciple', appended to
'The Church that was at Antioch', and so refers immediately
to St. Paul and his version of Christ's message; it is a statement
of how a man's followers may distort his meaning:

> He that hath a Gospel,
>   To loose upon Mankind,
> Though he serve it utterly—
>   Body, soul and mind—
> Though he go to Calvary
>   Daily for its gain—
> It is His Disciple
>   Shall make his labour vain.

The last two stanzas describe how the distortion comes about:

> It is His Disciple
>   Who shall tell us how
> Much the Master would have scrapped
>   Had he lived till now—
> What he would have modified
>   Of what he said before—
> It is His Disciple
>   Shall do this and more. . . .

> He that hath a Gospel
>   Whereby Heaven is won
> (Carpenter, or cameleer,
>   Or Maya's dreaming son),
> Many swords shall pierce Him,
>   Mingling blood with gall;
> But His Own Disciple
>   Shall wound Him worst of all!

There is, perhaps, a touch of the 'romantic' in the last stanza,
but even in so keenly felt a poem Kipling does not hesitate to
use the vernacular word 'scrapped'.

The outstanding 'actuality' poems, which justify putting
such poems in a different genre are of so great importance in
arriving at Kipling's philosophy of living that they have
already been quoted in part: the 'Hymn to Physical Pain' of
1929, and the 'Hymn of Breaking Strain' of 1935. They deal,

especially the first, with states of being described in 'The Burden', which belongs to 'The Gardener':

> Wherein no soul can aid,
> Whereof no soul can hear,

a subject less emphatically treated in 'The Comforters' (1912). The 'Hymn to Physical Pain' is an agonized poem, the actuality of a sense of guilt such as may overcome a man in his later years:

> The trusty Worm that dieth not—
> The steadfast Fire also

all is terribly portrayed, the only salve being extreme physical pain, although

> Thine is the weariness outworn
> No promise shall relieve,
> That says at eve, "Would God 'twere morn!"
> At morn, "Would God 'twere eve!"

the reference in the last two lines being to Deuteronomy xxviii. 67. Here we would seem to have, nakedly, not ideas about the Thing, but the Thing itself. The 'Hymn of Breaking Strain' of 1935 is not so agonizing, though it does deal with "our hour/Of overthrow and pain". In none of these poems is there any imagery; though written in more or less 'common measure', with rhyming 8, 6 or 8, 7 syllabic structure, there is nothing lyrical about them. Nor is the imagination invited to make journeys outward, but is impelled ever more within. One is tempted to call such poems 'granitic'.

It is by these poems, it can be maintained, that Kipling made a real contribution to the development of poetry; they are altogether original, and it would not seem that there is anything like them in the language. In many ways some of Hardy's poems resemble them, but there we are always conscious of a kind of 'poetic' overtone. To some extent this claim to uniqueness can be made for the 'thought' poems, though there we may sense precedents, especially perhaps in James Thomson's 'The City of Dreadful Night', a poem we know Kipling deeply responded to, not only quoting it, but using the title for his own prose writings. In 'romantic' poetry, especially in the ballad form as here regarded, he added to the old tradition, supplying examples notable in that kind, and which, like all his poetry, bear the strong impress of his individuality. He was never imitative, though he would not deny the roots from which his work sprang; he had too strong a sense of tradition. He definitely ranks among the poets, not merely as one in whose 'verse' there is a great deal of 'poetry'.

CHAPTER IV

Verse

Thus, the artless songs I sing
Do not deal with anything
New or never said before.
                    'A General Summary'

However invidious the distinction between verse and poetry
may be, some verse is clearly not meant to be poetry. It merely
conveys more pithily, more jauntily even, the sort of thing that
prose can tell you, or wishes you to know. It is more on the
level of every day. This is not to say that verse-writing is not
an art, since every craft becomes so if pursued devotedly
enough. There are plenty of borderline cases, easily exemplified
in Kipling's work alone. In which category are we to place
'The Dove of Dacca', somewhat mysterious, or the plain but
moving 'Ford o' Kabul River' with its repeated pulse-like
"Ford, ford, ford o' Kabul River"? With most poets the
distinction is easy to make; editions of Hood's poems are
divided into 'comic' and 'serious' poems; Macaulay's *Lays of
Ancient Rome* are verse; but 'The Jacobite's Lament' is poetry.
Sometimes, not in Kipling alone, verse is rescued from becoming poetry by the introduction of some incongruous word, as
when in 'Giffen's Debt'

> They raised a temple to the local God,
> And burnt all manner of unsavoury things . . .
> And blew into a conch and banged a bell . . .

Nevertheless there is an idea within the piece which might have
been made into a poem.

'Giffen's Debt', however, appeared in Kipling's first volume
of metrical expression (excluding the privately printed ones),
namely *Departmental Ditties*, which, no doubt, is generally
supposed to come under the heading of 'light verse'. But what

'light verse' is, it is not easy to determine, as may be seen by referring to Mr. W. H. Auden's Introduction to, and choice in, *The Oxford Book of Light Verse*, especially as the one example he gives of Kipling's light verse is 'Danny Deever'! But one of the suggestions that he makes is useful in this context, namely that light verse is written "when the things in which the poet is interested, the things which he sees about him, are much the same as those of his audience, and that audience is a fairly general one. . . ." This would include *vers de société*, of which Kipling wrote some entertaining ones, the most amusing being versifications of what might be called 'club gossip', such as would make a young man of nineteen or so eager to know life, feel that he really is knowing it. We can even now chuckle over the verses on Potiphar Gubbins or Boanerges Blitzen, or the unfortunate General Bangs, "that most immoral man", as did, no doubt, the readers of the newspapers where they first appeared. Already there is skill, if not mastery of verse; they have not the beautiful finish of, say, Calverley's *Verses, Fly-Leaves, and Translations*.

They vary, however, in depth; much that is serious is written "in jesting guise", as he says in that near-poem, the 'Prelude'. They have an aura of deeper meaning, sometimes a heartfelt comment on the burden the Englishman in India had to bear, or something verging on the scathing or bitter. So this collection of early verse is by no means to be ignored as an expression of Kipling's individuality. Very few are sheer 'light verse'; but that Kipling was well aware that such things were not poetry is attested, not only by the indifferently good 'Prelude', but by that real poem 'L'Envoi', which accompanied the second edition of 1886:

> The smoke upon your Altar dies,
> The flowers decay . . .

which demands a response quite different from the verses, though some of them are imbued with somewhat grim notions, as is 'The Undertaker's Horse', but are, clearly, designed to go no deeper than verse.

One could say that these verses are experimental. Certainly in these ditties, as Kipling very properly called them, he would seem to have been trying his hand at many forms: the ballad as in 'The Ballad of Fisher's Boarding House'; the ballade as in those 'Of Burial' or 'Jakko Hill'; the Browning sort of monologue in 'One Viceroy Resigns'; the sonnet in 'Two Months'; blank verse in 'Giffen's Debt'. He comes also close to the epigram in 'Certain Maxims of Hafiz':

The ways of man with a maid be strange, yet simple and tame,
To the ways of a man with a horse, when selling or racing that same.

But more especially he sought for metres that would suit him, often recklessly giving way to his predilection for rhyme, including internal rhyme, which even in his later years sometimes tended to be a little too intrusive:

As I left the Halls at Lumley, rose the vision of a comely
Maid last season worshipped dumbly, watched with fervour from afar;
And I wondered idly, blindly, if the maid would greet me kindly. . . .

continuing in like manner in the first three lines of the seven more stanzas of 'As the Bell Clinks'. Much the same, though to a lesser degree, occurs in 'Pink Dominoes': "Jenny and Me were engaged you see. . . ." But he also found the four-line stanza, and the six-line stanza with alternating lines of various syllabic value, which he afterwards used as only a master can. Sometimes the metre is too lilting, or the rhyme too pat, as to spoil such a set of verses as 'La Nuit Blanche', where the whole dread experience is put too much in the manner of 'light' verse. But on the whole, the performance as such is astonishing, and the experimentation was to bear fruit.

In these early stages we often find him putting the same feeling or notion in more than one form. There are two pieces written not long after he came back from India to live in London, in which he expresses his disgust at the place, the climate, the people, and their way of living. The first, 'In Partibus',[1] was printed at the end of December 1889. The opening stanza mentions the 'buses that run to Battersea and Bow and other places; the third tells us:

[1] In *Abaft the Funnel*. Not in Definitive Edition.

> The sky, a greasy soup-toureen,
>   Shuts down atop my brow.
> Yes, I have sighed for London town
>   And I have got it now:
> And half of it is fog and filth,
>   And half of it is row.

And later we read:

> It's Oh to see the morn ablaze
> Above the mango-tope. . . .

and so on. That, of course, with other parallels, is the theme of the popular 'Mandalay' of June 1890, well-known, partly, perhaps, because it is set to rousing, singable tunes. It is too familiar to need quotation, but the likenesses are fairly close throughout.

Probably his greatest successes in verse at this early period were the poems about private soldiers, notably in *Barrack-Room Ballads*, where he used the Tommies' vernacular; one need quote only the poem 'Tommy' itself, in which he expresses his indignation at the way he found that soldiers were regarded and treated in England:

> I went into a public-'ouse to get a pint o' beer,
> The publican 'e up an' sez, "We serve no red-coats here."
> The girls be'ind the bar they laughed and giggled fit to die,
> I outs into the street again an' to myself sez I:
>   O it's Tommy this, an' Tommy that, an' "Tommy, go away";
>   But it's "Thank you, Mister Atkins," when the band begins to
>   play. . . .

And later on:

> We aren't no thin red 'eroes, nor we aren't no blackguards too,
> But single men in barricks, most remarkable like you . . .

Since many of the verse pieces that he wrote in this mode are meant to be spoken by people whose natural speech is the vernacular, objections made to the over-use of this idiom seem beside the point. People declare that they would rather say "Follow me home" than "Follow me 'ome", and that everyone is at liberty to drop his aitches if and as he wishes to. But the piece, called 'Follow Me 'Ome' is obviously by a Tommy, and

written in his language, with his mentality. Not that most
people would have what at this time (1893) was Kipling's
sense of rhythm and form; we feel at once, though we need
not analyse, the generally anapæstic lilt of the stanzas, and the
slow-march effect of the refrain:

> There was no one like 'im, 'Orse or Foot,
>   Nor any o' the Guns I knew;
> An' because it was so, why, o' course 'e went an' died,
>   Which is just what the best men do.
>
>   *So it's knock out your pipes an' follow me!*
>   *An' it's finish up your swipes an' follow me!*
>   *Oh, 'ark to the big drum callin'*
>   *Follow me—follow me 'ome!*

Nor would one wish for a different idiom, seeing the kind of
verse it is meant to be, in 'Private Ortheris's Song', "My girl
she give me the go onest," with its chorus:

> Ho! don't you 'eed what a girl says,
>   An' don't you go for the beer;
> But I was an ass when I was at grass,
>   An' that is why I'm 'ere.

The effect of such a piece as 'The Ladies' would be lost if put
in correct middle-class language, with its refrain "An' I learned
about women from 'er" and the all too popular, even aphoristic
conclusion:

> *When you get to a man in the case,*
>   *They're like as a row of pins—*
> *For the Colonel's Lady an' Judy O'Grady*
>   *Are sisters under their skins!*

Such things are clearly verse and not poetry. And here, perhaps,
it should again be said that these pieces must be read in the
context of their time; and not only that, but also in the context
of the supposed speaker—of that time. To repeat, Kipling does
not himself rejoice in loot, nor in the cruelties of fighting
relished by the soldiers who 'wrote' the verses. There once more
his empathy gave him, so to speak, another voice.
   It is clear that the greater proportion of Kipling's metrical
output is verse, sometimes a little careless, and not poetry,

though 'poetry' will keep breaking in. There are, however, some very interesting examples of what might be called verse which has a meaning, makes an impact which prose cannot give. One is 'The Two-Sided Man', already drawn upon in explaining Kipling himself. Another can be offered 'We and They', a sermon against snobbery and racial discrimination: it ends:

> All good people agree,
>   And all good people say,
> All nice people, like Us, are We
>   And every one else is They:
> But if you cross over the sea,
>   Instead of over the way,
> You may end by (think of it!) looking on We
>   As only a sort of They!

And there is, of course, the well-known 'If', a poem in the long line of Stoical poetry beginning with Thomas Campion's 'The Man of Life Upright', expressed by many poets since, including Wordsworth in 'The Happy Warrior', and in Kipling's own day by Housman.

Then, to conclude, there is some verse, lightly written, but ramming home a point that demands ever more attention. It is remarkable that so early as 1933, in 'Fox-Hunting', he should have made so arithmetically accurate a forecast as is contained in the final stanza:

> When men grew shy of hunting stag,
>   For fear the law might try 'em,
> The Car put up an average bag
>   Of twenty men *per diem*.
> Then every road was made a rink
>   For Coroners to sit on;
> And so began, in skid and stink,
>   The real blood-sport of Britain!

Again, in 'The Muse Among the Motors', containing some twenty-five poems, successfully 'after the manner of' poets from the Greek Anthology to Stevenson, on motor-cars, the last piece 'The Moral' '(Author Unknown)' roundly states what other pieces had indicated, a theme which became the official slogan during Christmas 1964, 'Don't drink and drive'. The unknown author is evidently a car, and he—or it—concludes:

> I will make you know your left hand from your right.
> I will teach you not to drink about your biz.
> I'm the only temperance advocate in sight!
> I'm all the Education Act there is!

It is impossible to do more than indicate the immense variety of Kipling's verse or illustrate how often it verged upon poetry, not only in metre, diction, and imagery, but also in subject-matter, in 'hieroglyphic suggestion'. 'The Last Suttee' might well have become a poem, and so might some of the later satirical pieces, such as the withering, scornful 'Gehazi', blasting the Marconi scandals. One can only be astonished at the wealth of ideas, the invention in form, the *apparent* ease, the mastery.

I know that in quoting Kipling's poems I have omitted a number which many people regard as their favourites; I have left out many of my own. My experience constantly is that in thumbing through the pages of the Definitive Edition, I come across some piece or passage that delights me, or opens new vistas of thought or experience.

One may fitly end with what Mr. A. L. Rowse has written: "What is certain is that Kipling was the last poet to express the whole life of a people, and to speak directly to and for the people The poets of the 1930s talked about it, but Kipling did it."[1]

[1] *Sunday Telegraph*, 19 December 1965.

P

APPENDICES

Kipling's Stories and Essays Mentioned in the Text

Name of Story	Date of first publication	Collected
Among the Railway Folk	1888	*From Sea to Sea*
Army of a Dream, The	1904	*Traffics and Discoveries*
Arrest of Lieutenant Golightly	1886	*Plain Tales from the Hills*
As Easy as ABC	1912	*A Diversity of Creatures*
At the End of the Passage	1890	*Life's Handicap*
Aunt Ellen	1932	*Limits and Renewals*
Baa, Baa, Black Sheep	1888	*Wee Willie Winkie*
Bank Fraud, A	1887	*Plain Tales from the Hills*
Beauty Spots	1931	*Limits and Renewals*
Below the Mill Dam	1902	*Traffics and Discoveries*
Bertran and Bimi	1891	*Life's Handicap*
Beyond the Pale	1888	*Plain Tales from the Hills*
Black Jack	1888	*Soldiers Three*
Bread Upon the Waters	1896	*The Day's Work*
Bridge-Builders, The	1893	*The Day's Work*
Broken Link Handicap, The	1887	*Plain Tales from the Hills*
Brushwood Boy, The	1895	*The Day's Work*
Bubbling Well Road	1888	*Life's Handicap*
Bull that Thought, The	1924	*Debits and Credits*
By Word of Mouth	1887	*Plain Tales from the Hills*
Captive, The	1902	*Traffics and Discoveries*
Centurion of the Thirtieth, A	1906	*Puck of Pook's Hill*
Children of the Zodiac	1891	*Many Inventions*
Church that was at Antioch, The	1929	*Limits and Renewals*
Cold Iron	1909	*Rewards and Fairies*
Comprehension of Private Copper, The	1902	*Traffics and Discoveries*
Conversion of Aurelian McGoggin, The	1887	*Plain Tales from the Hills*

In the Interests of the Brethren	1918	*Debits and Credits*
In the Matter of a Private	1888	*Soldiers Three*
In the Pride of His Youth	1887	*Plain Tales from the Hills*
In the Rukh	1893	*Many Inventions*
In the Same Boat	1911	*A Diversity of Creatures*
Janeites, The	1924	*Debits and Credits*
Judgment of Dungara, The	1888	*Soldiers Three*
Judson and the Empire	1893	*Many Inventions*
Knife and the Naked Chalk, The	1909	*Rewards and Fairies*
Knights of the Joyous Venture, The	1906	*Puck of Pook's Hill*
Last of the Stories, The	1888	*Abaft the Funnel*
Letters of Marque	1887–8	*From Sea to Sea*
Letters of Travel	1920	*Letters of Travel*
Letters to the Family	1908	*Letters of Travel*
Lispeth	1886	*Plain Tales from the Hills*
Little Foxes	1909	*Actions and Reactions*
Love-o'-Women	1893	*Many Inventions*
Madonna of the Trenches, A	1924	*Debits and Credits*
Maltese Cat, The	1895	*The Day's Work*
Man Who Would be King, The	1888	*Wee Willie Winkie*
Manner of Men, The	1930	*Limits and Renewals*
Marklake Witches	1910	*Rewards and Fairies*
Mark of the Beast, The	1890	*Life's Handicap*
Mary Postgate	1915	*A Diversity of Creatures*
Matter of Fact, A	1892	*Many Inventions*
Minds of Men, The	1916	*Sea Warfare*
Miracle of Purun Bhagat, The	1894	*The Second Jungle Book*
Miracle of Saint Jubanus, The	1930	*Limits and Renewals*
Miss Youghal's Sais	1887	*Plain Tales from the Hills*
Moral Reformers, The	1899	*Stalky & Co.*
Mother Hive, The	1908	*Actions and Reactions*
Mrs. Bathurst	1904	*Traffics and Discoveries*
My Son's Wife	1917	*A Diversity of Creatures*
	(written 1913)	
My Sunday at Home	1895	*The Day's Work*
Old Men at Pevensey	1906	*Puck of Pook's Hill*
One View of the Question	1890	*Many Inventions*
On Greenhow Hill	1890	*Life's Handicap*
Only a Subaltern	1888	*Wee Willie Winkie*
On the City Wall	1888	*Wee Willie Winkie*
On the Gate	1926	*Debits and Credits*
On the Great Wall	1906	*Puck of Pook's Hill*

Wayside Comedy, A	1888	*Wee Willie Winkie*
Weland's Sword	1906	*Puck of Pook's Hill*
William the Conqueror	1895	*The Day's Work*
Winged Hats, The	1906	*Puck of Pook's Hill*
Wireless	1902	*Traffics and Discoveries*
Wish House, The	1924	*Debits and Credits*
With the Main Guard	1888	*Soldiers Three*
With the Night Mail	1905	*Actions and Reactions*
Without Benefit of Clergy	1890	*Life's Handicap*
Woman in His Life, The	1928	*Limits and Renewals*
Wrong Thing, The	1909	*Rewards and Fairies*
Yoked with an Unbeliever	1886	*Plain Tales from the Hills*
Young Men at the Manor	1906	*Puck of Pook's Hill*

A Guide to Further Reading

The books here mentioned are of recent date, and can be said to supersede earlier ones. An extensive bibliography is to be found in No. 19 of the *Writers and Their Work* series, published by Longmans, Green & Co. for the British Council: *Rudyard Kipling*.

For BIOGRAPHY the authoritative work is *Rudyard Kipling. His Life and Work*, by Charles Carrington (1955). A useful supplement to this is *Rudyard Kipling to Rider Haggard. The Record of a Friendship*. Ed. by Morton Cohen (1965).

For his WRITINGS, *The Art of Rudyard Kipling*, by J. M. S. Tompkins (1959) is of first importance, to which may be added *La Poétique de Rudyard Kipling*, by Francis Léaud (Paris 1959). An interesting study on a smaller scale is *Aspects of Kipling's Art*, by C. A. Bodelsen (1964). For his early development, *Kipling in India*, by Louis L. Cornell (1966) is to be recommended.

His POLITICAL ideas in relation to the Imperialism of his time are admirably elucidated in *The Vision and the Need*, by Richard Faber (1966).

Essays on Kipling are collected in *Kipling's Mind and Art*, ed. by Andrew Rutherford (1964), and give a fair impression of Kipling's position in the literary world since his death. *Kipling and the Critics*, ed. by Elliot L. Gilbert (N.Y. 1965), includes some of the earlier reactions from Max Beerbohm onwards.

Current criticism and comment may be found in the quarterly *Kipling Journal*, the organ of the Kipling Society, and in *English Literature in Transition*, Purdue University, Indiana, Vol. 3, No. 4, 1960, and Vol. 7, No. 4, 1964.

Some Rare or Invented Words
Used by Kipling

Kipling sometimes used words or terms in common use in the eighteenth century, which may still have been in use when he was young, such as 'powdering along' or 'smoking along' for going fast: or 'hirpling' for lolloping along uneasily. These will not be noted. Surprisingly in the *Jungle Book* story, 'Letting in the Jungle' he uses the term 'milling along' in its modern, almost slang connotation. Besides using fairly common 'rare' words, such as 'glairy' for sticky, viscid, he seems often to have invented some, mainly onomatopoeic, which may be baffling when referred to, but in their context are usually plain enough. He appears to have enjoyed this, especially when writing the stories he was going to read to his children; they are notably numerous in *Rewards and Fairies*.

BAFFED: Chil the Kite and his mate swooped down: "The two baffed under Mowgli's nose so close that a pinch of downy white feathers brushed away." *Jungle Books*. 'Spring Running.'

    The nearest approach in the *N.E.D.* would seem to be 'a blow with anything flat or soft'. The verb is 'to bark'.

BEAZLED: "I came back to the barge one day . . . fair beazled out." 'A Priest in Spite of Himself'; ". . . he fair beazled the life out of her." 'Simple Simon.'

BEWLING: ". . . the wind bewling like a kite in our riggin's." 'Simple Simon.'

BIVVERING: "Two kestrels hung bivvering and squealing above them." 'The Knife and the Naked Chalk.'

    N.E.D. To bive (O.E.) 'To shake, tremble.'

BRISH: "His stirrup brished Red Jacket's elbow." 'A Priest in Spite of Himself.'
"This hay's full of hedge-brishings." 'A Doctor of Medicine.' Probably a variant of 'brush'.

BULTING: "on besom black nights bulting back and forth off they Dutch roads . . ." 'Simple Simon.'
It might be a variant of 'bolting'; 'Besom' presumably means 'broom', here a dirty one.

CHUNAMED: "And so back through the chunamed courts." *From Sea to Sea.* 'Letters of Marque IV.' Covered over with chunam, a plaster made of shell-lime and sea-sand. *N.E.D.*

COAMINGS: "One looks down over the coamings . . ." 'With the Night Mail.' "The raised borders about the edge of the hatches and scuttles of a ship . . ." *N.E.D.*

CUTCHERY: ". . . the House of Rimmon, be it office or cutchery." 'Letters of Marque I.' Indian. "A hall or chamber of audience." *N.E.D.*

DEW-BLOBBED: "Dan took a few steps across the dew-blobbed lawn." 'Cold Iron.' Blob, i.e. bubble. *N.E.D.*

ELLE-WOMAN: "She is reduced to a shell—is a very elle-woman of an engine." *From Sea to Sea.* 'Among the Railway Folk.'
Possibly on the analogy of 'elle-maid', an elf-maid. *N.E.D.*

FLINDERS: "Then—*Pouf!*—the false flint falls all to flinders." 'The Knife and the Naked Chalk.' "Thin chips or splinters." *N.E.D.*

GARMED: ". . . they smarmed and garmed everything." 'The Mother Hive.' Probably an invention.

GASH: "Why they broke down and looked so gash." 'On One Side Only.' *Letters of Travel.*

GRIFF: ". . . as though I had been a griff but twenty minutes landed." *From Sea to Sea.* 'The Smith Administration.' The Serri Cabal.
Probably "a type of mulatto". *N.E.D.*

GUB: ". . . hove the pudden at me on the bowsprit gub by gub." "gubs of good oakum". Both 'Simple Simon.' Probably 'gob': "a lump, clot, of some slimy substance". *N.E.D.*

GYDON: ". . . the sole av my boot flappin' like a cavalry gydon . . .' 'Love-o'-Women.'

KELK: "a breadth of rampant kelk feigning to be lawful crop". 'An Habitation Enforced.' Kelk is the roe of a fish, hardly applicable here. Kipling may have meant 'kelp', "a kind of large seaweed". *N.E.D.*

KENCHES: ". . . the silvery-gray kenches of well-pressed fish . . ." *Captains Courageous.* V. "A box used in salting or packing fish." *N.E.D.*

LITHER: "I counted the lither barrels of twenty serpentines . . ." 'Hal o' the Draft.' Probably meaning 'evil'.

NESTY: "the nesty streaky water". 'The Disturber of Traffic.'

PAVISANDING: "forth she come pavisanding like a peacock—". 'Simple Simon.' Would seem to mean 'covered over' or 'protected'; the sentence goes on "stuff, ruff, stomacher and all". *N.E.D.*

PENK: "Wot makes the soldier's 'eart to penk, wot makes 'im to perspire?" 'Oonts'. (Poem.)

POLTING: "There was a middlin' lot comin' down-stream, too—cattle-bars an' hop-poles and odd-ends bats, all poltin' down together . . ." 'Friendly Brook' (and again later). "To knock, thrash, beat, bang." Now dialect. *N.E.D.*

PUTE: "only you and I chance to be pure pute asses". 'Hal o' the Draft.' "Pure, clean, mere." *N.E.D.*, which quotes this phrase.

PUT-LOCKS: "I was at Torrigiano's feet on a pile of put-locks." 'The Wrong Thing.'

QUIRT: ". . . the nigger had then and there laid into him with a peculiarly adhesive quirt . . ." *Kim.* VI. "A kind of riding-whip . . . having a short handle and a braided leather lash about two feet long." *N.E.D.* Since this is of American use, it is hard to see how an English soldier-boy in India could have known the word.

RAXED: "One by one the sea raxed away our three Boats"; "I raxed me a meal fra galley-shelves and pantries . . ." 'Bread Upon the Waters.' "Reach out for", Scottish, seems the derivation of Kipling's use. *N.E.D.*

RUFFLE (v): ". . . the Spanisher he ruffled round in the wind . . ." 'Simple Simon.' Probably means came round untidily, perhaps aggressively; to ruffle has also, rarely, meant "to furl a sail". This might be implied. *N.E.D.*

RUGG (v): ". . . when they get good hold and rugg you." 'The Manner of Men.' "To pull forcibly, violently or roughly; to tear, tug." *N.E.D.* There spelt 'rug'.

SCADDER: ". . . an' she just tongues him scadderin' out o' doors . . ." 'Friendly Brook.' Probably means 'scuttling'.

SCRATTEL: "I must have looked a sore scrattel." 'Brother Square-Toes." "He sure-ly was a pitiful scrattel—his coat half torn off, his face cut . . ." 'A Priest in Spite of Himself.'

SCUTCHEL: "I've brought you what I could scutchel up of odds and ends." 'Simple Simon.' ". . . 'er mother 'ad sent 'er round to scutchel up what vittles she could off of us." 'The Wish House.' 'Sneak, beg.'

SHRUCK: "She shruck too much for real doings." 'The Wish House.' Probably local for 'shrieked'.

SLOB: "we saw a man slouching along the slob . . ." 'The Conversion of St. Wilfrid.' "Soft mud on the sea shore." *N.E.D.*

SLIDDERING: "I was aware of Benedetto . . . sliddering up behind me." 'The Wrong Thing.' "To slide, to slip." *N.E.D.*

SKELPED: "we skelped our divoted way round nine holes . . ." 'The House Surgeon.' "To strike, beat, smack, slap." *N.E.D.*

SKITTERED: ". . . the engine skittered over broken glass like a terrier in a cucumber frame." 'My Sunday at Home.' "To skip or skim *along* a surface, with occasional rapid contact." *N.E.D.*

SPRUDEL: ". . . buccaneering's no game for a middle-aged man—but I gave that fellow sprudel!" 'Sea Constables.'

STOACHED: "The ground about was poached and stoached with sliding hoof-marks." 'Simple Simon.'

STOUSH: " 'Who's going to stoush us?' Orton asked fiercely." 'A Friend of the Family.' 'Hit, strike.' Australian. E.P. Vol. II.

STUBBING: ". . . obligin' with a hand at early potato-liftin', stubbin' hens, an' such-like." 'The Wish House.' "To remove the stub-feathers from (a fowl)." *N.E.D.*

SOUNDER: "a sounder of pig had gone into the Arti-goth patch". 'Bubbling Well Road.' "A herd of wild swine." *N.E.D.*

SPLUTTED: "Frankie had put in from Chatham, with his rudder splutted." 'Simple Simon.' Presumably 'split'.

SWOP-HOOK: ". . . because a man had left his swop-hook or spade there." 'Cold Iron.' "*Dial.*, a kind of reaping-hook for cutting crops close to the ground." *N.E.D.*

THUTTER: ". . . the old mill shook and the heavy stones thuttered on the grist." 'Below the Mill Dam.' "But they hung on behind while their teeth thuttered." 'Simple Simon.' "To make the spluttering or shaking sound suggested by the word", *N.E.D.* which quotes also from *Captains Courageous*, "a grinding, thuttering shriek".

TOT: ". . . walking wide of some old ash-tot . . . " 'Cold Iron.' "A dust heap or refuse heap." *N.E.D.* "We hid our horses in a willow-tot at the foot of the glebe." 'Hal o' the Draft.' "Anything very small" *N.E.D.*

TRINKLE: "Even in December people had no more than begun to trinkle back to town." 'A Priest in Spite of Himself.' "To trickle, or flow drop by drop." *N.E.D.*

TUTT-MOUTHED: "He was just a outrageous, valiant, crop-haired, tutt-mouthed boy roarin' up an' down the narrer seas . . ." 'Simple Simon.' *N.E.D.* gives under 'tutty' "irritable, testy, peevish".

VAMBRISHED: ". . . in a great smoky pat vambrished with red gun-fire." 'Simple Simon.' Apparently means 'defensively armoured'. See *N.E.D.* under 'vambrace'.

WEBSTER: ". . . quick as a webster unrolling cloth almost." 'The Wrong Thing.' A weaver (*obs*) *N.E.D.*

WERISH: "This Oxfordshire plague, good people, being generated among rivers and ditches, was of a werish, watery nature." 'A Doctor of Medicine.'

INDEX

INDEX

233